Comprehensive Guide to Emergency Preparedness and Disaster Recovery

Frances C. Wilkinson, Linda K. Lewis, and Nancy K. Dennis

Association of College and Research Libraries
A division of the American Library Association
Chicago, Illinois 2010

The paper used in this publication meets the minimum requirements of American National Standard for Information Sciences–Permanence of Paper for Printed Library Materials, ANSI Z39.48-1992. ∞

Library of Congress Cataloging-in-Publication Data

Wilkinson, Frances C.
 Comprehensive guide to emergency preparedness and disaster recovery / by Frances C. Wilkinson, Linda K. Lewis, and Nancy K. Dennis.
  p. cm.
 Includes bibliographical references.
 ISBN 978-0-8389-8548-9 (pbk. : alk. paper) 1. Libraries--Safety measures--Planning. 2. Emergency management. 3. Library materials--Conservation and restoration. 4. Library buildings--Conservation and restoration. 5. Academic libraries--United States--Case studies. 6. Emergency management--United States--Case studies. I. Lewis, Linda K. II. Dennis, Nancy K. III. Title.
 Z679.7.W55 2010
 025.8'2--dc22
            2010015094

Printed in the United States of America.

14 13 12 11 10   5 4 3 2 1

TABLE OF CONTENTS

DEDICATION

Fran, Linda, and Nancy dedicate this book with sincere appreciation and respect to all our colleagues at UNM who responded with intelligence and grace to the floods and fire over the last few years. Their work and endurance under extended and difficult circumstances are an inspiration. And to our often forgotten support system—family and friends—who were patient and generous, and listened to our long tales of the disaster stories. Thank you!

ACKNOWLEDGEMENTS

Fran, Linda, and Nancy gratefully acknowledge our colleagues, families, and friends for their encouragement, advice, patience, and support as we wrote this book. Our special thanks go to Mary Ellen K. Davis, ACRL Executive Director, for recruiting us to write this book; to Camila A. Alire, Dean Emerita of University Libraries at the University of New Mexico and Colorado State University for her guidance, knowledge, and expertise in disaster recovery; and to Martha Bedard, Dean of University Libraries at the University of New Mexico, for granting all three of us sabbaticals to do the writing.

We thank the many people who helped us to recover from our own disasters at the University Libraries (UL)—a fire at our Zimmerman Library in 2006 and two floods, one at our Centennial Science and Engineering Library in 2004 and another at our Zimmerman Library in 2007. Their help and support enabled us to restore our libraries and provided a great deal of the information that we are sharing in this book. They include the members of the library's disaster response assistance team (DRAT) as well as the many special people at companies and vendors who assisted with the Zimmerman Library fire and flood. BMS CAT was our primary vendor for collections salvage, removal, cleaning, restoration, and storage as well as providing smoke neutralization throughout the library. Several local companies provided us with other essential facilities services. Rockefellers Cleaning and Restoration Company performed the initial water removal, climate stabilization, and cleaning of library offices. Greg Hick's and Associates (architects) led the planning, design, and construction for the first floor and basement restorations. Maloy Construction, Inc., provided demolition of the first floor and basement damaged areas and rebuilt our enhanced first floor reference area. Britton Construction, Inc., was our general contractor for the basement renovation. Improve Group coordinated and installed the compact shelving in our basement and three sub-basement levels. Santa Fe Protective Services conducted the manual fire watch and provided security services throughout the building recovery and restoration process. Absolute Back Order Services, Inc. found print journals that we never expected to obtain. Roswell Bookbinders bound and stored materials for us for many months. EBSCO Information Services, ProQuest LLC, and Readex provided extended trials and expedited access to their electronic resources. They all provided invaluable support as we rebuilt our collections and restored our facilities. We also thank Wes Carlton for his guidance and assistance during our first flood at our CSEL branch—he taught us well so that we were better prepared for our next disaster at Zimmerman Library.

We express our admiration and gratitude to the UL employees who were part of the disaster recovery, especially those people who were displaced for almost two years while we recovered from the fire and flood. Their positive attitude and commitment to the UL in support of the recovery are an inspiration. A special thank you to Dan Barkley, Anne Schultz, Sever Bordeianu, and Kathy Gienger for their willingness to be the first UL employees to triage and assess collections immediately after the fire. Ed Padilla, UL Facilities Manager, Louie Perez and Bonifacio Anglada were the foundation of the recovery and rebuilding efforts for the UL. We thank Deborah Cole and the other members of the Fire/Watch Book Group for creating *The Zimmerman fire: (re)collections*, a compilation of interviews, essays, poetry, art, photographs, memoranda, and miscellany contributed by UL employees and the

UNM community about the Zimmerman fire. The book touches the heart and soul of everyone who views it.

We thank Bruce Neville for his leadership and organization during the post-flood recovery pack-back of materials at our CSEL branch. His work at CSEL laid the groundwork for our successful Zimmerman Library pack-out and pack-back. Their endurance, intelligence, and good cheer kept everyone going when energy and patience were dwindling away.

An incredible support team from UNM including Joel Straquadine, Manager of Facilities Maintenance at the Physical Plant Department (now University Safety Officer); Vince Leonard, University Fire Marshal; Bob Dunnington, Program Operations Director at Risk Management; Kathy Guimond, Chief of UNM Police and Director of Security; and Rick Henrard, General Manager at UNM Office of Capital Projects,. We thank Joel for supporting the UL at every turn, cutting through the bureaucratic red tape to get us what we needed, when we needed it. He is amazing! We thank Vince and Bob for their support, guidance, and liaison with the State Fire Marshal's office after the Zimmerman fire. We thank Kathy for her unflagging support and assistance at every turn, from notifying Fran immediately after the fire broke out all the way through the reopening of the basement. The library could not have a better friend! We thank Rick who kept the Zimmerman basement rebuilding project on time and on budget and helped us to create a new, inviting space for student learning and collaboration.

We thank our colleagues at Cal State Northridge, Colorado State, Tulane, UH Manoa, UI, and UNM who authored the case studies in Part IV of this book. These compelling stories document the tireless work and commitment of individuals and organizations who are dedicated to the protection and survival of libraries that have faced disasters.

In addition we thank our customers, the students and faculty who supported us throughout the recovery, learned new ways of working without their favorite paper journals or study areas, and reminded us how important libraries are to the customers. We are also deeply grateful to the individual and institutional donors from across the country who offered journals to replace our lost materials. Special thanks go to David A. Phillips, Curator of Archeology at UNM's Maxwell Museum, who helped us rebuild our archeology and anthropology collections by gathering donations in these areas through his many national contacts.

Several of our colleagues at the UL stand out for the assistance and support that they provided to us as we researched, wrote and edited this book. They include Linda Skye for her incredible knowledge of Microsoft Word and its many "features," Patricia L. Campbell for her superb photograph preparation assistance—she perfected it with her "M" dogs, and Randy Moorehead and his team for their speedy delivery of hard-to-find materials from interlibrary loan.

Our unending gratitude goes to Gail Lane and Roberta Innan, who read and edited every word of this book before we submitted it to ALA-ACRL. Without their expertise this book would not have taken shape. Any mistakes in it are ours alone. We also thank Katrina Wilkinson for suggestions on chapter titles, wording, and for spending hours online to find the perfect quotes to open each chapter.

And lastly, we thank Fran's at-home office staff, Chera and Asrai (the Ragdoll kittens) and Nancy's many furry friends for keeping our spirits up, providing endless entertainment, keyboarding numerous extra letters and symbols into the manuscript—we hope that we found them all—and for serving as paperweights for whichever documents we were trying to work on at the time.

INTRODUCTION

Disasters in libraries have been reported for eons. One of the more infamous was the fire that destroyed much of the Alexandria library in Egypt in approximately 48 BCE. Other disasters have occurred in libraries throughout history; they seem to be increasingly prevalent.

Library disasters can be caused by a number of possible events that are broadly categorized as either natural disasters or human-caused disasters. They include floods, typhoons, tsunamis, hurricanes, tornados, fires, earthquakes, landslides, mudslides, avalanches, volcanic activity, violent acts, and so forth. These disasters can bring damage to collections, equipment, and facilities and cause injury or death to library customers and employees. In some cases, librarians may receive warning that a disaster is imminent, but in most cases the disaster will strike without warning.

A 2005 survey conducted by Heritage Preservation of over 14,500 archives, libraries, societies, and museums found that 59% of respondents had collections damaged by light; 53% damaged by water; and 47% damaged by airborne pollutants. The study also found that 80% of the institutions responding did not have an emergency plan that included collections with a staff to carry out the plan.[1] ACRL's *CLIP Note #41: Emergency Response Planning in College Libraries*, a survey of small to mid-sized college libraries found that 75% of respondents had experienced an emergency, with several reporting multiple emergencies. Twenty-nine percent of responding libraries that had experienced a disaster reported that they did not have a plan in place to deal with the event. The most frequently cited disaster in that study involved water (61%), followed by weather (9%), and fire and mold (8% each) tied for third place.[2]

Awareness about the risk of a library incurring a disaster has increased since the tragic events surrounding Hurricane Katrina and the terrorist attacks on September 11th.[3] Based on the number of U. S. Disaster Declarations filed by states across America, not only is awareness of disasters increasing, but actual disasters are increasing.[4] A quick review of the library literature over the last couple of decades reveals that the number of articles and books written about the importance of disaster preparedness, response, and recovery planning is increasing as well.

About the Authors

Five years ago the University of New Mexico, University Libraries (UL), experienced its first significant disaster, a flood at the Centennial Science and Engineering branch library. Unfortunately, it was not the UL's last disaster. In a short 1 ½ years later a fire broke out in the Zimmerman Library, followed by a flood 1 ½ years after that. (For a description of those disasters see the case study section.)

The three authors of this book were extensively involved in the UL recoveries. Fran Wilkinson is the team leader of the UL's disaster response assistance team (DRAT), is the deputy dean of the UL, and also served as interim dean during most of the Zimmerman Library fire recovery. Linda Lewis coordinates collection development and management, and served as the DRAT associate coordinator for collections recovery during the Zimmerman Library recovery. Nancy Dennis is the associate dean for facilities and access services, and served as the DRAT associate coordinator for facilities recovery during the Zimmerman Library recovery. Fran, Linda, and Nancy, working with the DRAT, also initially compiled and continue to maintain the

UL's disaster plan. They know first hand what is required to successfully respond to and recover from library disasters. Throughout the recovery process, they turned to a number of colleagues, organizations, companies, books, and articles for guidance. Everyone was gracious and willing to share their expertise, wisdom, and advice. The outpouring of support from every sector was heartening. The authors intend this book to return some of that generosity by providing the reader with practical information about every step of the planning, response, and recovery process and by offering case studies from multiple libraries, each with different types of disaster experiences.

Organization of the Book

The *Comprehensive Guide to Emergency Preparedness and Disaster Recovery* is written primarily to address disaster planning, response, and recovery in medium to large sized academic libraries, experiencing moderate to large-scale disasters, but its content can be adapted for other situations.

The chapters are grouped into four parts, with an extensive appendix section. Part I addresses Disaster Preparedness with chapters on Disaster Prevention and Preparedness Planning; Writing the Disaster Preparedness, Response, and Recovery Plan; and Training for Disaster Preparedness and Response. Part II covers the Emergency Response with chapters about How to Respond When a Disaster is Imminent and How to Respond When a Disaster Strikes. Part III discusses aspects of Disaster Recovery and includes chapters on Collections Recovery: Working with Recovery Teams, Vendors, and Insurance Providers and Facilities Recovery: Working with Architects, Contractors, and Others as well as a chapter on Lessons Learned. Part IV presents seven case studies from six libraries, each by an author(s) who led or participated in the recovery at their library. The case studies include: California State University, Northridge: Sustained Upheaval: Rebuilding the Oviatt Library after the Northridge Earthquake; Colorado State University: Response and Recovery from a 500-Year Water Disaster; Tulane University: Hurricane Katrina; University of Hawaii at Manoa: Library Flood; University of Iowa: Flood; University of New Mexico: Zimmerman Library 2006 Fire That Led to the 2007 Library Flood: An Overview; and University of New Mexico: Zimmerman Library Fire: A Case Study in Recovery and Return of Library Collections. The Appendix features a Model Disaster Preparedness, Response, and Recovery Plan; a Model RFP for Disaster Recovery Services; and sections on disaster companies; journals; and societies and organizations. Also provided are an extensive bibliography and a glossary.

Notes

1. "Heritage Health Index" (Heritage Preservation, 2005). www.heritagepreservation.org/HHI/execsummary.html (December 3, 2009).
2. Marcia, Thomas, ed., *Emergency Response Planning in College Libraries* (Chicago: American Library Association, 2009), 7.
3. Ibid, 3.
4. Federal Emergency Management Agency (FEMA). http://www.fema.gov (October 1, 2008).

PART I: DISASTER PREPAREDNESS

Chapter 1

DISASTER PREVENTION AND PREPAREDNESS PLANNING

"By failing to prepare you are preparing to fail." — Ben Franklin

No one wants to think about a disaster happening in their library. At one time it may have been possible for librarians to expect that they could complete a long career without experiencing a major disaster; however, today a search of the library disaster literature will quickly dispel that hope for most librarians. In the last decade alone, academic libraries have experienced numerous disasters. These incidents range from relatively minor emergencies such as a water leak affecting only a small portion of the facility, to major disasters such as a flood or fire affecting the entire library facility. Even more extreme disasters such as hurricanes and floods impacting entire communities have been reported in the media more frequently in recent years. For example, using the search string "increase in natural disasters" in Google retrieves over four million hits.

Disasters come in many forms including floods, typhoons, tsunamis, fires, earthquakes, landslides, mud slides, avalanches, windstorms, hurricanes, tornadoes, mold outbreaks, pest infestations, human-caused violent behavior, and so forth. These disasters can potentially harm collections, facilities, library employees and customers in addition to disrupting library programs and services. Miller states, "It is human nature to hope that such situations will never strike, but such wishful thinking is no substitute for planning, which could ameliorate some of the worst aspects of disasters, even catastrophic ones."[1] For these reasons, having a comprehensive, frequently updated disaster preparedness, response, and recovery plan is critical to informing both library employees and the public, as well as to minimize the disaster's impact and to restore services and access to collections as quickly as possible.

The decision to produce or revise a library disaster preparedness, response, and recovery plan can be driven by either institutional or library administrators or by librarians in preservation, collection management, or other areas. If the decision comes from the library dean or director, usually a librarian is assigned to write the plan. If the idea comes from a librarian, then the library administration must be enlisted to support development of the disaster plan. Creating a comprehensive disaster plan requires an investment of human, financial, and time resources. The plan needs to have buy-in and support from employees in every area of the library as well as support from campus officials to ensure that the library's plan dovetails with the campus disaster plan. The library will have to work with and depend upon various campus offices in the event of a disaster.

Getting Organized and Ready to Write the Plan

When taking on the assignment of writing the library's disaster plan, reactions may span a wide range of possibilities. Emotions may range from enthusiasm about this great opportunity, nervousness about the amount of work involved, or near panic cause knowing where to start is difficult. Some librarians may feel all of those responses simultaneously. This section will describe the initial planning process that will enable the development of the library's disaster plan which includes reviewing the campus's emergency plan, securing support from the library's administration, appointing a disaster assistance response team, and conducting an environmental scan.

Review the Campus Emergency or Disaster Plan

Review the campus's disaster, emergency and/or safety plan when tasked with writing the library's first plan; revising an old, out-of-date plan; or revising a current, reasonably up-to-date plan. Due to the many recent crisis events taking place on campuses across the country, ranging from building damage to personal violence, almost all campuses have developed a disaster or emergency response plan. If your campus plan is not online or if it is password-protected for security reasons, contact the campus safety officer or police department to acquire a copy of it. Most campus plans will address overarching organizational priorities such as the general safety of students, faculty, staff and visitors and the campus infrastructure; however, they will probably not address the specific needs and priorities of the library. Work closely with the campus safety, police and fire departments to integrate the library's plan with existing plans. These offices can help identify regulations that affect the building, develop the disaster plan and ensure that the plans work together. In many cases, these offices can also help train library personnel about emergency preparedness and response. The purpose of the library's plan must focus on facilities, collections, and the people in those buildings.

Secure Support from the Library Administration

Developing a comprehensive disaster plan takes time and financial resources. The library's disaster response team must work closely with the library's administration to ensure that the administrators recognize the importance of developing a plan and that they support the work required. A plan will have limited effectiveness if it is not supported by the entire library, and the library administration should set the

tone by its commitment and financial support. The plan must be reviewed regularly, emergency response supplies must be purchased, and personnel must be trained. A plan is worthless if it is written and filed away; it must be kept current, which requires that the support from the library administration be explicit and ongoing. Setting a calendar for cyclical review and revision of the plan can be an organizational reminder to revisit the plan.

Every library faces more demands for time and money that it can meet. Be aware of the political and financial realities. Librarians responsible for facilities, collections, and safety must persuade the library administration, if those administrators are not already convinced, that disaster planning and prevention must be a priority among other vital needs of the library. Stress that planning and prevention can reduce the risks of loss and injury, making the library a safer place for people and collections. Planning and prevention can make the response and recovery less expensive and shorten recovery time. The costs of prevention are far lower than the costs of response and recovery. Acknowledge that the process of reviewing the physical condition of the library will undoubtedly identify things that need to be addressed; therefore, the needs will be documented and prioritized so that problems can be addressed in stages.

The library administration must provide visible support for the librarians responsible for the work of analyzing the status and needs of the library in preparation for compiling the disaster plan. An official charge to the individuals responsible for writing the plan should be prepared by the library's dean or director. Employees must be informed that disaster planning is a library-wide priority, and that the individuals who are writing the plan have the authority to request information, participation, and assistance from the rest of the library staff.

Budget. Creating and implementing a disaster plan requires time and money. The individuals who are preparing the disaster plan must work closely with the library administration to provide a budget for necessary expenses. During the initial stages of investigation and conducting the environmental scan, the major costs will be release time for library employees and for office supplies and copying. Hiring consultants to evaluate the library or assist in writing the disaster plan will usually engender additional significant costs for these services. The completed plan will require costs for copying and distributing in whatever formats are appropriate.

After the disaster plan is written, the costs will expand. Funds may be necessary for testing and training. Training on how to evacuate the building will not require additional money, but training to use emergency equipment such as fire extinguishers or to do basic preservation of collections could require payments to outside individuals or organizations. Some computer-based testing and training may be appropriate, but may require purchasing or leasing some types of software. The library must have basic emergency supplies within easily accessible storage locations. These supplies need to be inventoried and replaced as needed. Acquiring them and replacing them will be another category of expenses. Training and supplies must be a part of the library's annual budget, and should be considered as important as any other operating expense.

When a disaster happens, librarians may discover that they need items not included in the emergency supplies on hand. When writing the disaster plan, learn how items can be purchased while in the middle of a disaster. Know how minor and major expenses and purchases will be approved and processed within the library as well as within the larger organization. For example, who should be called on New Year's Eve to authorize a major purchase in response to a disaster?

Appoint a Disaster Response Assistance Team (DRAT)

Establishing a team that will respond to emergencies

is essential. This team is referred to in the literature under a variety of names including Disaster Response Assistance Team (DRAT), Library Emergency Response Team (LERT), Library Disaster Response Team (LDRT), and so forth. The team will respond to a library disaster and oversee its recovery and it will typically also be responsible for writing and revising the library's disaster plan. The library's dean or director will appoint the team members and charge the team. Library administrators and supervisors need to support the team members by adjusting their workload to allow them the time to carry out their duties on the team. The time required will vary widely depending on the size of the organization, the level of the planning process, and the extent of the disaster.

DRAT Member Characteristics

Identifying roles and responsibilities that need to be filled and matching the right library employees to meet those needs is critical to both writing the disaster plan and to a successful recovery. Prospective team members must have the right attitude and characteristics. They must be interested, enthusiastic, organized, flexible, adaptable, and willing to serve. They need to know the library and how it functions; meet deadlines and be prepared for meetings; be good listeners; respond quickly to questions; possess good interpersonal and communication skills; have the ability to see the big picture as well as being able to drill down into the finest details; and respect the abilities of other team members. While striving toward these lofty goals, they must not expect perfection in themselves or in others.

Team members need to be committed to staying aware of new trends and developments and participate in ongoing training to keep their skills current. For example, team members need to be aware of new or emerging services and products such as fire suppression systems, disaster recovery companies, technologies to treat damaged materials, and communication companies that can execute the library's emergency contact list when needed.

The individual who will lead the team must possess solid leadership, organizational, and communication skills. The leader must be confident, but never arrogant. This leader will need exceptional writing skills and sound organizational skills to lead the team in compiling the plan. This person must also be comfortable adapting to rapidly evolving situations that change as events unfold. The leader should be able to set an agenda, conduct productive meetings, and follow-up appropriately at every stage of the process from writing the disaster plan to the final recovery of any potential disaster and evaluation of the plan. This person must be able to prioritize and keep the team focused on the tasks at hand. The leader must listen well, ask questions with ease, solicit pertinent information, be able to make decisions quickly and not be defensive when second guessed, and be able to explain tasks to team members as clearly as possible. The team leader needs to have a calm temperament to help others remain calm—this will be challenging in the face of an emergency. Disasters can create tense situations, distractions, shock, grief, and conflict. The DRAT leader must be aware of the potential—even likelihood—of these heightened emotions, watch for them, and appropriately address signs of acute stress. The leader must not engage in conflicts personally and should help others to manage them or emerge from them quickly in a manner that will not distract the team members from their duties. The team leader should appreciate a sense of humor and, ideally, will possess one. In a crisis, everyone involved is likely to be more highly strung than usual and humor can help to reduce the tension.[2]

Who to Include on DRAT

Include not only administrative personnel on the team, but the people who have working knowledge of the library buildings, equipment, and collections. Be sure to know in advance any physical/health limitations that would curtail a potential DRAT member's involvement. For example, learn ahead of time if someone is sensitive to chemicals or smoke, if they have visual problems that make working in dim lighting difficult, if they have physical limitations that might make repeatedly climbing stairs difficult, and so forth.

DRAT should be a core team of people who have the knowledge to deal with various aspects of emergencies. To the greatest extent possible, try to match team members' functions with skills from their job assignments. These individuals need to possess some degree of leadership skill, the ability to make decisions under pressure, good verbal and written communication skills, emotional maturity, and the ability to avoid panic—at least publicly.

Depending on the size and complexity of the library and the nature of the emergency, the DRAT may consist of a relatively small core of individuals who perform multiple roles or the team may be quite large with team members having more narrowly defined roles. Team members should be prepared to take on additional roles outside of their normal roles in the event that other team members become incapacitated or they are otherwise unavailable to perform their assigned roles. The planning, emergency response, and disaster recovery phases will require differing levels of engagement for team members. For example, some team members will be more focused and commit more time during the emergency response phase while others will be more involved during the disaster recovery phase.

> **Disaster Response Assistance Team (DRAT) member roles might include the following:**
> - Library Dean or Director
> - DRAT Team Leader
> - Communications & Media Coordinator
> - Facilities & Security Coordinator
> - Human Resources Coordinator
> - Administrative & Financial Coordinator
> - Library Services Coordinator
> - Systems/IT Coordinator
> - Collections & Preservation Coordinator

DRAT Member Roles and Responsibilities

The roles and duties assumed by each of the DRAT members might include the following:

The Library Dean or Director determines the level of the library's response based on priorities and the scope of the disaster. This person works with the university media relations office and often serves as the library's primary contact with the media, approving all external communications. The dean or director is the library interface with the campus and the community at large. This person contacts donors, library friends, and other key supporters to provide initial information and regular updates regarding the disaster. The dean or director provides regular reports and updates to the provost and/or president or chancellor. This person may serve as the DRAT team leader, but more often the team leader role is delegated to a library administrator who will have the time to provide more hands-on leadership throughout the emergency response and disaster recovery process. Working with the administrative & financial coordinator, the library dean or director approves financial outlays.

The DRAT Team Leader coordinates all activities of the team. The team leader generally oversees the preparation and revision of the disaster preparedness, response, and recovery plan. The team leader coordinates the library's response to the disaster with members of the library's administration, the communications & media coordinator, and others as appropriate. The team leader also manages the recovery and salvage operations and other associated recovery activities. The team leader must be able to make decisions quickly in the middle of a disaster. This person is charged with staying current on recovery procedures by reading pertinent literature and attending meetings, workshops and conferences on relevant topics. In addition, the team leader may coordinate the ongoing training of the team. The team leader keeps notes on lessons learned and at the conclusion of the disaster, reviews and updates the plan as needed. If no disaster occurs, the team leader reviews the plan regularly (at least annually) to keep it current and works with the human resources or communications coordinators to keep emergency contact information up to date.

The Communications & Media Coordinator operates the library communication center. This person ensures that the communications center has necessary equipment and supplies to respond to the emergency, including a dedicated telephone line, fax machine, computer with Internet access, and basic office supplies. The coordinator may be the person who contacts the library staff with instructions when a disaster occurs outside of normal working hours. Working with the human resources coordinator, the communications & media coordinator may develop and maintain the phone tree containing contact information for staff. This person often contacts nearby libraries, consortia to which the library belongs, appropriate library organizations, as well as donors and friends of the library on behalf of the library dean or director. The coordinator may also be responsible for communicating with other campus departments and emergency services. In order to carry out these tasks, the individual responsible for communications coordination must have not only the office phone numbers and e-mail addresses for all the people who should be notified, but also the home and cell phone numbers and any alternate e-mail addresses. The communications & media coordinator may be the one who provides updates regarding the disaster on the library's Web site and on its informational telephone recording and may also prepare FAQ sheets or organize staff booths providing information about the disaster. Working with the library dean or director and the university media relations office, the coordinator liaises with the media, prepares press releases, and is the first point of contact or spokesperson for questions handled by the library about the disaster from external entities. In addition, this person may serve as the official recorder for documenting major decisions, activities, the time line, and other matters involved with the disaster, thus preserving the historical record. The coordinator may also serve as the photographer to help document the disaster and the subsequent recovery effort through photographs and film.

The Facilities & Security Coordinator will work with the campus police, physical plant and other emergency response personnel to stabilize the library's environment. This person must be familiar with the library building, infrastructure and systems as well as with library evacuation procedures. This individual must know the locations of the utility emergency shut-off controls, alarm system controls, emergency exits, and fire extinguishers. The facilities & security coordinator should be familiar with the library's emergency supplies and where they are located as well as knowing where larger, rarely needed equipment and supplies are located around the campus. If rodents, snakes, or other pests are hiding in damaged areas of the building, the coordinator will notify anyone working in the area that extra precautions will be needed. This person may also arrange for protective equipment, such as dust masks and respirators, as well as the training needed to use them safely. The facilities & security coordinator may also monitor the safety and security of disaster recovery workers as well as possibly arranging for water and food for workers when they are unable to leave the disaster site easily. This person may need to arrange for receipt of incoming and outgoing mail and other materials and for transportation and storage of materials. If the building is shared with any non-library entities, the coordinator will need to communicate with them about the facilities.

The Human Resources Coordinator will have several roles that evolve throughout the disaster response and recovery process. This person should work with the communications & media coordinator to keep an updated list of contact information for all library personnel, including home phones, cell phones, and alternate e-mail addresses. One initial role, in cooperation with the communications & media coordi-

nator, is to ensure that all staff are aware that a disaster has taken place and to understand where they are to report and what hours they will work. If some or all employees are covered by a bargaining union, the coordinator will need to know the union contract provisions and may have to work with human resources at the parent institution if these employees will need to work non-standard schedules. The human resources coordinator may be called upon to hire temporary staff quickly. Disasters create high levels of stress, grief and other emotions. Staff jobs will change at least temporarily and in major disasters, staff may be displaced from their regular work sites for months or even years. This coordinator will need to be aware of these reactions and situations, and may arrange for counselor assistance, training, and other needed support. In addition, this person will respond to the offers of assistance from the community and will coordinate any volunteers who are used. Libraries are typically a major employer of student workers. Since student employees do not receive any type of paid leave, the coordinator may need to work closely with them to find other positions on campus to mitigate their lost income.

The Administrative & Financial Coordinator will be the point of contact for all financial and contractual matters. At the onset of the disaster, the coordinator will work with the campus budget office and other campus offices to determine who has the authority to approve various expenses. Working with the library dean or director, this coordinator will either authorize and approve disaster response and recovery expenditures or work with other campus offices to accomplish this duty. The coordinator will oversee expenditures such as authorizing additional supplies and equipment purchases or rentals, working with the human resources coordinator to authorize temporary personnel expenditures, and may authorize recovery vendor invoices. This coordinator may also serve as the library's liaison to insurance investigators if the parent institution does not handle this process through a central campus office.

The Library Services Coordinator will plan strategies to provide post-disaster library services to customers after the disaster. If the entire library building must be closed, this person arranges for space in alternate locations to provide basic information, reference, and possibly interlibrary loan services. For example, library services may be temporarily relocated to another library on campus, to a classroom with Internet connectivity, or even to the campus student union building. Immediately after the disaster, this coordinator will work with the communications & media coordinator to develop basic talking points as well as more detailed information about the disaster.

The Systems/IT Coordinator initially will assess library systems to determine what damage the equipment, software, and data sustained. This person will lead the restoration of online services as quickly as feasible. In cases where the library building will be closed for some time, the coordinator will work with other library personnel to arrange systems access at alternative locations. If some staff will be temporarily working from home, the coordinator will consult with them to determine what equipment, software and connectivity may be needed. This person, working with the administrative & financial coordinator, may also determine the value of destroyed computers, servers, and other equipment and negotiate pricing for replacements.

The Collections & Preservation Coordinator (sometimes referred to as the Salvage Coordinator) assesses damage to the collections and directs triage efforts determining which materials can be saved as is, which require restorative treatment, and which are beyond restoration. This coordinator oversees the inventory of the disposition of each type of material and determines priorities for replacement and salvage. The collections & preservation coordinator may work with the insurance carrier to determine replacement value for lost materials. This individual is the point of contact with book, journal or other vendors during the process to replace lost items.

The coordinator may plan and manage the removal activities—pack-out—and the return activities—pack-back—of materials and also maintains an inventory of damaged and discarded materials.

Once the library administration has identified the roles and the responsibilities for each disaster response assistance team member and appointed the right people in the organization to fill the roles, the information should be included in the appendix of the disaster plan. This list of each committee member and their responsibilities will help to reduce confusion regarding who does what during an emergency or disaster.

Conduct an Environmental Scan

Before the newly appointed DRAT begins the process of writing the library's disaster plan, the team members should conduct an environmental scan of their library and campus community in order to determine the condition of their library. Some emergencies are completely unexpected and could not have been prevented. Many others can prevented or at least be less damaging if steps are taken at an earlier time to identify and correct problems. Environmental scans are meant to review the organization, gather information, analyze the data and evaluate the options.

The environment within and surrounding a library is complex. Conducting an environmental scan enables DRAT members to gather information about all aspects of the physical building, the collections and equipment, and the manner in which the building is used. If the library has done a previous environmental scan or disaster plan, start by reviewing those documents to learn what conditions have been previously identified. Schedule meetings with staff in all areas and ask them about existing and potential problems. Involve student workers as well. They notice situations and potential problems while shelving or performing other tasks that staff may not have seen. Do not assume that DRAT members can recognize all problems, or that all problems have been documented and reported. Ask a friend or colleague from another library to walk through the library building in order to identify areas of concern that may have overlooked. The local police and fire departments may be available to review the library building for vulnerabilities. Their expert advice can be extremely helpful in identifying vulnerable areas and determining which areas should receive immediate attention.

The scan should consider the structure of the building, the security of the building and safety of the people using it, the area surrounding the building, the security of technological resources and equipment, and how collections are handled. The following are some examples of the types of questions that might be asked to gather the information needed for the environmental scan:

Structural building conditions:

- Are there any known problems such as places where water always leaks when it rains? Have there been previous problems with cracks in the walls? Have there been past disasters that could have damaged the building's structural integrity? Are there stains from water leaks? Are there areas of cracking plaster or missing ceiling tiles? Are there any leaks from toilets, sinks, water fountains, pipes, etc? Is the roof inspected regularly?
- Where are the controls for utilities? Can you shut off the water or power if necessary?
- Are the utilities adequate? Do they meet the current code requirements? When you added computers, did you verify that you did not overload electrical wiring capacity? Are you using overloaded extension cords or surge protectors instead of adding appropriate electrical outlets? Are all electrical panels easily accessible?
- If your building has historical, cultural, or architectural significance, do you have documentation of the building, interiors, and its furnishings? What are the restrictions involved in its use or renovation?

- Does any portion of the library have classified materials? What protocols determine access in case of an emergency?
- Are any doors always kept open? In fires, closed doors may limit the spread of the fire or smoke; installation of fire doors that automatically close when alarms are activated may be required.
- Are library building plans current and accurate? Do they show all alarms, exits, rooms, doors, etc?
- Are there areas in the building that are isolated, where library personnel are present infrequently? If so, what security is provided for that area?
- Are all building keys or access codes accounted for?
- Are chemicals stored correctly? Some libraries may have specialized materials for photographic collections; most will have cleaning supplies. All materials that could be hazardous must be stored safely.
- Are there signs of pests, insects, rodents, mold, or mildew?
- Are any areas of your building undergoing renovation? Be aware that construction will create dust that can set off alarms, and sparks that can create fires. Be aware of what is being done, and know that any construction may have unanticipated side-effects or consequences.
- Is there a current inventory of all furnishings and equipment? Does it include documentation of the value of these items?

Alarms and other emergency response capabilities:

- Are there alarms for fire, smoke, carbon monoxide, humidity, temperature, motion detectors and water leaks? Are all alarms checked regularly? Not all areas will need the same level or type of alarms. For example, a rare book collection may need more extensive alarm systems than the general book stacks and employee work areas.

- Can the alarms be heard in all areas of the building? Do they also have visual and auditory warnings? Do they automatically notify police or fire personnel?
- Are there sprinkler systems or fire suppression systems located in the library? Are they checked regularly?
- Are there sufficient fire extinguishers? Are they checked regularly?
- Can emergency response vehicles reach the building readily? Are non-emergency vehicles parked too close to the building's exits, making access difficult for fire trucks?
- Are the exits clearly lit and marked? Are any of them blocked with boxes or equipment? Are emergency exits properly secured in order to allow use only in case of emergencies?
- Are there accurate, visible signs to assist people in exiting the building?
- Are escape plans prominently displayed that provide information vital to fire safety, escape, evacuation, and rescue of the facilities occupants? (See ISO 23601:2009, "Safety Identification—Escape and Evacuation Plan Signs" for more information.)[3]

Surrounding the library building:

- Are there trees near the building with branches that could damage roofs? Could falling branches break windows?
- Is landscaping near the building? If so, does the water drain away from the library rather than seep into the foundation?
- Are all gutters, eaves and drains open and clear?
- Is construction scheduled nearby that could result in interruptions in delivery of utilities, increased dust, broken water mains, or blocked traffic?
- Are statues or pieces of art or other works of cultural significance located in the library building or on the library grounds? Do they belong to the library or to another campus organization? Is documentation of the condition and value of these items available? Are they on loan from another institution? If so, is a loan agreement on file? How are they insured? Is there photographic or visual documentation of these works?

Communication and technology:

- Do cell phones work in all areas of the library building? If not, investigate technology that will boost the signals, or get alternative devices such as short-wave radios.
- Are all work phones programmed with the emergency numbers for campus or city police?
- Are the technical systems, local databases and financial information backed up regularly? Are the servers in a secure location?

Small equipment:

- Is there a kitchen? What types of appliances exist in the kitchen?
- If there is a microwave, coffee pot, or stove, never leave it unattended while it is in use. Burning popcorn can set off fire alarms or possibly start a fire. Make sure all coffee pots, stoves, and space heaters are turned off when not in use. Is there a fire extinguisher near cooking equipment?
- Are space heaters or fans permitted in the library? If so, they should have UL (Underwriters Laboratory http://www.ul.com/global/eng/pages/) approval. Limit use to space heaters with automatic shut-off switches to prevent potential fire in case they fall over.

Collections:

- Are current inventories of library collections, realia and art on file? Does documentation exist for both the original costs and the current replacement value of special items?
- Are boxes stacked so high that the top boxes are difficult to reach? If so, move them because boxes stacked in this manner can fall and injure people.
- Are materials, boxes, carts, or equipment blocking doors or halls? If so, move them and store them appropriately.

- Are materials shelved on the floor? If so, move them because they will be damaged if a flood occurs. Use shelving that has a raised platform as the bottom shelf.
- Are materials located on the very top shelves? In the event of a water leak, the materials will be damaged more than might have happened if there had been an empty top shelf that shielded the books. In addition, the fire suppression system may not work properly if it does not have sufficient clearance.
- Is all shelving braced properly so that it will not fall over? If not, correct the situation.

Correcting Existing Problems to Prevent a Disaster

Preventative measures and addressing existing problems can either prevent a library disaster or help the recovery process progress more quickly, allowing the library to resume services sooner. After conducting the environmental scan and gathering all the information available regarding conditions in and around the library, DRAT members must prepare a report analyzing the results of the scan and a compilation or listing of all problems identified in the scan. The DRAT report provided to library administration will suggest options and potential solutions regarding the problems and concerns identified in the scan. Other units such as the campus risk and safety office, the physical plant department, or the central landscaping unit should also be apprised of these issues.

Most environmental scans identify some situations that can be corrected easily and inexpensively. Recommendations to resolve other more costly and complex problems identified by the scan can be implemented in stages as funds become available. Try to move from awareness to mitigation, or when possible complete prevention, as quickly as can be achieved given library and institutional priorities and funding capability.

Facilities. Preventing a problem is almost always easier and less expensive than recovering from a disaster. Some potential problems with the facility can be addressed easily. For example, identifying the locations of hazardous chemicals and addressing their proper storage should be fairly straight forward for most libraries and involve little if any expense. Other situations may be more complicated, but still fairly affordable. For example, if the library is surrounded by extensive landscaping that sometimes causes water to pool at an entrance, a project to completely re-do the entire landscaping may not be reasonable. Obtaining a supply of sand bags or requesting that a small retaining wall be built to protect the area might be an acceptable solution, at least for the short term. Building a small wall will be much less expensive than replacing large areas of flooring and shelving, or dealing with the problems that would result if someone fell because of the wet sidewalk. Still other situations, such as the need for fire suppression systems or additional shelving to reduce overcrowding, will require substantial time and money.

DRAT members should identify the approximate costs of the various options for resolving the problems. Some problems that are too expensive to resolve quickly will be reported and should be included in the long-range planning for the library and its parent institution. The DRAT report will include documentation about the problems and recommendations for resolving them.

The library will need to keep records of the problems that have been identified and report them to appropriate officials and departments in the parent institution. When campus administrators, such as the provost and president, change, the library administration should provide the new administrators with information concerning the library's needs. This step will be especially important if a disaster occurs, because senior campus administrators will be called upon to answer questions not just regarding the disaster itself, but about any circumstances that could have prevented or mitigated the disaster. For example, in the case of a fire in the library, knowing that the library had asked for funding for a fire suppression system, but that the request was in a university deferred-maintenance queue, would be helpful information for central administrators to have when answering questions from the public, legislators, donors, the media, etc. Assisting these people in providing intelligent, accurate information is always imperative to avoid confusion and misinformation.

Collections. When a disaster happens, one of the first questions will be "What was the value of the lost items?" If the library does not have an accurate, current inventory of all its collections, equipment, and furniture, that question is very difficult to answer. A thorough inventory is extremely time-consuming, especially for a large library, but all libraries should have at least the basic information about their facilities and collections. DRAT members should identify any existing lists and records to determine what needs to be updated. An inventory of the rare books should include documentation that clearly identifies the items and their value. If a complete inventory of a large circulating collection has not been done recently, a map of the collection that shows what is in each area should be created. Look at the shelves and approximate how many volumes are in a section of shelving. Take photographs of sample shelving areas to document density and number of shelves per section. Then, for example, if a disaster happens on the 2nd floor in the southwest corner and 10 sections of shelving are lost, librarians will know what call numbers were involved, and approximately how many pieces were lost.

Communicating concerns. Some library organizations may be reluctant to have problems exposed to the parent institution. The library administration may feel that publicizing problems will reflect poorly on library management. Some libraries may believe that the parent institution will never provide funds for major expenses to correct problems. Some parent organizations may think that the library's concerns are not valid, or believe that other campus needs must take a higher priority. The DRAT team leader may need to meet privately with the library dean or director to discuss the reasons behind the reluctance. The team leader must stress to the library's administration, and the library administration should stress to the parent organization, that preventative measures are cost effective, averting some disasters completely and significantly minimizing others.

Planning a New Building or Remodeling an Existing One

When renovating an existing building or planning a new building, work closely with campus planning and construction personnel in order to incorporate features that will protect collections, personnel and buildings. Architects and contractors will know the requirements of the current building codes, but librarians will know current library operations and needs. Working together will result in a building that can minimize the impact of potential disasters.

Prepare a checklist of questions that will assist the library team and other members of the building design team to design library spaces that are safe and secure. Refer to these questions often during the various stages of construction. The checklist is intended to serve as a valuable tool for planning and programming existing and new library buildings or spaces.[4] Some areas to consider when preparing the checklist include alarms, fire suppression systems, exits, areas of refuge, emergency shut-off controls for utilities, and so on.

Alarms are created to alert occupants to emergencies, and they need to be located throughout the building. All areas need smoke and fire alarms that are easy to see and hear. Some areas may also need water detection systems, humidity monitors, carbon monoxide detectors or motion detectors. Work with architects and contractors to install the proper alarms in the various parts of the building.

Fire suppression systems such as wet-pipe sprinklers and fire doors that can be closed in case of an emergency can control or limit the spread of a fire. Work with architects to design features that will reduce the damage caused by a fire or smoke. Several different types of fire suppression systems are available. Work with the fire department and the campus safety office to identify the best systems for the library.

Emergency exits must be clearly marked, well-lit, and easily accessible. During renovations, make sure that exits remain clear and that any temporary emergency exits are clearly identified. When designing new library buildings, include easy access to the facility for emergency vehicles. If the fire trucks cannot get close to the building, a great deal of damage could be sustained before the fire is extinguished.

In an emergency, elevators usually will not function except when overridden by authorized emergency response personnel. Individuals who cannot be evacuated from the building via the stairs need to have areas of refuge where they can remain until emergency personnel can rescue them. Designated refuge areas are often located in stairwells. Procedures to help people reach these areas of refuge and to notify emergency responders about their locations must be included in the library's evacuation plans.

Knowing how to turn off the utilities quickly during an emergency situation can be vitally important. Many buildings now have the ability to shut off the water from outside the building as well as shutting off the supply to specific fixtures. Make sure that the controls are readily accessible for authorized personnel, that library personnel know what to do, and that emergency responders know where the controls are located.

Construction and renovation activities nearly always have unexpected interruptions and unanticipated side-effects. Construction may create dust that can set off fire alarms if the work area is not properly contained. Renovation can lead to the discovery of issues that must be corrected such as outdated wiring. A spark can start a small fire. Workers can leave doors open, allowing dust to get into the HVAC system. Removal of flooring can lead to the discovery of flooring material containing asbestos that must be contained or removed. Construction trucks can block emergency access for emergency personnel and fire trucks. Working closely with the project managers on a daily basis is necessary in order to track the schedule and to keep library personnel safe and informed.

The library should have input on any contracts for renovation of an existing building or for building a new facility. Attempt to negotiate items that protect the library during these projects. Insist that security and management personnel from the contractors be present whenever construction is being done, that construction areas should be sealed off by temporary walls and plastic to reduce the spread of dust, and that the construction company manager and the library facilities manager check the progress daily to verify that work is progressing safely.[5]

Conclusion

Disasters—either major or minor—happen somewhere every day, usually with little or no warning. The librarian whose career will not include a disaster of some kind is very rare and very lucky. All librarians and all libraries should be prepared, while continuing to hope that they will be one of those few that escape unscathed. Library administrators must support the creation of a disaster response team and the writing of a disaster plan. Evaluating the library's existing circumstances can result in the correction of problems that would lead to major emergencies in the future. Designing new buildings and renovating existing ones to include safety and security measures will prevent or reduce problems later. Planning is the core responsibility of a disaster team and is essential for the successful operation of the library.

Notes

1.   William Miller, "Natural Disasters in the Academic Library," *Library Issues* 28, no. 3 (2008): 1-2.

2.   Heritage Preservation, *Field Guide to Emergency Response* (Heritage Preservation, Inc., 2006): 12.

3.   "Safety Identification—Escape and Evacuation Plan Signs: ISO 23601:2009." (International Organization for Standardization). http://www.iso.org/iso/catalogue_detail?csnumber=41685 (October 10, 2009).

4.   William W. Sannwald, *Checklist of Library Building Design Considerations* (Chicago: American Library Association, 2009), vii, 181-183.

5.   Barbara Buckner Higginbotham, "Practical Preservation Practice: Managing Emergencies: Small Construction Projects," *Technicalities* 19, no. 9 (1996): 1, 12-14.

Chapter 2

WRITING THE DISASTER PREPAREDNESS, RESPONSE, AND RECOVERY PLAN

"Divide each difficulty into as many parts as is feasible and necessary to resolve it." —Rene Descartes

Well-constructed disaster preparedness, response, and recovery plans can minimize security and safety concerns in addition to reducing the risk of loss of life, facilities, and collections;[1] however, writing such a plan can seem overwhelming. Information is available in books, articles, and bibliographies in print and on the Internet, as well as through various consultants, institutes, agencies, library and other professional associations, and other entities to aid libraries in developing a plan. In addition, a plethora of programs, workshops and seminars are offered at library conferences and through other continuing education and professional enrichment venues.[2] New topics and fields that deal with disaster planning and recovery are rapidly emerging, including emergency control management, business continuity management, systems interruption and recovery management, incident management and the like.

In fact, so much information is available—some of it contradictory—that many people become even more confused about where to begin. Although most plans cover similar topics, a library's plan should be customized and tailored to that library's specific needs. In writing a first plan, adapting another library's plan, or using a fill-in the blanks sample plan is a good starting point. See Appendix A for a model disaster preparedness, response, and recovery plan. Contacting other near-by libraries that have disaster plans can also be a good beginning strategy. Many state library associations have a committee or interest group that can assist or make referrals to professionals in other libraries to assist with writing the initial plan. As an existing plan is

revised and updated, consider adding topics or sections to make it more comprehensive and library specific.

One way to simplify the overwhelming process of writing the first plan or extensively revising an existing plan is to divide the process into a series of stages. Preliminary steps to take before the actual writing begins may include gathering necessary date and conducting research. Next, organize the key elements to be covered, articulate the steps, and project a time line for evaluating and revising the plan. Once those steps have been outlined, writing the plan should be somewhat less daunting.

Before Beginning to Write the Disaster Plan

As discussed in Chapter 1, review any existing campus disaster, emergency and/or safety plans, garner the support from the library's administration, have a disaster response assistance team (DRAT) in place with each member's role carefully delineated, conduct an environmental scan, and address any disaster prevention issues. Once these actions are completed, the next step is to articulate the purpose for the library's specific plan, determine who will write and distribute the plan, and agree on which major categories will be covered in the plan. Addressing these often overlooked steps in the planning process can help to avoid misunderstandings and confusion later.

Determine the Purpose of the Disaster Plan

Having a clear, agreed-upon understanding of the library's purpose for its plan will enable the individual or team who will write the plan to deliver a useful, understandable, well-organized document that meets the needs of the people who will use it. The purpose should include the following elements:

To assign responsibility. Who is responsible for which tasks both initially during the emergency response, and later during the disaster recovery stage? Most libraries will assign a team of individuals to deal with disasters. Individual team members must understand their roles in the team and their attendant authority and responsibility. In addition to each team member's primary role, the team member will usually have one or more back-up roles.

To provide communication. Communication is perhaps the single most important objective in any disaster plan. Provide communication between, among, and across the right people at the right time. Without it chaos will abound and costly mistakes will occur. Everyone involved in a disaster, at every level, is responsible for providing the best, most complete communication possible.

To establish contact with contractors and consultants who specialize in disaster response. Negotiating a contract with local and national disaster recovery services before a disaster strikes saves time and cost later. Faster response to an emergency can minimize damage to and loss of collections and equipment. See Appendix for a Model RFP for Disaster Recovery Services.

To document emergency response processes and procedures. For example, the plan should state where the library's temporary command center will be established, how library employees and others will receive the latest information about the disaster, how library services will be provided, etc. Documentation after the disaster occurs should include dates and actions associated with the disaster and its subsequent recovery as well as photographs and other visual and audio recordings.

To anticipate possible disasters and develop measures to reduce their impact. Prepare a list of possible disasters and instructions about how to respond to them, keeping in mind the local environment. For example, an earthquake is more likely to occur in California, while a hurricane may be more predictable in the gulf coast area. Identify ways to minimize the damage to collections and to provide alternative services to customers using various disaster scenarios.

To ensure that library services are reestablished as quickly as possible after a disaster. For example, the library may arrange for temporary space for staff in another building or for reference services to be performed in a central location on campus such as a classroom with Internet connectivity, the student union building, or another centrally located venue.

To identify the location of disaster supplies and equipment. These items should be kept on hand or in a known, readily available location and documented in the plan. All supplies should be reviewed on a regular basis and refreshed as needed. Some larger or expensive equipment may be housed offsite, be available through another campus department such as the physical plant, or be provided as part of a contract with a recovery vendor.

To establish priorities to determine the order in which collections, equipment, and other materials are to be rescued and removed from damaged facilities. Know the value of the collections and locations of equipment, such as the server hosting the library's catalog. Prepare a prioritized list of the collections and equipment to be salvaged. Include descriptions and locations of these materials so that rescue workers not familiar with them can locate and identify them. Include this information in the plan.

To solicit feedback at multiple levels to evaluate the effectiveness of the library's disaster plan. The DRAT members should provide feedback on the plan. Each time the plan is used, even for small water leaks, it should be reviewed for potential improvement. Feedback from others on campus as well as other librarians who have experienced a disaster should be solicited. All contact information should be reviewed and updated on a regular, scheduled basis.

Who Should Write, Revise, and Distribute the Disaster Plan

Although some discussion continues about whether a person or a team appointed by the library's administration is best to write the library's disaster plan, conventional wisdom suggests that having a team develop the plan is prudent. Matthews et al. conducted an analysis of literature and other sources regarding disaster management and emergency planning in libraries and concluded that "Disaster plans should always be a joint effort, composed by a small team and not left to one person…. Teams help to provide a range of experience and expertise so that the plan does not have one particular focus."[3]

Libraries may choose to have their DRAT members draft their disaster plan, with review and final approval from the library administration or dean or director. Typically, the DRAT team leader is designated to guide the team throughout the process of writing the plan, just as this individual coordinates the team's efforts during a disaster. DRAT members are knowledgeable about the library's facilities, collections, and staff. These individuals were chosen to serve on DRAT because of the expertise that they bring to the group due to the library positions that they hold, such as preservation officer, communications specialist, facilities manager, human resources coordinator, collection development manager, IT director, as well as senior members of the library administration.

The DRAT members are also well suited to revise the plan as needed. These are the individuals who will be called upon to execute the plan in case of a disaster and as such, they will be in the best position to accurately gauge which parts of the plan work well and which areas should be revised. They have a vested interest in ensuring that the library has the best plan possible to meet its specific needs. The DRAT members are also tasked with keeping abreast of the latest literature and trends in the disaster preparedness, response, and recovery field. In addition, they will also engage in ongoing training to maintain and enhance their knowledge and skills in case of an emergency. Thus, they are most appropriate to revise the plan as needed.

Once the plan is written and after each major revision the library's dean or director or other designated library administrators will review and approve the plan. After the plan is approved it will be distributed widely. The library administration and library public service areas should have either electronic access to a copy of the plan or a paper copy of it. DRAT members should have a paper copy of the working plan at work, at home and in their car. They should also save the plan on their Net-Book or other electronic device and to one or more document storage systems such as Google Docs. As existing technologies improve and as new ones emerge supporting larger text files, other non-paper based, green options for accessing the plan will be preferred. Team members should keep their copies in a readily available location where they can access it at a moment's notice. They should also review the plan often so when a disaster strikes they are familiar with what to do and how to locate the information that they need quickly.

In addition to these obvious people, provide a copy of the library's plan to the central campus emergency planning group or committee, as well as to the person (such as the Provost) to whom the library reports. The library's plan should have not only the support of the library administration, but the support of appropriate individuals in central campus administration as well. Also, other campus units such as the campus police, physical plant, and the local fire department should receive a copy. Offering a tour of the library facility to appropriate staff in these units to familiarize them with the library prior to a flood, fire or other event can save time, frustration, and possibly lives in the event of an emergency. Encourage campus police, physical plant staff, firefighters to visit the library at least annually and whenever these key personnel have changed or when there have been changes in the library facility. Their review of and input on the plan could be particularly valuable.

What Key Elements Should Be Included in the Disaster Plan

The contents of a disaster preparedness, response, and recovery plan will vary. Each library will determine what is most useful for its plan. The literature and most library organizations provide numerous examples of content that a library may wish to include. Most library plans include some version of the following sections:

- Introduction and Statement of Purpose
- Contact Information—including who to call and what to say, identifying both library emergency contacts and contact information for other campus offices
- Disaster Supplies—list of supplies and locations, both internal and external
- Salvage Priorities—for collections, equipment, and other materials
- Informational/Fact Sheets—with instructions about building evacuation as well as best practices about how to respond to various kinds of disasters and measures to reduce their impact
- Appendix
  » List of Disaster Response Assistance Team (DRAT) members, including their roles and responsibilities
  » Building floor plans including exits, areas of refuge, locations of fire alarms and fire extinguishers, utility shut-off valves, salvage priorities, etc.
  » Contact information for local, regional, and national disaster recovery and other related vendors, noting if any of these vendors has a pre-contract arrangement with the library or parent institution; also include contact information for insurance providers, if appropriate
  » Forms for documenting the disaster

  » Links to campus emergency, safety, and disaster plan(s)
  » Environmental scan or library building survey
  » Distribution, review, and update schedule for the plan

Many libraries choose to prepare more than one version of their disaster plan. These versions may include a master version, a working version, and a version that does not include personal contact information.[4] The master version of the plan contains all the information discussed above. The master version might also include disaster response reports, and miscellaneous notes. A copy of this version is typically held in the dean's or director's office or with the DRAT team leader.

The working version of the plan—distributed to the DRAT and appropriate library service points—is a portable, stripped-down, utilitarian copy that includes only the key categories such as contact information, the location of supplies, salvage priorities, fact sheets, and the building survey and floor plans. Another version for the public, without information such as the home and cell phone numbers of the campus central administration and library staff, may be prepared for informational purposes. For example, this version of the plan might be shared with interested individuals, such as general library staff and other libraries requesting a copy of the plan to use as a model for creating their own plan.

The library administration will need to determine if their disaster plan will be located on its Internet or Intranet Web site. Some libraries choose to make their plan public on their Web site, but do not include contact information such as individual's home or cell phone numbers. They may choose to either provide the master version of their plan with the introduction and appendix or a shortened version. Other libraries include the master plan with home and cell phone contact information on a password protected library Intranet. Still other libraries choose to only provide the plan in paper format. Regardless, best practices suggest that all members of the DRAT have a paper working copy available both at work and at home. During a disaster DRAT members may not have easy access to a computer with working, wireless Internet capability. Also, since disasters often strike outside of normal working hours, DRAT members should keep a copy of the plan at home in a readily available location.

Writing the Disaster Plan

Perhaps the most common mistake that DRAT members can make is trying to develop a disaster plan that attempts to cover every possible detail and scenario. Attempting to do so is a monumental and likely hopeless task that will consume far too many resources, and with the need to maintain the normal business of the library such a process is likely to lose all momentum and be abandoned. Disaster plans must have flexibility as their defining feature. Remember at every stage to keep the planning process fairly simple and straightforward to avoid preparing overly complicated, detailed, and expensive disaster recovery plans.[5]

Once the library administration has clearly articulated the purpose for the library's specific disaster plan and who will write and distribute it, and the DRAT members have agreed on the key elements to be covered, the DRAT is ready to begin gathering data and writing the various sections of the plan. These major areas will include contact information, disaster supplies, salvage priorities and informational/fact sheets with instructions about how to respond to various kinds of disasters as well as an annotated floor plan section located in the appendix of the disaster plan.

Communication with the Right People at the Right Time

"If you do nothing else right, you must have near-perfect communication, following a disaster. Otherwise you will be managing two disasters."[6] Any library that has experienced a disaster would no doubt agree that good communication is essential when responding to and recovering from a disaster of any size.

A disaster communication plan will include at a minimum a contact list, sometimes referred to as a phone tree, containing contact information for disaster response assistance team members, library administrators and other campus officials. A comprehensive communications plan may also include information about where the library's disaster command center will be established with alternative locations in case the first choice is not available; a central telephone number to call that will provide regularly updated information to library staff and customers; where to set up information booths or signage such as sandwich-boards around campus announcing locations for both physical and virtual alternative library services; where and how public services such as reference will be provided as well as where to pick up interlibrary loan materials; and how customers can regain personal items left in the library when it was evacuated.

The communication plan may also include a section listing people and organizations to be notified of a disaster such as the various consortia and organizations to which the library belongs, major acquisitions vendors, and institutional and private delivery companies, as well as donors and other friends of the library. The plan should include a form for documenting the disaster including major decisions, activities, the time line, and other matters pertaining to the disaster. The communication plan should identify and provide contact information for local or regional experts who can provide assistance. For an example of a city cooperative approach, see the San Diego/Imperial County Libraries Disaster Response Network (SILDRN)[7] or the Los Angeles Preservation Network (LAPNet).[8] The plan should also discuss how to deal with the media if this service is not provided by the parent institution. Even if requests by the media for information are not handled by the library, write a brief blurb about the disaster and follow up with small updates on the recovery process for the state library association newsletter, appropriate library discussion lists, and public Web sites. Having this information readily available will help the library's dean or director, the communications & media coordinator, or other campus officials respond quickly and accurately to inquiries by the press or other media.

Preparing the contact list. Identify all individuals who need to be contacted in the event of an emergency. This list will include library administrators, DRAT members, key members of the campus central administration, as well as any managers of other operations that share the library facility such as tutoring services, commercial coffee shops, etc. Contact anyone who should not learn about the disaster from the media such as significant donors or political representatives. Prepare a sample script of what information will be told to the individuals who are contacted. Include what has happened, how they will get additional and/or updated information, and where and when they should report for work.

Disasters often happen at night, on weekends, or holidays—times when people are not at work and may be difficult to reach. The contact list or phone tree should include multiple methods of contact for each person including home, cell, and work phone numbers as well as pager numbers for those few individuals who still have them. Include work and personal e-mail addresses for each person. Also include instructions about posting information on Facebook and other social networking sites that are reserved for library employees. Despite the ubiquity of computers, some people still do not have a computer with Internet access at home or they do not regularly check their e-mail from home. The plan should include ways to confirm that the intended person received the communication.

Only in fairly small libraries will one person be assigned to call and/or e-mail every contact on the list. Develop a plan for who will call whom and designate a back up for each person tasked with making the calls in the event of illness, vacation, or some other reason. No matter how detailed the contact plan is, something will likely go wrong. The most important aspect of the process is to remain flexible and communicate with others when problems arise.

Disaster Supplies

The disaster plan should include an inventory of all disaster related supplies, where they are located, and a time line for reviewing and refreshing them. Lists of recommended supplies for libraries abound in the literature and on the Internet, including the Federal Emergency Management Agency (FEMA)[9] and Homeland Security Web sites.[10] The exact supplies required will vary by library depending on its size, type, geographic location and environment. Larger libraries will need greater numbers of supplies and specialized libraries will need more focused supplies. Supplies needed for unique materials can be found on the Library of Congress[11] and National Archives Web sites.[12] Depending on the environment where the library is located, having additional or supplemental supplies on hand such as plastic or poly sheeting, i.e. Visqueen®, in areas where water leaks or flooding are more prevalent, may be advisable.

Regardless of the type of library or its location, having basic supplies readily available in multiple locations can ameliorate the impact of small emergencies like roof or water leaks. Emergency supply kits such as the Rescubes® and its slightly larger counterpart ReactPaks® are convenient and designed to be compact and easily portable. They can be purchased from various library supply vendors. See Appendix B for a list of companies. These kits are a good, basic start to ensuring that supplies are readily available when and where they are needed. As a matter of basic safety, supplies like first-aid kits and flashlights should be provided to all public service areas.

Having a more extensive selection of supplies available centrally at one library branch on campus can significantly reduce damage in even a moderate disaster. Store supplies in containers that are portable, such as in large, clean plastic trash containers with wheels or provide fold-up cubes on wheels to make transporting them easier. Where feasible, several libraries may enter into a collaborative arrangement and agree to store a cache of supplies in a central area where they can be shared. This arrangement can prove especially advantageous for smaller libraries that are geographically near one another such as those in a major metropolitan area. In a larger or more wide-spread disaster, appropriate supplies are useful to rescue workers once they are allowed back in the building after a fire, major flood, earthquake, etc.

The plan should also include locations to obtain additional or specialized supplies and equipment. Some larger or expensive equipment such as industrial fans, large humidifiers or dehumidifiers, portable generators, water pumps, or fork lifts may be housed off-site or be provided by a campus department such as the physical plant. Be sure to determine which emergency equipment is available on campus, as well as which equipment can be rented or provided by local vendors, and include that information in the disaster plan. In the event of a major disaster, the library may hire—or have pre-contracted with—a large national commercial disaster recovery company that will arrange for nearly all supplies from latex gloves to fork lifts.

All supplies should be labeled with the date they were purchased, and they should be checked on a regular basis, preferably quarterly but at least annually, and refreshed as needed. When storing supplies, consider arranging them into more frequently and less frequently used categories and labeling and storing accordingly.[13] For example, paper towels are likely to be used more often than plastic sheeting.

As part of the supply inventory in the disaster preparedness, response, and recovery plan the library should include a time line for checking supplies to determine if supplies are still viable and specify a replacement plan. In the event of an emergency ensure that batteries for flashlights are not expired, rubber gloves and/or booties are not crumbling from age, and plastic sheeting to shield books from water is not used up from a previous water leak. Staff need to know where the supplies are located and have access to them. All efforts should be made to avoid stumbling around searching for a flashlight when the lights go out or discovering that the locked supply closet key is assigned to someone who is not available.

Core supplies. Core supplies that most libraries should have consist of command center supplies, general supplies, first aid supplies, safety supplies, and specialized supplies for major disasters. Some duplication of supplies within the categories may be needed. For example, the command center may be located at a considerable distance from the location where the safety supplies may be located. Core supplies include:

- Command Center Supplies:
  » Identification—badges and/or badge holders, brightly-colored vests
  » Communication and safety devises—cell phones, walkie-talkies, megaphone/bullhorn, whistles, air horns, caution tape
  » Documentation—tape or digital recorders, disposable digital cameras, cam-corders and supplies, portable flash drives
  » Technology support—regular and heavy-duty extension cords in various lengths, surge protectors
  » Miscellaneous—folding chairs, blankets, emergency snacks and bottled water, cash and/or credit card access
- General Supplies:
  » Paper and writing implements—clip boards with paper, larger paper for signs, posterboard, pens, pencils, markers
  » Tape—transparent tape, duct tape, masking tape, caution tape
  » Cleaning and sanitary supplies—paper towels (without dyes that can leave stains),

white towels, rags, sponges, mops, brooms, buckets, garbage bags, all purpose-cleaners, antimicrobial soap, alcohol-based hand cleaner, eye wash, toilet paper, disposable wipes, wet-dry shop vacuum

- » Scissors, utility knives with extra blades
- » Tools such as screwdrivers, hammers, nails, crow bar
- » Plastic crates, folding wheeled carts, wheeled garbage cans
- » First Aid Supplies, per ANSI Z308.1-2003:[14]
- » Adhesive tape
- » Adhesive bandages and sterile scissors
- » Antiseptic
- » Burn treatment
- » Gloves
- » Sterile pads
- » Absorbent compresses
- » Bandages in variety of sizes
- » And may also include: eye covering that can be attached, eye wash, cold packs, rolled bandages

- Safety Supplies:
  - » Lighting—flashlights with extra batteries, small temporary hanging lights
  - » Protective clothing (in various sizes)—rubber or nitrile rubber gloves, disposable latex gloves, booties to cover shoes in various sizes, safety-toed boots, protective coats/smocks, disposable overalls, plastic aprons, hard hats, protective safety glasses and eye covering
  - » N-95 respirators (which many people call dust masks, but these respirators are fitted to the face and have double elastic bands to hold them in place) and NIOSH-compliant respirators
  - » Object protection, drying, packing and salvage—plastic sheeting in large rolls, unprinted newspaper to protect surfaces and wrap materials, blotting paper, waxed

paper, transparent tape, packing tape, scissors, clothes line and pins, cardboard sheets and boxes, plywood

- Moderate to major disaster—supplies typically not stored in the library (supplied by recovery and salvage vendors or available through campus physical plant or other campus areas):
  - » generator, industrial fans, large humidifier/dehumidifier, large water pumps, portable devices that measure moisture in solid objects such as Aqua Boy®, pallets, fork lift, crane, freezer space, extensive temporary emergency lighting, sandbags, etc.

Salvage Priorities

Salvage priorities typically include collections, equipment, and files. The salvage priorities section of the library's disaster plan will be highly specific to each library's situation. Collections vary greatly from library to library, and equipment or files that are deemed vital to one library may be less important to another library. Priorities change over time as well, so priorities must be reviewed and updated to remain current.

The member(s) of DRAT, typically the collections & preservation coordinator, will work with other collections personnel, library IT personnel, and library administrators to determine the salvage priorities for their library. These key people must agree on what will be the top priority materials to be salvaged and what items will be a lower priority or not rescued at all. The larger the scale of the disaster, the more important these priorities become. Identify first, second, and third level priority for collections, equipment, and files to be rescued as well as develop a list of collections that have the lowest priority to be salvaged. Remember that overarching priorities must be determined for the library as one entity, not just for each department within the library.

Writing the salvage priorities section of the disaster plan can be one of the most daunting areas to develop. A good place to start is with the library's collections, which typically represent one of the parent institution's most valuable capital assets. Even broader, when the university is the flagship for the state, the library's collections may be the most valuable asset in the state. Begin by determining what collections the library owns. Do inventories exist of all the collections of the library including books; journals manuscripts; papers from famous authors, politicians and the like; media including CDs, DVDs, photographs, maps, artifacts, art; and so forth? Libraries can use their online public catalogs to identify most items that are owned; however, some items may not be in the catalog. Inventories of some special collections such as rare leather bound or autographed books, art exhibition catalogs, manuscripts, scrapbooks, papers, artifacts, and the like may be available in in-house databases or only in paper card catalogs or accessions lists. In order to prioritize collections to be rescued the library must know everything it owns.

Once there is a clear picture of what collections are owned, determine the value of these collections. This information will be required to submit an insurance claim for destroyed items. If the value of the collections is not known and the team does not know how or where to get such information, meet with the campus risk management, accounting unit, or other appropriate office to assist with valuing the collection. The institution or the state may have values already established. If not, librarians and risk management personnel may work together to determine an agreeable formula for valuing the library's book and journal collections, such as multiplying the number of volumes by some dollar figure that includes the average cost of a book or journal with the other associated costs for replacement—reordering, cataloging, processing, etc.—built into the figure. Rare or unusual items such as some special collections or art will typically require an appraisal by a trained professional.

Libraries will typically place a higher priority on collections that are unique, difficult or impossible to replace, areas of specialty for their campus, items of local, regional, or historical importance, and/or highly valuable. Other aspects to consider when assigning priorities for salvaging collections include whether the material is available in another format. For example, many government documents are available online, and if the library is not a federal depository, it may consider not replacing the paper copy.

Determine which materials require immediate attention to avoid their destruction such as leather-bound books, vellum or clay-coated paper (such as used in many art books), or water-soluble inks. Consider whether rescuing the items and restoring them would cost more than replacing the items. Although all collections owned by the library have some value, consider identifying collections that are a last priority for rescuing because either they can be replaced for less cost than restoring them or because they no longer have significant importance to the campus curriculum.

Collection priorities are the most involved to develop because providing collections is central to the library's mission and they constitute the most valuable asset the library owns; however equipment to provide access to the library's increasingly electronic collections cannot be overlooked in the salvage priorities section of the library's disaster plan. The library's IT unit should maintain an inventory of all public and staff PCs, printers/scanners, library servers, and other technology. The library should also maintain a list of equipment such as security systems for collections like sensitizers/desensitizers for materials checked-out at circulation, in-house binding equipment such as spiral binding machines, fax machines, and so forth. Also, each piece of equipment should have a value assigned to it on the inventory list.

Furniture is another asset to include in the salvage priorities. While most library furniture is fairly generic and can be easily replaced, some furniture may be historical, rare, custom-made or have some other significance that makes it a priority to be rescued.

Some library files may also be important salvage priorities. Know what is legally required to be kept. If the library is the official archive for some types of documents, those will obviously be a high salvage priority. In some libraries, administrative files such as financial records, contracts and memoranda of understanding, and personnel files may be considered a major priority; however, with advances in technology, now many such files are kept electronically, backed-up, and/or not housed onsite at the library. Increasingly, these types of paper files are no longer necessitating the same salvage priority that they once held.

After the first, second, and third level priorities and the lowest level priorities are determined, include in the plan how to identify and where to locate these items. Floor plans should be illustrated with the locations of the salvage priorities, but include as many specific identifiers as possible in the narrative form in the plan such as: the second server from the top on the rack in the southwest corner of room 323 on the third floor of the Jones Library or the fore-edge books on the first range of shelving in the special collections unit, room 119 in the northeast corner of the Martinez Memorial Library. Some libraries have identified unique or valuable items—especially equipment or files having high salvage priorities—by marking them with a colored dot to aid rescue workers in identifying them.

Insurance. Maintaining current inventories of library collections, equipment, and facilities and working in conjunction with the institution to agree on valuation of the collection are critical steps to prepare the library to deal with insurance claims after a disaster.[15] In almost every case, the library is insured as part of the parent institution's policy. Although typically insurance coverage is negotiated through a central purchasing office and claims are handled by the risk management unit for the institution, the DRAT and other library administrators

should know which company insures the institution and examine the insurance policy to understand coverage and requirements. Know the amount of the deductible and who pays it (the library or the parent institution); whether fine arts, artifacts, and highly valuable items are covered or if they require a rider or separate policy; what documentation will be needed to file a claim such as formal appraisal for rare items; what kinds of incidents are covered such as arson or floods and are there any restrictions; and any other information that may be specific to the local area or situation as part of the planning process before the disaster strikes.

Possible Disasters and Measures to Reduce Their Impact

A comprehensive disaster plan should address the various types of emergency situations or disasters that a specific library might face. Remember, one cannot anticipate every scenario and trying to do that is generally unproductive. Start this part of the planning by preparing a list of possible disasters, keeping in mind the local environment. For example, a tornado is more likely to occur in some parts of Oklahoma or Kansas, while a fire may strike anywhere. Identify ways to minimize the damage to collections caused by various hazards, provide basic instructions for assessing damage and triaging materials, and anticipate methods to provide alternative services for customers using various disaster scenarios.

In any emergency, obviously the safety of people should come before collections and facilities. To ensure that the evacuation plan functions efficiently and effectively, it should be tested periodically, be evaluated regularly, and have enhancements made when practical.

Disaster plans should include basic information about how to address each emergency scenario that is relevant to individual libraries. Create tip sheets for these scenarios providing clear and concise step-by-step instructions. These instructions should highlight the problem and describe immediate action steps as well as salvage steps to take later in the recovery process. Remember, the point of these scenarios is to provide information that is clear and easy to follow. Do not try to include every conceivable scenario or every possible response, action, or remediation step.

Building Survey and Floor Plans

Depending on the severity of the disaster and for safety reasons emergency responders such as firefighters and police may not authorize DRAT members to enter the library for hours or even weeks or months after the event. Most emergency responders will not be familiar with the library facility, even if they have been given a tour or used library services at some previous time. They must rely on floor plans. Once the initial emergency is contained, recovery workers and library staff must use floor plans to identify which materials to rescue and in what order of priority. For these reasons, up-to-date floor plans that are clearly coded for easy interpretation are vital to the library's successful recovery operation.

As part of the planning process, DRAT should conduct at least a basic building survey and preferably a more complex environmental scan. See Chapter 1 for suggestions on aspects to consider when preparing an environmental scan. DRAT members will use the input provided in the building survey or environmental scan to annotate building floor plans with the information needed to assist emergency responders and recovery personnel. The member(s) of DRAT who are assigned this task, typically the facilities & security coordinator, will begin by obtaining an accurate set of the floor plans for each area of the main library and all branch libraries as well as any offsite archival or storage facilities.

Each of the floor plans should be annotated with the following information:

- Structural Building Markers—the location of entry/exit points, windows, stairwells, elevators, shut-off controls for utilities, drains, sump-pumps, etc.

- Safety Systems and Equipment—the location of master fire alarm panel, fire detectors, fire alarm annunciators, hand-held fire extinguishers, fire suppression systems including the type of system (water-based or other), water detection equipment, carbon monoxide or other detectors, as well as emergency areas of refuge for people remaining in the building
- Supply Caches—the location of all disaster supply cabinets, closets, or other storage areas; also note the location of all flashlights and first aid kits
- Salvage Priorities—the location of collections, equipment such as computers and servers, and other materials to be salvaged and the order of priority for rescuing them
- Areas Surrounding the Building—on plans depicting the façade of the building, note the location of landscaping, gutters, external drains, fire hydrants, or other objects that emergency responders might need to know about

Since information on multiple aspects of the library's systems and collections will be illustrated on the floor plans, libraries should color-code the information and provide a detailed legend for all codes so that emergency responders can quickly identify the information they need.

Embedding Disaster Awareness in the Library's Organizational Culture

Unless a library's disaster plan is current, accurate, widely available, and supported by the parent organization, it is completely worthless. Moreover, the value of the plan cannot be realized unless everyone in the library knows that a disaster plan exists, knows where it is, and knows how to use it. Educating the staff about the importance of disaster preparedness can take time unless the organization has recently experienced some kind of disaster. Trying to build support for a plan that deals with a hypothetical future that may never happen is difficult since the plan lacks immediacy. Unfortunately, only a disaster in or near the library will convince some people that they have a responsibility to plan and prepare. DRAT members must work with the staff in all areas to share information about preparedness, prevention and response, answer questions, and help staff to understand the importance of planning for a disaster.

Fire and evacuation drills are important, but training needs to go beyond that. All personnel should be trained so that they can act effectively in an emergency. Many libraries offer first-aid training, or training in the use of fire extinguishers. Some organizations conduct digital scenarios or role-playing exercises in order to train staff how to respond. Others use scenarios in training meetings, where the group can ask questions such as "If the main exit were unavailable, how would you evacuate our building?" Explore all options to increase awareness in the library. Different people possess different learning styles—visual, verbal, and hands-on—so try to develop as many training delivery methods as practical and effective. See Chapter 3 for more information about training.

Evaluating and Revising the Plan

Unless the disaster preparedness, response, and recovery plan is current it has little value and will provide only limited assistance in an emergency. Given the critical importance of the plan, library administrators must create a mechanism to ensure that the plan is evaluated and updated regularly, specifying who will update it and how often it will be reviewed.

Evaluating and revising the library's plan will typically be the responsibility of the DRAT and the process is usually led by the DRAT team leader. Some parts of the plan may remain fairly stable, while others will need more frequent revision. For most libraries, all parts of the plan should be reviewed at least annually or after a disaster occurs. DRAT members may find it useful to create a checklist containing each section of the disaster plan— contact information, supplies, salvage priorities,

etc.—and the date by which each part should be evaluated and revised if necessary. Instead of using a paper checklist to accomplish these tasks, DRAT members may find it more efficient to set up a shared drive so that any DRAT-authorized member can access an electronic file of the disaster plan and make updates at any time. These updates can be flagged for later review, comment, and approval by other DRAT members. Regardless of the method used to update the plan, the date that the section was last reviewed and the date that any needed changes to the disaster plan were distributed to plan holders should also be recorded.

Generally the part of the disaster plan that will change most frequently is the emergency contact information. People change jobs within the library, resign and move to other jobs, retire, and change their phone numbers. To ensure that contact information is current, the DRAT team leader will usually ask the human resources coordinator or the communications & media coordinator to verify contact information and update it monthly. As personnel databases become more sophisticated a mechanism may be installed that will automatically generate updates when an employee's information changes.

Disaster supplies will need to be monitored and checked on a regular basis, preferably quarterly, but at least annually. As part of the supply inventory section of the disaster plan, the library should include a time line, with specified dates, for checking supplies to determine if they are still viable. The plan should include a mechanism and budget for replacing supplies such as expired batteries, dried-out plastic or rubber items, and so forth as well as for replacing any items that have been used during a previous emergency.

Salvage priorities for collections, equipment, and other materials may not change as often as contact information, but they should be revisited at least annually. Many library disaster plans were written with an emphasis on print collections. These plans need to be updated with greater emphasis on recovery from unplanned interruptions to electronic services. In addition, the systems/IT coordinator for DRAT should participate in reviewing salvage priorities for equipment. As technology evolves, equipment salvage priorities will change. Avoid wasting the precious time of emergency workers by making sure that items on the salvage list are still priorities.

Informational/fact sheets containing instructions about the building evacuation process as well as best practices about how to respond to various kinds of disasters and measures to reduce their impact typically change less often than the other sections of the disaster plan; however, they too should also be reviewed annually.

For some libraries, building surveys and floor plans may not change significantly for many years; however, they still need to be reviewed at least annually, not just when significant renovations occur. Even minor changes can make a major difference when responding to a disaster. Moving a door or a range of shelving or repurposing a room or office can create confusion for emergency rescue workers, delaying action and thus endangering people or causing increased damage to facilities. In addition to structural changes, floor plans should be kept up to date to depict the location of fire extinguishers and fire alarms.

Information in the plan's appendix may become outdated. For example, new preservation techniques may emerge, disaster response vendors and contractors appear or disappear, insurance coverage may change, training opportunities may present themselves, and so forth. All this new information should be incorporated into the disaster plan.

Conclusion

Writing a disaster preparedness, response, and recovery plan is a daunting process for most librarians. The process requires significant time, and human and financial resources; however, no library should be without one. Most disaster plans amass information on whom to contact and how to reach them, where recovery supplies are located with a time line for reviewing and refreshing them, salvage priorities, information on best practices when responding to various kinds of disasters, and annotated floor plans to assist emergency response personnel. While the type of disaster plan and the specific information included in it will vary slightly by library, having a clear, concise, comprehensive, and easily accessible plan that is regularly evaluated and revised as needed is critical in the event of a disaster. A well-constructed disaster plan will guide the actions of the disaster response assistance team, reducing response time and minimizing the impact of many disasters.

Notes

1. Diane Lunde and Patricia A. Smith, "Disaster and Security: Colorado State Style," *Library & Archival Security* 22, no. 2 (2009): 111.

2. Julie Todaro, *Emergency Preparedness for Libraries* (Lanham, MD: Scarecrow Press, 2009), 77-78.

3. Graham Matthews, Yvonne Smith, and Gemma Knowles, *Disaster Management in Archives, Libraries and Museums* (Farnham Surrey, England: Ashgate Publishing LTD, 2009), 123.

4. Stephen Henson, "Writing the Disaster Response Plan: Going Beyond Shouting Help! Help!" *Proceedings of the 9th Annual Federal Depository Library Conference, October 22-25, 2000* (Washington, D.C.: FDLP Desktop, 7). http://www.access.gpo.gov/su_docs/fdlp/pubs/proceedings/00pro28.html (October 10, 2009).

5. Brian D. Voss, "What Would Ozymandias Think About Disaster Planning?" *EDUCAUSE Review* 41, no. 2 (March/April 2006): 76-77.

6.   Camila Alire, Personal Conversation with Fran Wilkinson, Albuquerque, NM, May 1, 2006.

7.   San Diego/Imperial County Libraries Disaster Response Network (SILDRN). http://orpheus.ucsd.edu/sildrn/ (October 10, 2009).

8.   Los Angeles Preservation Network (LAPNet). http://www.usc.edu/org/LAPnet/ (October 10, 2009).

9.   Federal Emergency Management Agency (FEMA). http://www.fema.gov (October 10, 2009).

10.   Department of Homeland Security. http://www.dhs.gov/index.shtm (October 10, 2009).

11.   Library of Congress. http://www.loc.gov/index.html (October 10, 2009).

12.   National Archives and Records Administration (NARA). http://www.archives.gov (October 10, 2009).

13.   Todaro, *Emergency Preparedness for Libraries*, 106.

14.   American National Standards Institute, First Aid Kits - ANSI Z308.1-2003. http://www.ansi.org (October 10, 2009).

15.   Lunde and Smith, Disaster and Security, 111.

Chapter 3

TRAINING FOR DISASTER PREPAREDNESS AND RESPONSE

"Excellence is an art won by training and habituation." —Aristotle

All libraries include education as one of their core missions. Beyond instructing library customers on how to access library collections, programs and services, education should include training for library employees on new technologies, collections, policies, and procedures as well as training that enables library employees to respond effectively to emergencies including disasters. Employees who are able to react appropriately to work-based emergency situations may help to minimize the extent of the damage and perhaps save lives, facilities, equipment, and collections.

The Critical Importance of Disaster Preparedness and Response Training

Training library staff in how to prepare for and respond to a disaster serves two fundamental goals: to enhance the confidence of the staff responding to a disaster and to identify gaps or deficiencies in the library's disaster preparedness, response, and recovery plan.

Training provides employees with the skills to react instinctively to emergencies when they do not have time to consult the library's disaster plan. Emergencies can quickly develop into major crises. Training can prepare staff to respond without panic and can give staff the tools to handle situations confidently when these employees absolutely must perform under pressure.

The process of designing and offering training sessions will keep the disaster plan current and fresh in the minds of library staff. In addition, it may reveal gaps in the library's disaster plan and identify sections of the plan that need improvement. For example, when conducting an evacuation drill, employees may discover that a recent addition of shelving obstructs sight of emergency exit signs.

Implementing Disaster Preparedness and Response Training

For any training program to be successful, library administrators and supervisors must provide ongoing support of training for library employees by explicitly communicating the importance of training through both words and actions at all levels of the organization—they must "walk the talk." Administrators lead by example by attending the training sessions and requiring that all personnel participate in the training program. They can work to create a culture that encourages staff participation and establishes the benefits for the individual as well as for the organization.[1] The importance of active participation in the library's training offerings—including disaster preparedness and response training—cannot be over-emphasized.

Attending disaster training should become part of every employee's job. While more advanced and/or specialized training may be provided to the library's disaster response assistance team (DRAT), basic disaster training should be provided to all library employees. Special training sessions should be conducted during any renovation or remodeling projects as well as after the projects are completed.

Supervisors should work together with employees to develop their annual goals and identify needed training to ensure high quality performance in the event of a disaster. Successful completion of identified training would become part of the employee's performance evaluation.[2] In addition, training on emergency procedures and disaster preparedness and response ought to be part of the orientation process for all new library employees. Conduct training sessions shortly after employees are hired, and repeat them after employees have become more settled in their assignments and work areas.

Everyone can benefit from training—administrators, DRAT members, managers, librarians, student employees, volunteers, and custodians. Emergencies often happen outside of normal business hours. Training is imperative for staff covering night, weekend, and holiday shifts so that they will be prepared to handle emergencies. For example, employees in the library at midnight need to know how to respond appropriately to emergency or disaster situations because most library administrators are not on campus at that hour to take charge. Ideally, every library employee regardless of status or rank is responsible for watching for potential disasters and knowing how to respond to them correctly.

Types of Disaster Preparedness and Response Training

Emergencies and disasters in libraries involve people, facilities and collections. The library's disaster preparedness and response training program should include procedures for evacuating everyone from the library building including customers with special needs, training in first-aid, security of facilities and equipment, and preservation of collections.

Safety. The safety of all people in the library comes first; therefore, training for library employees should include protocols for evacuating the library building and administering basic first-aid. All library staff must know the basic protocol for evacuating the library building in case of a fire alarm, flood, human-created violence or any other

emergency. Public service or facilities staff are typically the ones assigned to oversee the evacuation process, ensuring that both library customers as well as other staff have vacated all areas of the building. Evacuation training must identify alternative evacuation routes. For example, if a fire is on the north side of the library, staff must know if there is an exit through the south side of the building and how to access it. This training should include actual evacuation drills.

Once the library's customers and staff have been safely escorted from the library and entrances have been secured to prevent customers and staff from re-entry, employees must know what to do next. For example, are library employees at liberty to leave the area? If so, when do they need to return? Whom do they need to contact? Is there a designated location for staff to gather to await further instructions? In addition to procedures to evacuate the building of all library customers and staff, safety training should include identifying locations for library employees to meet to await further instructions and a verification process to determine that they reached their designated rendezvous location. If library employees work in multiple departments such as catalogers who also work in public services, they must know the evacuation routes for both areas, and know which rendezvous location they should use.

Some libraries appoint a person, sometime referred to as a safety warden, for each unit or each floor of the library to oversee the evacuation of employees in their area. In this instance, procedures would be established for staff to check in with the safety warden (or the back-up) at a predetermined rendezvous point, to ensure that all staff have exited the building. Procedures will vary among libraries, but establishing some type of protocol in advance can resolve confusion during and immediately after an evacuation. This sounds very obvious, but a large building may have several evacuation routes and multiple potential rendezvous points. All staff need to know the procedure to follow.

Most libraries provide basic first-aid training for their employees, especially for public services staff. The library's DRAT members should also be trained to administer first-aid. While such training is never a replacement for emergency medical professionals, it is an increasingly important skill for library employees to possess.

Ask the central campus administration about institutional policies and available training in this area because policies and regulations will vary. Ideally, the library should have employees trained in basic first-aid available at all times the library is open. If the library has portable defibrillators, staff must be trained in their proper use. Some libraries do more extensive training, providing full CPR (cardiopulmonary resuscitation) and AED (automated external defibrillator) training. If the library's parent organization has emergency personnel who can respond rapidly, such training may be prohibited or not considered to be a high priority. If the library facility is more isolated, the need for personnel who can administer first-aid may be a critical need.

The training required for library staff to operate or wear specialized safety apparatus will vary by institution. For example, some institutions mandate a health screening and completion of a training workshop to wear N-95 respirators (which many people call dust masks) or to wear other NIOSH-compliant respirators. To operate some types of equipment certification or licensing may be required. Check to determine what types of training, certification, or licensing is needed prior to encountering an emergency situation or disaster.

Facilities. After the library customers and employees have been safely evacuated as a result of an emergency or disaster, the security of the library facility itself must be addressed. Library administrators, building managers and members of DRAT should know how to use emergency equipment and supplies such as emergency weather radios or fire extinguishers (although employees should never place themselves in danger by attempting to use equipment rather than leave the premises). They should receive training concerning the location and operation of emergency controls for utilities and emergency systems such as alarms and fire suppression systems. When new preservation or emergency equipment is acquired, the staff should receive instruction on its use as soon as possible. Employees need to be properly trained to handle any chemicals such as those that might be used in cleaning or in library preservation labs. All staff should have training about basic computer security. They must know what options exist to save and securely back up information that they are responsible for maintaining. The library or campus information technology departments may provide such information. If so, they should share it widely in all ongoing software/hardware training sessions as a matter of responsible computer use. Knowing data storage options whether on portable flash drives or on network devices is important, but not to be determined in the middle of an emergency. Storage devices may be listed in the Salvage Priorities section of the disaster preparedness, emergency response, and disaster recovery plan and IT personnel should be familiar with the safe removal of those devices if time allows during the evacuation.

Collections. Some library staff, including DRAT members, must be trained in collection preservation techniques.

"Historically, the Libraries have turned to the Preservation Lab for the coordination of response and recovery operations. In designing an in-house disaster training program, the emphasis was on developing familiarity with the initial response procedures so that every staff member felt comfortable handling emergencies or disasters as part of a team or by themselves. We also wanted staff to be able to handle all levels of activity, as most incidents were small such as a wet newspaper delivered on a rainy day, or damp books returned by students from a variety of mishaps."[3]

In case of a disaster involving water, many people may be needed to assist in the preliminary triage of damaged collections. Staff who have received basic disaster preparation and response training will be more able to identify materials that can be readily salvaged. Larger libraries need to arrange for more extensive training in conservation methods.

Scheduling Disaster Preparedness and Response Training

Scheduling training is always challenging. Identifying a time when most library staff can attend training while providing coverage to keep at least minimal library services such as circulation and reference open can be difficult. In addition, identifying and reserving an appropriate training venue can pose complications. For example, fire extinguisher training is typically done in an outside location such as a parking lot or other open space. Training in preservation for collections may require the use of a sink or large workspaces. Specialized training must be scheduled at a time when the required area is not in use, but during hours when staff are available. Balancing these competing time constraints is not an easy task.

The time periods required for training vary by the type of training desired. For example, training for handling emotions during a disaster, stress reduction, or book handling can last from an hour to half a day. A basic first-aid and preparedness training offered by the American Red Cross may require only 1½ hours to conduct while their full first-aid, CRP, and AED training may last a full day.

To facilitate training participation by all assigned employees, multiple sessions of training should be offered at staggered days and times. In a large organization disaster preparedness and response training might need to be repeated over several months to ensure that everyone who needs training has the opportunity to receive it.[4] Training must be repeated at intervals in order for people to remember details. Most disaster training should be scheduled annually. Some training, such as building evacuation drills should be scheduled more often, perhaps quarterly or at intervals mandated by the parent organization. Specialized training, such as the certification programs for first-aid training offered by the American Red Cross, must be repeated at specified intervals in order for staff to remain certified.

Budgeting for Disaster Preparedness and Response Training

Library administrators are responsible for identifying ongoing funding for the disaster preparedness and response training program. Too often, due to shrinking library budgets, training funds are the first to be cut; however, informed and knowledgeable employees are pivotal to the success of the library. Every effort should be taken to avoid funding cuts for library training programs.

Specific costs for the disaster preparedness and response training program will vary depending on the type of training. For example, the only costs in evacuation drills are the costs of the staff time and interruption in services. Many types of training will require that supplies be purchased; however, these costs should not be extensive. When training is offered by the parent institution, costs may be minimal. Outside groups such as the American Red Cross may be relatively inexpensive, depending upon your location. Fees for national groups such as the American Institute for Conservation of Historic and Artistic Works will be more expensive if the trainers must travel to the library.

Resources Providing Disaster Preparedness and Response Training

The library's parent organization may offer emergency preparedness and response training as well as safety training. Sometimes campus health and safety divisions, fire departments, or campus police will create training workshops for libraries on how to handle emergencies. Some organizations may provide additional training courses that highlight potential risks and promote prevention such as stress reduction, injury prevention, and various other health and safety offerings.

Regional consortia or organizations such as the American Institute for Conservation of Historic and Artistic Works (AIC),[5] Western States and Territories Preservation Assistance Service (WEST-PAS),[6] the Northeast Document Conservation Center (NEDCC),[7] or regional library networks such as Amigos[8] or Lyrasis[9] offer courses or publish materials about preservation techniques. The American Library Association (ALA) provides information on the need for training in several documents on their Web site.[10] The Federal Management Emergency Agency (FEMA) provides a guide for business and industry containing information about emergency management that includes safety information as well as information related to specific hazards.[11] The American Red Cross provides extensive information regarding safety training options. The American Red Cross Web site includes information on training options for adults and children, emergency preparedness techniques, disaster supplies recommended to have on hand, and so on.[12] Local Red Cross agencies often have their own Web sites that provide information about the training that they provide with costs, schedules and contact information. They typically offer a variety of training that includes basic and advanced first-aid, CPR (cardiopulmonary resuscitation), and AED (automated external defibrillator) as well as a wide range of other safety training.[13] See the Appendix of this book for additional information about societies and organizations that provide assistance.

Methods Used in Disaster Preparedness and Response Training

Learning styles varying considerably from person to person. For example, some individuals learn well from role-playing exercises; others prefer a more structured lecture-style approach and others prefer more individualized online sessions. When identifying the most effective methods of training, consider the type of instruction best suited to meet the needs of the audience being trained. An evacuation drill that requires staff to leave the library and meet at an assigned location is the best way of testing that capability. Assembling all staff in a room and lecturing them about the exit doors will be much less useful. Such evacuation drills are comparatively short, and result in minor disruptions of services. Conducting a full-scale practice in which all library services are moved to another facility is too complicated, disruptive and time-consuming to be practiced as part of emergency evacuation. Obviously, identifying and conducting training that is more dynamic than lectures and less extreme than full-scale relocation of all library services is critical to respond successfully to an emergency or disaster. There are a variety of team building and decision making exercise scenarios that can be adapted to fit library disaster training needs. Consult with library administration, the potential audience, and those who will conduct the training to identify the best options for training methods.

Another effective strategy is to schedule meetings with individual groups to discuss the library's emergency and disaster plans. Create scenarios in which a member of DRAT presents a hypothetical disaster and leads the group in a discussion of options. Ask facilities managers to address a problem such as a broken water pipe in the basement that has soaked the carpet for 10 feet around the area. The group should identify how they should react and who should be notified. As the group identifies potential solutions, they may also identify challenges; such discussions can help planning teams identify where the library may be vulnerable.

The published materials on emergency preparation, disaster response, first aid, and preservation of materials are extensive. Training sessions can provide library staff with core reading and video materials. *Library conferences and societies frequently offer training on various aspects of disaster prepara-tion and response and on preservation techniques. Ask your colleagues in regional groups about such possi-bilities.* See the Appendix of this book for selected resources.

In addition to the more traditional training methods, some companies have created games that include disaster scenarios which can be used for training purposes. See Disaster Game[14] or Stop Disaster Game[15] for examples. *Virtual worlds such as Second Life[16] can be used to create training scenarios. Many companies and organi-zations have begun using such virtual worlds in order to conduct training that would be too ex-pensive or too dangerous to do in an actual physi-cal environment. Second Life is a web-based environment in which users can create environ-ments and visit worlds created by other users. Companies and organizations are using Second Life to test situations that would be too expen-sive or hazardous to attempt in the real world.[17] Second Life does require fast computers, high bandwidth, and considerable time to fully learn the system. Because conversations in Second Life can be overheard by others in the virtual envi-ronment, detailed information concerning build-ing security should not be included.[18]* Presently, virtual environments offer considerable poten-tial, and equal drawbacks, for disaster training. DRAT members should learn about develop-ments and keep their library administration in-formed about options.

Evaluating the Disaster Preparedness and Response Training Program

Emergency and disaster preparedness and response training cannot be a static process. Training topics and sessions need to be evaluated regularly for effec-tiveness by soliciting feedback from participants. Just as libraries are constantly changing, training must be a continual process. Changing circumstances in the library may require different kinds and/or more frequent training. For example, if the library is un-dergoing a remodeling project, specialized training to address potential hazards or identify new emergency exits from the building should be required.[19] Use the feedback from the evaluation process to revise the library's disaster response training program as well as the disaster preparedness, response, and recovery plan.

Conclusion

Training and planning for emergencies must have the explicit support of the library's administration and become part of the library's organizational culture. The library's disaster preparedness and response training program should include evacuation of the library building, training in first-aid, security of facilities and equipment, and preservation of col-lections. Training should be offered frequently and evaluated appropriately to fulfill obligations of safety for library staff and customers. All staff must partici-pate in appropriate training in order to improve their personal safety and security as well as enhance the ability of the organization to deal with emergencies and recover from disasters.

Notes

1. Frances C. Wilkinson and Linda K. Lewis, "Developing a Safety Training Program," *Library & Archival Security* 21, no. 2 (2008): 81-82.
2. Ibid, 83.
3. Diane Lunde, "Preservation: Staff Training for Disaster Response," *Colorado Libraries* 34, no. 4 (2008): 29.
4. Wilkinson and Lewis, Developing a Safety Training Program, 82-83.
5. American Institute for Conservation of Historic and Artistic Works (AIC). http://www.conservation-us.org (No-vember 16, 2009).

6. Western States and Territories Preservation Assistance Service (WESTPAS). http://westpas.org (November 16, 2009).

7. Northeast Document Conservation Center (NEDCC). http://www.nedcc.org (November 16, 2009).

8. Amigos. http://www.amigos.org (November 16, 2009).

9. Lyrasis. http://www.lyrasis.org (November 16, 2009).

10. The American Library Association (ALA). http://www.ala.org/ (November 16, 2009).

11. Federal Management Emergency Agency (FEMA). http://www.fema.gov (November 16, 2009).

12. The American Red Cross. http://www.redcross.org (November 16, 2009).

13. Wilkinson and Lewis, Developing a Safety Training Program, 81.

14. Disaster Game. http://www.stopdisastersgame.org/en/home.html (November 16, 2009).

15. Stop Disaster Game. http://www.stopdisastersgame.org/en/home.html (November 16, 2009).

16. Second Life. http://secondlife.com (November 16, 2009).

17. Kristine S. Condic, "Using Second Life as a Training Tool in an Academic Library," *The Reference Librarian* 50, no.4 (2009): 338.

18. Ibid, 345.

19 Wilkinson and Lewis, Developing a Safety Training Program, 83-84.

PART II: EMERGENCY RESPONSE

Chapter 4

HOW TO RESPOND WHEN A DISASTER IS IMMINENT

"It wasn't raining when Noah built the ark." —Howard Ruff

Library leaders prepare for emergencies and disasters in a variety of ways depending on the type of disaster and whether they have prior warning of its approach. Disasters in academic libraries comprise a number of possible events broadly categorized as either natural disasters (sometimes referred to as acts of God) or human-caused disasters (sometimes referred to as man-made disasters). However, even these historically accepted categories are becoming blurred to some extent by the changing nature and growth of cities with diverse building patterns impacting water flow and drainage and affecting a slowly shifting topography. Some forest fires are started by humans, but when they burn for miles, are affected by other factors, and spread to buildings they are sometimes viewed as natural disasters. Thus, some disasters historically considered natural might also be considered human-caused.[1] Nonetheless, these two general categories prevail when discussing disasters at a macro level.

Numerous categories and lists of disaster types at a micro level exist in the literature, such as weather-caused, unexpected outcomes or secondary disasters, mass movement, geographical, and human-caused disasters. Each of these categories overlaps considerably with one or more other categories. For example, weather-caused disasters might include water damage and flooding from heavy rains, rivers overflowing, levees breaking, typhoons, tsunamis, and hurricanes, any of which can lead to an unexpected outcome or secondary disaster such as mold outbreak and/or pest infestation. Mass movement disasters include earthquakes, landslides, avalanch-

es, and the like. Geographical disasters usually refer to disasters more common to specific areas such as earthquakes, landslides, mudslides, avalanches, volcanic activity, wildfires, tornadoes, typhoons, tsunamis, and hurricanes. Human-caused disasters result from events that occur as a result of carelessness or malicious intent include arson, tampering with water pipes to cause flooding, explosions from bombs, gunfire causing injury or death to persons as well as damage to materials and facilities, and so forth.

While most disasters strike without warning, sometimes libraries may have anywhere from a few minutes to a few days of notice that a disaster is imminent. Most disasters in the United States for which libraries may have prior warning are weather related such as approaching hurricanes or impending floods from rising river water, levees breaking, and related events. Other types of disasters where librarians may have some notice include tornados as well as human violent behavior such as bomb threats.

Any of these disasters could profoundly affect library facilities, infrastructure supporting resources and services, staff, and customers as well as the library's parent institution and the surrounding community. Recovery from these devastating events can take months or even years from which to recover. While librarians can do nothing to prevent a hurricane from making landfall or to hold back a rising river, even minimal time to prepare before the disaster strikes can allow dramatic improvement in the outcome of the library's response.

Disaster Response Actions

Some of the strategies that library leaders will employ as they begin responding to a looming emergency are similar for all types of disasters, while other approaches will differ significantly, depending on the type of disaster expected. For example, when any disaster is anticipated, library administrators will mobilize the library's disaster recovery assistance team (DRAT) members to action and will work with appropriate officials at the parent institution to coordinate preparedness activities.

DRAT members will call an emergency meeting and consult the disaster preparedness, response, and recovery plan for guidance as an initial, standard response protocol. They will also formulate the disaster-specific actions to take which will vary depending on the exact nature of the emergency. Each member of DRAT will be responsible for a specific area of the plan and will work quickly and flexibly to take action and to address any last minute developments.

Core Responses for Most Disasters

In any emergency situation, the safety of library customers and staff always takes precedence over collections and facilities. When disaster responders receive prior warning that a weather event is approaching, the parent institution will inform the library of the overarching steps, such as moving people to a designated area of refuge or evacuating the entire building. In all cases, the library will defer to the parent institution for instructions on how to proceed.

As discussed in depth in Chapters 2 and 5, the library's disaster preparedness, response, and recovery plan will inform DRAT members about internal actions to take. Unfortunately, the reality is that the library's plan is often not completely up-to-date. Phone numbers change; disaster supplies are used and not immediately replenished; salvage priorities shift; and floor plans may no longer be accurate due to minor remodeling, the expansion of shelving ranges, and the like.

In rare cases where the plan is completely current, situations arise that were not anticipated in even the most flexible plan. Most librarians agree that attempting to plan for every contingency is generally ill-advised. Thus, the DRAT members will first evaluate and then adjust the disaster plan; however, the overall plan will provide much needed guidance during this highly uncertain and stressful time.

Regardless of the type of approaching disaster, the initial steps that DRAT will take when preparing to respond to an emergency are fairly standard. These actions include initiating communication with all appropriate parties, checking disaster supplies, establishing a disaster command center, securing and backing up technology and virtual services, revisiting salvage priorities, and reviewing floor plans for accuracy. DRAT will not have the luxury of time, so each of these tasks will have to be executed quickly.

Communication. Communication is perhaps the single most important factor when responding to a disaster. The assigned DRAT member, typically the communications & media coordinator or the human resources coordinator, will begin preparing for a pending disaster by reviewing the library's crisis communication plan. Although the coordinator will be generally familiar with the communication plan, emotions will be peaking and some aspects of the plan could easily be forgotten or overlooked. For example, the contact information contained in the plan, sometimes called the phone tree, for library employees and designated campus officials might not be current. If needed, the coordinator should update it to the extent possible given the time available. The communications & media coordinator should prepare a script covering the information to be shared with library staff along with a reminder of where and when to check in after the disaster subsides. This information should also be provided via a library-wide e-mail list or other methods.

If possible, the coordinator or the dean or director will contact the various consortia and organizations to which the library belongs to inform them of the potential interruption of services. The library dean or director may also choose to contact one or more high-profile donors, especially ones who have given significant collections to the library, to reassure them that all appropriate measures to protect the collections are being taken. Also, the coordinator or the acquisitions head should notify major acquisitions vendors and book binders who may be located at a distance and thus not be aware of the pending disaster to instruct them to halt shipments of materials to the library. Communication with these groups will continue to be important after the disaster during the recovery process.

Contact any disaster recovery vendors and contractors with which whom the library has a contract so that they can develop contingency plans for assisting the library in the recovery process. In a major disaster, libraries that do not have such contracts are at a distinct disadvantage and may even be unable to save collections which might otherwise have been saved.[2] If the library does not have contracts with such vendors, check with the parent institution's central administration to determine if they have disaster recovery vendors under contract. If the parent institution does not have such agreements, the library should secure authorization to contact disaster recovery vendors either as soon as they know a disaster is approaching, if time permits, or immediately after the disaster strikes. See Appendix D for a model RFP for disaster recovery services as well as for a list of selected companies.

Change the recording on the library's main phone numbers to provide information and instructions to customers, donors, and any affiliate operations that share library facilities. Include in the recorded message how and when updates are likely to occur. The library's Web page and any other sites such as the library's Facebook page should also be updated to contain all pertinent information.

The library can reach the greatest number of people by arranging for multiple channels of communication with colleagues and constituents. Providing this information, with timely updates as events unfold, not only provides good customer service but will foster good relationships later as the library recovers from the disaster.

Disaster supplies. An assigned DRAT member will check the disaster recovery supplies inventory in order to determine which items are currently available and where they are located. If additional supplies will be required, they should be procured if time permits. Also, depending on the nature of the approaching disaster, it may be prudent to change the location of recovery supplies. Library staff who will assist with the emergency response should be notified of any changes made in the location of supplies, be provided with a list of available supplies, and be given direct access to the supplies regardless of their location.

Command center. The library dean or director or the designate will identify a command center in case all or parts of the library's physical facilities are incapacitated or unavailable. If the pending disaster is likely to be more localized, it may be possible to use a branch library or another building on campus as the command center. If the disaster is thought to affect the entire area, the command center might be located at a branch campus in a near-by town. If a major disaster is predicted, such as Hurricane Katrina, no command center will possible for some time or the command center may be determined by university administration such as was the case at Tulane University.

The communications & media coordinator should notify all library employees and central campus administrators of the location of the command center and any alternate locations where it may be housed along with any phone or fax numbers at the site. If practical, a DRAT member can retrieve and move appropriate supplies and equipment to the command center. These items might include communication and safety devices such as walkie-talkies, megaphones and air horns; technology support such as extension cords and surge protectors; documentation materials such as audio and video recorders and digital cameras; and other miscellaneous items such as folding chairs and bottled water as well as general supplies such as pens, paper, tape, scissors, cleaning and sanitary supplies, and so forth. For a list of suggested supplies, see Chapter 2.

Technology and virtual services. All academic libraries have plans for backing-up their virtual services. The systems/IT coordinator will ensure that all systems are secure and backed-up. Some libraries, like many businesses, are contracting with external organizations to archive their data electronically. Implementing this procedure ensures that data will be held at an additional location and be available to the library quickly and easily.[3]

In addition to ensuring that library data is backed-up with multiple copies distributed to different secure locations, the coordinator will also consider the safety of the hardware that hosts and serves the data. For example, if library servers are in a particularly vulnerable location the coordinator may temporarily move them to a safer site when possible. If the servers for the library's OPAC, interlibrary loan system, or institutional repository are located in the basement level or ground floor of the library and a flood is expected, relocating the server to a higher floor or another building would be practical. When possible, servers should not be located in the basement at any time but sometimes, due to space or financial constraints or other issues, this placement is unavoidable.

In all cases, library IT staff should develop and test protocols as part of a planning process to systematically take down servers and physically move them to a safer, more secure location. In most if not all cases, the data on servers, desktop PCs, and back-up drives is more valuable than the hardware it is stored on. In locales where disasters with regional impact are likely, such as areas prone to hurricanes, libraries should make pre-arrangements to secure data and to store and distribute it outside the re-

gion. Contact the campus IT department for information regarding participation in regional storage networks. When a disaster is looming or when the library is in the midst of a recovery effort is not the time to determine how data will be secured.

Salvage priorities. The collections and preservation coordinator, sometimes referred to as the salvage coordinator, will quickly review the library's salvage priorities, concentrating on collections. If any collections have been moved, withdrawn or added, the coordinator will communicate these changes to the other DRAT members and note how these changes could impact the library's salvage priorities. For example, if a new, rare, and expensive special collection has been added since the library's disaster preparedness, response, and recovery plan was last updated, that collection may become the first priority for rescue, lowering the previous first priority in the queue. If a flood is expected to damage unique materials that are housed in the basement, it may be feasible to relocate the materials to a higher floor. See Part IV for a case study on flooding at the University of Iowa libraries for an example of such preventative actions. If a library has added a new digital archive of journals or documents, salvaging existing print counterparts may not be a priority. The collections & preservation coordinator must know what materials are not priorities to be saved. The system/IT coordinator will conduct a similar process for the library's technology such as PCs, servers, microfilm reader-printers, copy machines, and other electronic items.

Floor plans. The facilities and security coordinator will review the library's floor plans, note any changes that have been made or that are in progress since the plans were last updated, and communicate these changes to library staff and other emergency responders. Often, the campus master plans are not updated until a construction project is complete. Also, in some cases there may be some lag time between when a minor remodeling project is finished and the master plan is revised. Communicating any changes on the floor plans regarding the layout of the library facility is a critical step because emergency responders will depend on the accuracy of the floor plans to navigate an unfamiliar building. DRAT members who work in the library each day still may not be familiar with the arrangement of all floors and areas throughout the library. Even minor changes to a pathway such as blocking a door could prove costly or even deadly during a disaster.

Specialized Responses for Various Disaster Types

While it is impractical for libraries to develop a plan of action to respond to every disaster scenario, DRAT members should be familiar with generally accepted best practices to guide their actions in the event of an emergency. Depending on the geographic location of the library, some types of disasters will not be of concern, while other types will be of particular concern. For example, libraries in Colorado are unlikely to experience a tsunami and have no need to consider response scenarios for such an event, while libraries in coastal Louisiana are at risk of having a hurricane reach land. Each library will develop informational sheets with tips to inform responders about ways to reduce the impact of the various disaster types that are most likely to take place in their area. Basic information on four types of events—hurricanes, floods, tornados, and bomb threats—follows.

Hurricanes. A hurricane is a tropical storm with winds that have reached a constant speed of 74 miles per hour or more causing torrential rains, high winds, and storm surges. Even more dangerous than the high winds of a hurricane is the storm surge which is a dome of ocean water that can be 20 feet at its peak causing severe flooding. Hurricane season in the United States spans from June through November each year.[4] Hurricane Katrina of 2005 is by far the costliest and the third deadliest hurricane to strike the United States.[5] See Part IV for a case study on Hurricane Katrina's effect on Tulane University libraries.

A hurricane watch means that hurricane conditions pose a possible threat typically within the next 36 hours, while a hurricane warning means that a hurricane is likely to come ashore in 24 hours or less. A hurricane watch calls for preparation and increased awareness on the part of the library, while a hurricane warning means it is imminent requiring immediate action to protect life and property.

As soon as a hurricane watch is announced, the library should enter an advanced stage of preparedness. If your campus does not provide regular information about the approaching storm, assign DRAT members to monitor the situation using emergency weather alerts or local media bulletins. Provide regular updates to staff via the library's e-mail list, Web site, or both. If the hurricane watch is announced at night or during other times that the library is closed, mobilize the contact list to advise staff of the approaching hurricane and any steps the library is taking in preparation for its arrival.

The exact actions the library will take to secure and close the facility will vary; however, the following steps are a good starting point:[6]

- Secure collections, files, papers, PCs, servers, etc.
- Fill all library vehicles with gasoline and park them in the securest location available
- If the library has an arrangement with an off-site storage facility to move its highest priority collections out of the danger zone, contact the company and begin packing the materials immediately
- Pack any secondary priority materials located in the basement or on lower floors and move those collections to higher floors when possible
- Move the remaining collections away from windows and cover the collections with plastic when feasible

Floods. Water damage occurs in approximately 85% of all emergencies,[7] whether from flooding as a result of an overflow from a body of water, accumulation from a storm, heavy rain accompanying a hurricane, or from numerous other sources. As with hurricanes, major flood watches and warnings will trigger preventative action from DRAT members. Many of the same steps taken to prepare for a hurricane should be initiated when preparing for a flood. For example, staff should pack collections and electronic equipment located in basements and on lower floors and move them to higher floors when possible. Time permitting, refer to the salvage priorities plan and move as much equipment as possible to higher floors. Anticipate what equipment would be required to set-up alternative service locations such as public PCs, COWs of laptops (with spare power cords and batteries), scanners, copiers, printers, monitors, and the like. This may be the only equipment available for an extended time if other equipment is damaged or destroyed. See Part IV for case studies on water damage and recovery efforts at Colorado State University, Tulane University, the University of Hawaii, and the University of Iowa libraries.

Tornados. A tornado is a violently rotating column of air that extends to the ground and picks up dust and debris as it travels. Occurring most frequently in areas east of the Rocky Mountains in the United States during the spring and summer months, tornados can reach speeds of over 250 miles per hour, causing great destruction. In an average year over 800 tornados are reported.[8]

The approach of a tornado is often preceded with little warning because tornados can develop very quickly. Tornados are typically announced by air raid sirens. These sirens indicate that a tornado has been sighted and may be approaching the campus; however, in some locales, air raid sirens may also indicate the approach of a severe storm or hurricane. In the event of a tornado, library security staff should direct customers and other library staff to a designated underground shelter or to an interior room or hallway with no windows. No one should leave the shelter until the all-clear siren is sounded or until they are instructed by a security officer. Librarians, working with campus safety officers, should develop a plan to assist persons with limited mobility and wheelchair-bound individuals to a safe location or if the event occurs too quickly to do this, then get them to a designated area of refuge.

Bomb threats. Libraries, once considered to be quiet places to engage in scholarly pursuits, are not immune to human-caused violent behavior such as bomb threats. When a bomb threat is received, the person receiving it should try to maintain a calm voice and attitude. Pass a note to the nearest staff member to call the police immediately. Ask the informant to tell you when the bomb is going to explode, what kind of bomb it is, and where it is located.[9]

Record the time the threat was received and when the call ended. When possible, write down the exact wording of the threat. Also note if the caller appeared to be familiar with the building or area when describing the bomb's location. In addition, pay careful attention to any details that the caller might reveal during the call. These might include:

- Voice characteristics: loud, soft, high pitched, deep, raspy, whispered, intoxicated
- Speech: fast, slow, distorted, stutter, lisp, nasal, slurred
- Language: well-spoken/educated, foul/profanity, taped, message read by caller
- Accent: local, regional, foreign
- Manner: calm, pleasant, angry, irrational, incoherent, deliberate, emotional, righteous, laughing, crying, disguised, deep breathing
- Background noises: voices, party, music, public address (PA) system, house noises, baby crying, animal noises, street noises, machinery, computer noise, planes/trains/buses

Remember that even the smallest detail may be helpful to emergency personnel later.

Conclusion

Most disasters strike without warning, but some events such as hurricanes, floods, tornados, and bomb threats may provide anywhere from a few minutes to a few days notice that a disaster is imminent. With preparations, libraries that have even a short time before a disaster strikes can significantly improve their response; reduce the impact of the disaster on library customers, staff, collections, facilities, and infrastructure; and shorten the time required for recovery and resumption of normal operations. An informed, well-trained disaster response assistance team and a current disaster preparedness, response, and recovery plan make this kind of preemptive response well worth the time and effort.

Notes

1. Julie Todaro, *Emergency Preparedness for Libraries* (Lanham, MD: Scarecrow Press, 2009), 5.

2. William Miller, "Natural Disasters in the Academic Library," *Library Issues* 28, no. 3 (2008): 2.

3. Mario Amato, "What Today's Businesses are Doing to Protect Their Future," *Disaster Recovery Journal* 22, no. 3 (Summer 2009): 70.

4. "Definition of a Hurricane" (Louisiana Homeland Security & Emergency Preparedness). http://gohsep.la.gov/factsheets/DefinitionOfaHurricane.htm (December 5, 2009).

5. Eric S. Blake, "The Deadliest, Costliest, and Most Intense United Sates Tropical Cyclones from 1851 to 2006 (and Other Frequently Requested Hurricane Facts)" (National Weather Service, National Hurricane Center, NOAA Technical Memorandum NWS TPC-5, Updated April, 2007). http://www.nhc.noaa.gov/Deadliest_Costliest.shtml (December 5, 2009).

6. "Before the Storm: The Countdown" (Lyrasis). http://www.lyrasis.org/Preservation/Disaster%20Resources/Before%20the%20Storm.aspx (December 5, 2009).

7. Heritage Preservation, *Field Guide to Emergency Response* (Heritage Preservation, Inc., 2006), 35.

8. "A Preparedness Guide: Including Safety Information for Schools." (Department of Commerce, National Oceanic and Atmospheric Administration National Weather Service). http://www.nssl.noaa.gov/edu/safety/tornadoguide.html (December 5, 2009).

9. Miriam, B. Kahn, *Library Security and Safety Guide to Prevention, Planning, and Response* (Chicago: American Library Association, 2008), 72.

Chapter 5

HOW TO RESPOND WHEN A DISASTER STRIKES

"When in danger or in doubt, run in circles, scream and shout." —Robert A. Heinlein
"Or maybe not." —Anonymous

The safety and security of library customers and personnel, as well as its collections, equipment, infrastructure, and buildings, are paramount at all times and remain the first priority during an emergency. Library administrators must address these concerns at every stage of library planning, design, construction, or remodeling as well as while creating a library disaster plan. Once all prudent safety, security, and planning measures have been taken, library administrators and disaster response assistance team (DRAT) members are as prepared as possible to respond vigorously when a disaster strikes.

Disaster response can be defined as "the procedures and processes whereby a team of trained individuals responds to a disaster and determines how to best recover the damaged materials so that 'business as usual' can resume as quickly as possible."[1] Depending on the type and severity of the disaster, the length of the emergency response phase will vary from a few days to a few weeks or more before it shifts into the disaster recovery phase. Generally, emergency response entails the activities conducted from the point of learning of the disaster and mobilizing the DRAT until the initial disaster clean-up is underway. The disaster recovery phase includes the activities that allow the library to resume normal operations[2] such as restoring damaged books, purchasing replacement materials or equipment, and renovating the library facility. Due to the complex nature of dealing with a disaster, no exact, clear-cut, or linear time frame exists to delineate when the response phase ends and the recovery phase begins and in reality, it does not really matter as long as progress is being made to restore library services. The emergency response phase begins with library leaders setting the tone for action and setting the library's disaster preparedness, response, and recovery plan in motion.

Setting the Tone

From the first moment that library leaders, including the library's DRAT members, become aware of the disaster, they must strive to set an appropriate tone. Their words, voice control (articulation, volume, speed, and rhythm), facial expressions, gestures, manner, mood, behaviors, and actions will impact everyone they encounter and can make a major difference in staff morale and confidence. Interaction with non-library partners will be significantly and positively impacted by a calm, professional demeanor projected by library response leaders. The tone they set during the emergency response phase establishes a climate and atmosphere that will shape the emerging organizational culture, and have an impact on the ultimate health and recovery of the library.

Everyone involved in the emergency response will be experiencing a rush of emotions and spiked adrenaline levels. The larger and more widespread the disaster, the more those individuals within the institution will be affected. Fluctuating emotions will cause stress and even feelings of guilt in the library dean or director and members of DRAT as these individuals work long hours and make extraordinary efforts to begin rebuilding the library.[3] A positive tone reassures staff and encourages them to work together and to support one another.

Questioning why the unimaginable happened, feelings of loss and violation, and concerns about whether the library can ever be truly restored, are natural. Most libraries represent so much more than just a building on the campus. They are often considered the heart of the campus, embodying its history, and featured in stories and memories recalled by current students and faculty as well as alumni. Due to all these factors, setting the right tone is essential. Library leaders will feel extra concern because they know that the tone they set through their words and actions are so critical to so many. They must resist the strong impulse to respond to every concern immediately. Although some situations must be addressed at once, when possible they should take a few minutes to think carefully about the consequences of each decision and seek input from their staff and other advisors.[4] Library leaders must remember that they are making history and shaping the library for years to come with every decision they make.

Over time, the shock of the disaster and long working hours in poor environmental conditions in which to work will cause most people to function at a reduced capacity, though they will likely not be aware of the change. Nurturing a culture that maintains the health and stamina of those involved in the response and recovery effort is paramount. The dean or director and the DRAT team leader will need to monitor the situation closely and take steps to promote the well-being of everyone involved, including themselves. For example, they might bring in snacks and beverages for DRAT members and other staff responding to the emergency; remind these responders to take breaks; make sure that they have some time for themselves to sleep, workout, and attend to personal affairs, family, and pets; and when possible, encourage humor.[5]

Perhaps the most critical aspect of the recovery, one that is often overlooked in the rush to address the rescue of collections, equipment, and facilities, is the emotional state of the people who are working day in and day out to restore the library. "At the heart of every disaster is the impact on people and their lives…immediately after a disaster, and for a long time thereafter, most people will suffer emotional trauma."[6] Remember that these individuals have experienced a loss, and they will react in many different, sometimes erratic, ways. The degree and the timing of these reactions will occur will vary greatly. Predicting who will be more affected is not possible because people's behavior is governed by their personal characteristics and memories that the disaster may have awakened about previous losses.[7]

Some people will need time to mourn the loss of the collections and/or facilities, while others will experience a desire to move on quickly, even becoming frustrated or unsympathetic to those individuals who are not yet ready to take that step. Others may feel isolated or inadequate. Still others may experience difficulty expressing their emotions. Some will experience troubles at home either as a result of their emotional reactions or due to their increased duties and long, unpredictable work hours. If the disaster affected the entire community, reactions may be further intensified due to the possible loss of their homes and the displacement of their family.

If the campus offers a counseling assistance program, arrange to have counselors work with anyone interested in their services.[8] If not, work with campus human resources or other offices to provide counseling services for those people who are interested. Arrange for no-cost open sessions where counselors are available on site to meet with staff. The dean or director or the DRAT team leader should consider setting the tone that counseling is helpful and that no stigma is attached to attending one or more of these sessions. Continue to facilitate counseling throughout the disaster response and recovery process because some people experience delayed reactions to stress or other emotions, especially around the anniversary of a disaster or other milestone.

Finally, remember to set a positive tone by fostering a spirit of camaraderie, acknowledging employee efforts, regularly thanking staff for their work, and celebrating even small triumphs at every stage of the response and recovery process. Remember that responding to a disaster is only the first step. Recovering from a disaster is a slow process, involving many people, and the right tone will facilitate healing and make a significant difference in the outcome of the recovery.

Emerging Leadership

Library leaders will need to be vigilant and nimble as they work with emergency responders, other library staff, campus administrators, and the public. They will need to rely on people outside the disaster area for assistance as well as possibly using consultants to advise or assist with some response and recovery activities.

The library disaster will bring out the best traits and abilities in some people, allowing their leadership potential to emerge or grow, while the disaster will have the opposite effect on other people. Many well-seasoned library administrators may never have dealt with a large-scale disaster, and they will need to stretch their knowledge, skills, and abilities to lead the disaster response and recovery.

Even library administrators who have led through a disaster and are quite knowledgeable about the steps to take to respond appropriately and recover successfully from a disaster cannot and should not try to direct every aspect of the process themselves. Leaders who try to manage, much less micromanage, the disaster response will prove frustrating for everyone involved and may even be impediments to the disaster recovery efforts of their teams. Instead, leaders must "seek to coordinate not to control."[9] New and seasoned leaders alike must comprehend this principle and seek to coordinate with first responders such as police officers, firefighters, and/or other professionals.

Coordinating with as opposed to attempting to control every decision or action of DRAT members is especially important. The disaster response

leadership must also "involve appropriate task delegation and labor division."[10] DRAT members will already know the tasks that they have been assigned during emergency response; however, "larger more complex tasks [must] be divided and handled by the most appropriate staff person or unit."[11] DRAT members will need to coordinate with many other responders within the library, throughout the campus, and outside the campus. They will need to consult with the library dean or director and the DRAT team leader; however, "when disaster strikes, immediate action is essential, and bureaucracy must be waived."[12] Library leaders must "permit decision making."[13] DRAT members must have the autonomy to make some decisions and take actions without prior approval. Planning prior to the disaster, including creating a mechanism to delineate the process by setting parameters for decision making, sets the tone for managing during the emergency and facilitates the conditions for leadership to emerge and grow which can greatly enhance the team's ability to respond dynamically to the disaster.

Setting the Disaster Preparedness, Response, and Recovery Plan in Motion

A disaster strikes the library and the phone call that no library dean or director ever wants to receive has come. The building has flooded; or it is on fire; or an earthquake, tornado, or hurricane has struck; or a mold outbreak has been detected; or some other equally horrifying disaster has taken place. Whether the disaster is fairly minor, localized in a small area of the facility, or large-scale, having an impact on the entire library, campus, or beyond, now is the time to put the library's disaster preparedness, response, and recovery plan into action.

Library administrators will mobilize the library's DRAT members to action and work with appropriate officials at the parent institution to coordinate response activities. DRAT members will assemble for briefing about the situation. They should refer to the disaster plan for contact information, salvage priorities and so forth. Each DRAT member will have one or more pre-assigned areas of responsibility; however, the team will also need to begin formulating the specific actions that members will take to respond to this unique disaster. Team members will need to work quickly and flexibly to carry out the functions of their coordination roles.

Specific measures taken to respond to the disaster include evacuating and securing the building, communicating with all appropriate parties about the disaster, documenting the response and recovery process, establishing a temporary command center, setting-up alternative physical and virtual service points, and assessing and triaging the damage to the facility, infrastructure, and collections.

Evacuating and Securing the Building

In an emergency situation, the safety of library customers and staff always takes priority over rescuing collections and facilities. If a disaster occurs during the hours that the library is open, trained library personnel will immediately evacuate the facility using established protocols. Staff must know all exit and alternate exit routes, areas of refuge for the disabled, rendezvous sites for staff, basic first-aid, and so forth. If the emergency consists of a fire, staff may initially respond by remembering and following two increasingly well-known acronyms: R.A.C.E. and P.A.S.S. R.A.C.E. stands for *Rescue* anyone in danger, *Activate* the fire alarm, *Contain* the fire by shutting a door, and *Extinguish* the fire. P.A.S.S. provides the basic directions of using a fire extinguisher: *Pull* the pin, *Aim* the nozzle, *Squeeze* the handle, and *Sweep* the spray at the base of the fire. Library staff should attempt to use a fire extinguisher only if they have had training, are comfortable using it, and the fire is fairly small. See Chapter 3, Training for Disaster Preparedness and Response, for more information on building evacuation and emergency response procedures.

Once all library customers and staff have been safely evacuated, the building must be secured to the degree possible given the damage it has sustained. In almost any significant emergency event, the campus police will arrive quickly to assist either with the evacuation and secure the building or to take over the process entirely. Other personnel from various units, agencies, and organizations will also arrive quickly. These responders include at a minimum persons from the campus physical plant and from risk and safety units as well as campus officials such as the provost or president, and representatives from the campus media relations office.

Police officers, other campus officials, or external agencies will often be the ones to determine who enters the building, for what purposes, when they are permitted to enter, and for how long. For example, when the disaster is fairly localized to the library building such as a small fire, firefighters will arrive within minutes and take control of the building. Even a relatively minor fire will take time to extinguish fully. Firefighters will also check to determine if the fire caused any related damage that could pose danger such as releasing chemical fumes from burned materials or damage to electrical outlets or wiring. (Figure 1)

If the fire appears to be human-caused, the library will likely be declared a crime scene and be off limits to librarians while the possible arson is being investigated by the fire department or other agency. If the disaster is caused by water, such as a burst pipe or valve, the utility company will be at the scene. If the flooding was human-caused, either by tampering with a valve or by faulty installation of a pipe or other part of the water delivery system, again the library may be declared a crime scene. A crime scene investigation can take from a few hours to a week or more to complete. If the disaster is a large-scale, weather-caused event, such as a hurricane, affecting the campus or the entire community the response will involve multiple agencies including FEMA and/or Homeland Security. During any of these situations the library administration will not be in charge of the building.

Figure 1: Charred Wiring Closet

Regardless of which entity has possession of the library building, once the immediate danger is over—the fire has been extinguished, the water and electricity have been shut-off, or the weather-caused event has passed—and emergency responders have left, the facility must be secured. Any broken windows or doors should be covered and the building should be cordoned off with caution tape or temporary fencing. (Figure 2)

Appropriate signage should be prominently displayed on multiple locations outside the library perimeter, stating that the library is closed and providing instructions about where to obtain additional information. Because "vandalism is one of the tragic aftermaths of disasters so a library with broken windows and broken doors will be tempting to those who are predatory during a disaster,"[14] se-

curity guards should be stationed at the library until normal security systems and alarms are restored.

Communicating with One and All

Communication is perhaps the single most important aspect to consider when responding to and recovering from a disaster. Disaster communication begins with emergency responders, campus officials, and library staff and continues with other libraries and affiliated services, the public, and the media. Without clear and timely communication, chaos will abound, costly mistakes will occur, unnecessary delays will ensue, and everyone involved will experience additional stress.

During a crisis, library leaders must communicate effectively; however, a successful communication strategy cannot be only top down from the dean

Figure 2: Caution Tape and Signage on Library Doors

or director, the DRAT team leader, or the communications & media coordinator. Everyone involved in a disaster, at every level, is responsible for providing the best, most complete communication possible. They must strive to communicate effectively and efficiently, anticipating the needs of the audience and adapting to rapidly occurring events. Frequently changing information is inherent during disaster response and recovery situations.

Emergency responders and campus officials. Library leaders and staff onsite at the time of the disaster or who arrive soon after the disaster occurs should make their presence known to the emergency responders at the disaster scene, introduce themselves if needed, provide contact information, and offer their assistance. To the extent possible and practical, they should help the external responders

to understand the library building. They should provide any available floor plans and inform responders of where the most valuable collections are located, if the building has a fire suppression system and where sprinkler shut-offs are located, evacuation routes and any unusual features of the facility that might hinder movement, as well as any other information that might prove useful.

Depending on the type of disaster, the library dean or director may not be in control of the building. Although emergency response officials such as local police and fire marshals or persons from national agencies will generally coordinate with library administrators, remember that the library facility itself is university property and while the library dean or director has oversight for the collections, equipment, and staff, they are essentially tenants in the building. Librarians must permit the "proper exercise of decision-making," avoiding clashes over organizational domains between themselves and others.[15] Library deans or directors and/or DRAT members and rescue contractors will need to enter the building in order to begin assessing the damage and start the triage of collections and equipment. They must coordinate closely with the officials who control the facility to arrange their entry to the building. Physical plant personnel will typically coordinate with appropriate individuals or agencies to address stabilizing the library building.

In addition to attending to collections and equipment, DRAT members may be able to make an arrangement for limited or escorted access to the library to retrieve urgently needed items that were left in the building when it was evacuated such as borrowed interlibrary loan books, any paper class reserve materials, payroll or other records that are not available electronically, file servers, and similar equipment or materials. Also, some library customers will have left behind personal items such as bags, back-packs, keys, medication, or laptop computers in their haste to exit the building. They will be very anxious to get these items back. Library officials will need to arrange a mechanism to accomplish this retrieval as soon as reasonably possible.

After the initial disaster event is contained library leaders will continue to communicate regularly with campus officials about disaster response and recovery activities and progress, especially with the person to whom the library dean or director reports. During this time and throughout the remediation process, staying in contact, discussing the direction the process is taking, and securing support and/or approval is vitally important.

Library staff. Communicating with all library staff as soon as possible after the disaster strikes is essential. The form of the communication will vary depending on the type and severity of the disaster. If the disaster is widespread over the entire city, such as a hurricane or earthquake, communication

infrastructures may be damaged so that telephone and Internet access systems may be down, rendering those modes of communication unavailable. If the area has not been evacuated, DRAT members can post initial information and updates at a pre-arranged location for library staff to read as soon as it is safe to do so. The campus will also have established protocols to provide information during a major disaster. The library should coordinate its efforts with campus communications.

If the disaster takes place when the library is open and the disaster is localized to the library building or a few surrounding buildings, such as a fire or flood, the employees on duty will obviously know about it, but will not necessarily know the next steps to take after they evacuate the building. For example, should they go home or wait at a designated rendezvous location for further instructions? A DRAT member be appointed to provide this information to the staff as soon as reasonably possible.

If the disaster involves only the library building and/or a few other nearby buildings, but happens when the library is closed, the dean or director or the DRAT member(s) who were notified of the disaster will activate the contact list, sometimes called the phone tree. This list will include other library administrators, DRAT members, key members of the campus central administration (if they have not already been notified), as well as any other managers of operations that share the library facility. Most campuses now have centralized communication broadcast methods that can send mass e-mails to students, faculty, and staff as well as sending text messages to the cell phones of those individuals who register for the service.

This centralized communication is useful for spreading basic, initial information to the entire campus community; however, it does not replace the need to communicate more specific information to library employees. The communications & media coordinator or designate will prepare a script that includes what has happened, how employees will receive updated information, and where and when they should report for work. The coordinator should take a deep breath and try to remain calm when contacting people. Remember that individuals have differing emotional reactions to bad news, but most will be shocked, confused, and/or have many questions about the emergency.

The phone tree should include multiple methods of contact for each person, including home and cell phone numbers. If no one answers the phone, the coordinator should use voice mail or text messaging if available to reach them. In addition, the coordinator will send an e-mail to the library's all-employee list as well as post information on the library's Web site, Facebook page, and/or any other social networking sites the library uses.

Only in fairly small libraries will one person be assigned to call every person in the library. Often the coordinator will contact the unit head or designate and that person will call others in the unit, including student employees whose contact information may change frequently and be maintained only in the unit.

The communications section of the disaster plan will prove invaluable; however, remember that no matter how detailed the contact plan is something will likely go wrong. The most important aspects of the process are to remain flexible and coordinate with others when problems arise.

After learning the details of the disaster, one of the next questions most staff will have is about their jobs. If the disaster is severe, they may ask if they still have a job. If the disaster is less severe or localized to the library building, and staff are told not to report back to work for a few days or longer, they will need to know if they will be paid for those days or have to use their annual leave. If the parent institution does not have a pertinent policy, check with the campus human resources director to determine how to answer these questions. If it will be days, weeks, or longer before the library building reopens, the human resources coordinator should arrange for alternative worksites for employees such as other library branches on campus, other campus buildings, or arrangements to telecommute from home when possible. In addition, the coordinator should make special efforts to locate work-study employment with other campus departments for library student workers who are displaced as a result of the disaster. Most often students will be paid only for the actual hours they work.

The contact made with employees in the hours or days immediately following the disaster is just the beginning of the disaster communication process. Regular, ongoing communication in multiple formats must be provided throughout the response and recovery process, including:

- Holding library-wide meetings called by the dean or director where information can be shared and staff can ask questions; these meetings might take place almost daily at first and as the recovery progresses, moved to a weekly or monthly schedule
- Establishing a central phone number with recorded updates providing the latest information
- Frequently updating staff through e-mail as well as via Web sites and social networking sites with photographs to show progress to those staff not directly involved in the response and recovery efforts as well as to document the process

Providing information to staff throughout the response and recovery process is imperative, not just to facilitate and move forward the recovery of the collections and facilities, but for the morale of everyone involved whether they work in the library that experienced the disaster or in a branch library on the campus. "Any kind of major disaster which hits an organization can be devastating, even to those staff members not directly involved in the disaster response and recovery. In fact, their lack of involvement can work against good staff morale. Therefore, communication with all library staff is critical."[16] Also, as the recovery continues, remember that many staff are either displaced themselves or are sharing their space with staff who are displaced, making working conditions far less than ideal. Stress levels will be unusually high; therefore, setting a positive tone, recognizing staff accomplishments, and celebrating milestones are more important than ever.

Other libraries and affiliated services. The library dean or director and members of DRAT should communicate about the disaster with their professional networks including people from the various organizations to which the library belongs as well as local or regional library experts who can provide assistance. The support and advice of these individuals and groups can prove invaluable when responding to a disaster. For example, talking to a librarian at another institution who has gone through a similar disaster can provide more useful information and reassurance than any article, book or Web site. Also, a consultant may be brought in to provide expertise on specific aspects of the process such as triage of damaged materials or organizing the pack-out if that knowledge is not available in-house.

Acquisitions vendors, consortia, other local libraries, and service representatives such as delivery companies should also be apprised of the disaster so that they can better serve the library. For example, depending on the nature of the disaster, the library may wish to cease interlibrary loan deliveries temporarily or it may ask that the library be given priority by lending libraries when filling requests for material. Other local libraries may need to prepare for customers displaced from the damaged library. The acquisitions librarian may ask vendors to hold materials and/or invoices or to ship them to a temporary address. Delivery companies will need to know where to deliver packages.

The public. The public will want to know the details of what happened in the disaster, how the library was damaged, what was lost, when will it reopen, and other related information. Many people will want to help by volunteering their time or donating cash or materials to the library. Alumni of the university, previous donors, and friends groups may be especially concerned. They feel an allegiance to the library and they have an important stake in the library's future success.

While the media will provide information to the general public, the library dean or director or the designate such as other library administrators, the development officer if the library has one, or the communications & media coordinator should personally contact major donors and friends of the library as soon as reasonably possible after the disaster to provide reassurance and to answer their questions. Beyond information regarding the disaster, frequently asked questions can address how to volunteer to help and how to make donations. The library should prepare a script to answer these questions.

Depending on the type of disaster, the specific situation the library is in, and the policies of the library and/or its parent institution, volunteers may or may not be desirable. If the parent institution permits volunteers and the library has the available staff to train and monitor them and ensure their safety, the human resources coordinator should create a list of the kinds of tasks volunteers are needed to perform. When community members contact the coordinator to volunteer their time, this person should always be gracious, explain what type of help is needed, listen to what kind of assistance potential volunteers are offering to provide, and note any special knowledge, skills, or abilities they may possess. Then, if appropriate, make arrangements with them to volunteer.

Many people will contact the library about making donations. Some individuals will want to contribute money. The library administration should establish an account for such cash donations to be deposited. Maintaining separate financial records for disaster recovery donations will allow library administrators to track donations and to account for how they were used.

Other individuals will want to donate books, journals, and other materials to the library. Once the library has an inventory of which materials were lost in the disaster, the collections & preservation coordinator, working with other library employees, will determine which materials should be replaced and in what format. For example, in today's digital age some paper collections will be replaced with electronic versions, while other collections may not be replaced at all if the university's core curriculum has changed significantly. The coordinator should prepare a list of needed items and make the list widely available. The library will want to ensure that any donations that it accepts are needed. Donations of materials that are inappropriate take time to dispose of and may create public relations problems. Determine if other area libraries are accepting donations and refer potential donors who offer materials not needed by the library.

In addition to knowing what materials are needed, the collections & preservation coordinator, working with the facilities & security coordinator, will need to determine when and where donations can be made. Depending on the degree of damage to the library, accepting donations of material may be impossible until repairs to the building are completed. If donations are accepted before the building is repaired, the coordinators will need to identify where donations can be delivered, processed, and stored until the facilities recovery is complete.

The media. When a disaster happens, the media will descend upon the dean or director or anyone in the library who they believe may have information, asking innumerable questions usually all at the same time. At some institutions all questions and requests for interviews from the media must be referred to the campus media relations office, while at other institutions that office will handle some media requests and the library's spokesperson, typically the dean or director or a designate who can represent the library well, will handle selected questions and interviews.

The library dean or director should decide well before a disaster how to present the library to the media and, as soon as possible after the disaster, this person should consult with the campus media relations director to determine what information will be publicized and who will provide it. If the library will be authorized to speak with the media, inform library staff that they should decline to speak with the media on behalf of the library about the disaster, and instead refer them to the library's spokesperson.

Ideally the spokesperson for the library would have had some media relations training about how to talk to reporters. This person should be comfortable speaking in public and be able to remain composed; be polite, personable, and quick-witted; be knowledgeable about the library; and be able to speak intelligently about the disaster and its impact on the library facilities, collections, programs, and services. Preferably, the spokesperson(s) would have met with representatives of the local newspapers, television stations, and radio outlets as soon as they were given their initial assignment. When a disaster strikes it is much easier for the spokesperson to work with media contacts with whom they have already established a relationship.

If the library spokesperson has not made these preparations and is dealing with the media for the first time, or if they have had a bad experience with the media in the past, they may be tempted not to answer any questions or to provide interviews. This tactic would be a major mistake. Remember reporters have a job to do and deadlines to meet, so they need information quickly to meet those demands. If the library spokesperson or campus media relations staff do not provide immediate information "reporters and their networks will send out inaccurate news."[17]

Media interest will be at its peak during and immediately after a disaster, which is exactly when the spokesperson will have the least information. If the disaster involves a crime, the authorities may insist that some information cannot be released to the media. The library spokesperson must not be pressured into speculating or revealing information that must remain confidential; however, the spokesperson should avoid the phrase "no comment." Instead, even if the information is slight, provide what can be shared about what happened, what the potential damage may be, what preventative measures were in place, what is known about the disaster's impact on the library, and how and where alternative library services will be provided. Also, give some interesting sound bites about the library. These might include the physical size of the building(s), the size and nature of the collections, the number of library personnel, the community the library serves, and any special services it provides. The media needs to have information to set the stage for their stories; therefore, the library spokesperson will want to provide interesting facts and figures for them to use.

Once the immediate crisis passes, the library spokesperson should continue to provide information throughout the recovery process. Provide brief updates on the recovery to the state library association newsletter, appropriate library discussion lists, and public Web sites. The communications & media coordinator should also keep a file documenting all the information that is published or broadcast about the library's disaster. Finally, remember that the media can be a valuable asset in providing information about the library to the public, helping libraries to better serve their communities.

Documenting the Response and Recovery

At the time a disaster strikes, everyone involved believes that they will never forget the details; however, as time passes, dates and the sequence of events begin to blur. Library leaders will need to ensure that every aspect of the disaster is carefully documented. This information will be sought by library users, staff, donors, the media, campus officials, insurance providers, architects, building remediation contractors, and in time, publishers and historians. In the midst of responding to an emergency, carefully recording

details on the form provided in the library's disaster plan is usually the last task on anyone's mind; however, doing so is a critically important activity to preserve the historical record. A digital voice recorder and/or camera may also be used as a supplement to the paper or electronic form.

The communications & media coordinator or designate and as many other DRAT members as practical should use a documentation form to record major decisions, activities, the time line, and other matters involved with the disaster. If the library's disaster plan does not contain a documentation form, the following initial information should be recorded: where the event occurred, what happened, when it began, when it was contained, who learned of it first, who was contacted, what happened next, and any other pertinent information.

Documentation should continue throughout the emergency response and disaster recovery phases. One method is for each DRAT member to write a sentence or two about each day's activities in an electronic or paper journal or a blog. The specifics of what occurred and when can be forgotten as the disaster response and recovery move forward. For example, the details and dates of even small matters can become important later for insurance or other purposes. Capturing this information when it is fresh will prove invaluable later.

In addition, the communications & media coordinator or designate should document the disaster and its subsequent recovery effort through photographs, video, and audio recordings. This person should also seek out photographs and related materials taken by others, noting who took them, where they were taken, and on what date so that permission to use them can be secured when needed.

Establishing a Temporary Command Center

The library's communications plan may include information about where its disaster command center will be established with alternative locations in case the first choice is not available. If the plan does not specify this information, the library dean or director, in consultation with other librarians and/or campus central administration, will designate where the command center will be located. If the library is sufficiently damaged that all areas of the facility must be closed, it may be possible to use a branch library or another building on campus as the command center. Of course, if a major disaster affects the entire area, such as Hurricane Katrina did, there can be no command center for some time and it may be located far away from the site of the disaster.

The location of the command center should be central to all disaster response operations since it will serve as the major coordination point for these activities. The communications & media coordinator should notify all library employees and central campus administrators of the location of the command center along with the phone numbers at the site. As soon as possible, DRAT members should move appropriate supplies and equipment needed to conduct business operations to the command center. DRAT members will check in at the center each morning and touch base with others throughout the day. The center will quickly become the hub for sharing information and for decision making.

Setting-Up Alternative Service Points

Once the building has been evacuated and secured, the immediate emergency has been contained, appropriate individuals and groups have been contacted, and a temporary command center has been established, DRAT members will begin restoring critical library services. The systems/IT coordinator and staff will determine if the library's servers

Figure 3: Alternative Reference Site in UNM Student Union Building

Figure 4: Information Referral Tent at UNM

which provide the public catalog, library Web site, institutional repository, and various other electronic materials, are functioning. If they are not, the coordinator and others will need to take appropriate action to restore them.

Other priority services include providing reference and information services, access to electronic class reserves, making circulation available for customers to return materials and to retrieve them if items can be paged from the damaged building(s), offering interlibrary loan borrowing and lending, and providing instruction to customers about alternative methods to access library materials. The library services coordinator will work with other public services librarians to provide customers with alternative locations for these post-disaster library services.

If the entire library building is closed but the disaster did not have an impact on the entire campus, the coordinator will arrange for space in alternate locations. Library services may be temporarily relocated to another library on campus, to a classroom, or even to the campus student union building; however, each of these services will require some infrastructure support. For example, reference service will require Internet connectivity (hardwired or wireless) to access electronic ready-reference collections, databases, the library's catalog, and various electronic full-text journals and books. Telephone availability is not required if cell phones are provided to reference staff. (Figure 3)

If the library branch where the disaster occurred cannot be accessed to page materials and deliver them to an alternative circulation desk, interlibrary loan will become the primary option for customers to access books and journal articles. In addition to computers with Internet connectivity, the interlibrary loan operation will require space to receive, disseminate, pack, and return material. Identifying a suitable location to provide instruction will become especially important during disaster recovery as customers rely even more heavily on electronic materials, some of which they may not have used previously. If a room with sufficient desktop computers for student instruction is not available, consider borrowing laptop computers from other campus units or groups or arranging for instruction sessions by embedding librarians at computer labs around campus.

Once alternative locations for key library services are identified, the library services coordinator will work with the communications & media coordinator to disseminate the information. Methods might include setting up information booths or signage such as sandwich-boards around the campus announcing alternative locations for both physical and virtual library services. (Figure 4)

This information should also be provided through the library's central recorded phone message, its Web site, its Facebook page or other social networking sources, and via campus broadcasting e-mail and text systems.

In addition to setting up alternative service points, library administrators and/or the human resources coordinator will arrange alternative worksite locations for displaced library staff. Begin the process by determining what kind and how much space and infrastructure is needed; identify which

Figure 5: UNM Library Staff in Protective Gear

Figure 6: Water Damaged Books

staff have to be centrally located, such as staff who provide reference, circulation, interlibrary loan and instruction services; and consider which tasks can be performed remotely.[18]

Assessing and Triaging the Damage

Once emergency and other safety personnel have determined that the library building is secure and any investigations at the site have been completed, the building will be released and library DRAT members will be authorized to reenter. Depending on the condition of the building, anyone entering certain sections will be required to wear protective clothing, hard hats, safety glasses, and/or respirator masks. Campus safety personnel will advise library staff of the type of gear, if any, that must be worn in each area of the library. (Figure 5)

Disaster recovery vendors have likely been working in the building to stabilize the facility all along, but at this point vendors who handle recovery of collections and/or equipment will begin working with DRAT.

Regardless of the circumstances that caused the disaster and whether it was natural or human-caused, most problems arise from water, mold, mud, soot, smoke, ash, pests or some combination of these factors. DRAT members must be familiar with each of these factors and the problems they pose in order to protect themselves from harm as they begin the assessment and triage process.

Water damage—whether resulting from a burst water pipe or a storm or from water used to fight a fire—is the most prevalent cause of damage. Water that is contaminated by hazardous chemicals or sewage poses additional concerns and requires special handling by trained professionals from outside the library. Materials exposed to salt water will also require special treatment. A survey in *ACRL Clip Note #40: Emergency Response Planning in College Libraries (2009)* reported that water was the most frequently cited emergency by college libraries, reported by 61% of respondents.[19] (Figure 6)

Mold is a fungus that feeds on organic materials, producing a superficial growth on various kinds of damp or decaying organic matter. Paper, of course is organic. Mold comes in many forms, but librarians are typically most concerned with mold spores that germinate in the presence of moisture such as direct water exposure or by extreme environmental factors such as temperature and humidity. Mold will cause decomposition of materials and will pose a threat to human health if left untreated. At best mold growth will leave behind discoloration on treated materials. Mold was reported by 9% of college libraries in the *Clip Note* survey.[20] (Figures 7 & 8)

Mud comes in a variety of types, containing different mineral components. For example, flooding in coastal regions may carry mud with high concentrations of sand and salt, while river flooding will contain sand and silt. Remediation will vary depending on the type of mud involved in the disaster. Mud can be quite slippery, and contaminated mud, like mold, will pose a threat to human health.[21]

Soot and ash, which are left behind after a fire, are quite destructive to collections, furnishings, computers, and buildings. Soot is greasy and acidic. Made up of very fine particles, soot will stick to almost any surface and permanently adhere to

Figure 7: Mold Damaged Books

Figure 8: Mold Damaged Walls

them if these surfaces are not quickly and correctly cleaned and treated. Ash is very abrasive and will easily scratch objects while they are being cleaned.[22] These contaminants can find their way into computers and servers, eating away at their circuit boards, causing damage that can take months to reveal itself. Fire is tied with mold as the third most frequently cited emergency in college libraries, after water and weather.[23] (Figures 9, 10, 11)

Pests can pose health concerns for people and can destroy collections. After a flood or other disaster, facilities are more vulnerable to infestation. Rodents, snakes, birds, and other creatures can damage collections as well as electrical wires and other components in buildings by chewing or nesting in them. Pest droppings, parasites, and disease can pose special hazards to library recovery workers.

In addition to being aware of these potential dangers, DRAT members should thoroughly re-familiarize themselves with the several sections of the disaster plan including informational/fact sheets, floor plans, and salvage priorities for collections, equipment, and other materials before conducting their initial walk-through of the building. They should bring supplies to document the damage including digital cameras, visual and audio recorders, and forms or paper and pens to take notes. The initial walk-through of the building will be a stressful and emotional time for most librarians, and they cannot rely solely on their memories of the damage to make salvage and recovery decisions.

After the initial walk-through, DRAT will often form two or more response teams, each dealing with a different aspect of the response and recovery.

Figure 9: Soot and Ash Damaged Books

Figure 10: Soot Encrusted Shelves

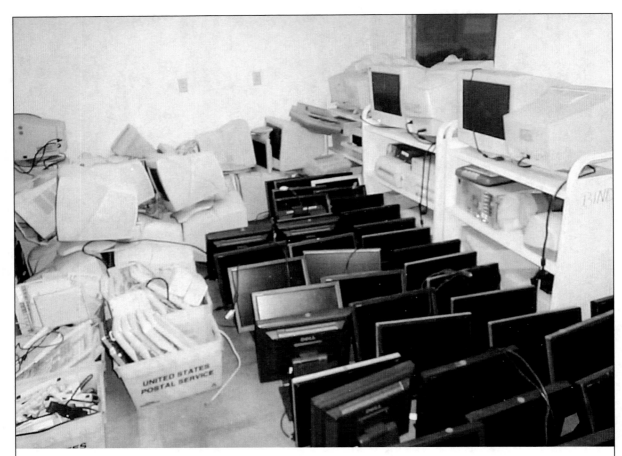

Figure 11: PCs Being Inspected for Soot and Ash Damage

These teams typically include a facilities team, a collections team, and possibly an equipment team if it is not included in either of the other teams. The library, or its parent institution on behalf of the library, will usually contract with one or more disaster recovery vendors who provide services to rebuild the facility, to rescue and repair collections, and to assess and repair equipment such as PCs and servers, as well as security gates, circulation and bindery devices, and the like. If copiers and printers are leased, the company that provides them will address them separately. If they are owned, they will be included with other library equipment.

The facilities assessment team will include library facilities personnel and campus physical plant staff, as well as disaster recovery personnel who partner with insurance adjusters to provide the resources and expertise necessary to respond to the disaster. Significant emergency response activities will be initiated to assess the damage, secure the building and surrounding areas and stabilize the facilities and structure. Securing the building as soon as possible by erecting fencing and hiring security personnel is imperative. Negotiating local road closures and defining work-staging areas will soon follow. If no electrical power is available near to the library, generators should be acquired and installed for immediate use. Remember to make arrangements for including ongoing refueling of these generators.

Within the library, begin by assessing air quality, and if needed, start treating it with air-scrubbers. Dehumidifiers or humidifiers may also be needed to restore proper humidity levels throughout the building. Roofs should be inspected for possible leaks and

Figure 12: HVAC Filters Before and After Replacement

windows for breakage. If they cannot be repaired quickly, determine the risk of ongoing damage to collections, equipment, and furnishings by continued exposure to outside elements such as rain, snow, or wind. Identify methods of protecting materials or moving them to dry secure locations within the damaged or adjacent buildings. If the damage to the building is so extensive that collections cannot be accessed, protected or secured, inform the parent organization and insurance adjustor of the risks and potential loss. For example, a $1000 a-day rental for a crane and operator used to lift out boxes, cabinets, or vaults may be significantly less expensive than the loss of a priceless collection.

Depending on the nature and extent of the disaster, a range of response and recovery activities instrumental in stabilizing the building infra-

structure could include: demolition of unstable structures; water extraction and/or mud removal; accelerated drying of structure or contents; debris removal; smoke neutralization; decontamination due to mold, chemical or biological spills; and extensive cleaning of all surfaces such as walls, ceilings, floors, plumbing, HVAC systems, furniture, and equipment. (Figure 12)

If the disaster is extensive, the stabilization portion of the response and recovery process benefits most from the experience of seasoned professionals employed by disaster recovery companies. These project managers' primary focus is to stabilize facilities, assess damage, and restore services as soon as possible. If damage is extensive and widespread and no contract or prior arrangements have been made with a disaster recovery company, strongly encourage the parent organization or insurance representatives to contact one of these companies for an initial consultation. Typically, such companies respond within a matter of a few hours. Many of these firms monitor potential disaster causing situations 24/7 and are known to contact library or facilities management personnel unsolicited very early on in the emergency response process. See Appendix of a list of disaster recovery companies and see Chapter 7 for more information about working with architects, contractors, and other recovery professionals regarding facilities.

The collections assessment team will begin by documenting as precisely as possible what items were damaged or lost, what it would cost to repair or restore them, what is desirable to be replaced with an exact duplicate or what is acceptable to be replaced in alternative formats or editions, and what will not be replaced. The building may still be damaged, limiting access to the surviving collections, records, and work areas, creating difficult conditions in which to work. Once collections can be reviewed, the team can begin the process of identifying what can be salvaged and what is a complete loss. Begin by identifying what types of materials were involved (paper, photographs, microforms, etc.); what caused the damage (water, smoke, etc.); and whether any of the materials were unique or extremely valuable. Depending on the library's ex-

pertise, outside consultants may be needed to assist with special formats and unique materials. Attempt to stay organized, patient, and calm, even when presented with the unanticipated events that are an inevitable part of disaster response. See Chapter 6 for more information about working with recovery teams, vendors, and insurance providers regarding collections.

Conclusion

The disaster emergency response phase includes all the activities conducted from learning of the disaster and mobilizing DRAT until the initial disaster cleanup is underway. The length of this phase will vary considerably before the disaster recovery phase begins. Emergency response starts with library leaders setting the tone for taking action by acknowledging emotions and providing support as well as guiding the process while allowing leadership to emerge at all levels. Emergency response continues by setting the library's disaster preparedness, response, and recovery plan in motion. Specific measures taken to respond to the disaster include evacuating and securing the building, communicating with all appropriate parties about the disaster, documenting the response and recovery process, establishing a temporary command center, setting-up alternative physical and virtual service points, and assessing and triaging the damage to the facility, infrastructure, and collections.

Notes

1. Kahn, Miriam, B., *Disaster Response and Planning for Libraries.* (Chicago: American Library Association, 1998), 2.
2. Ibid, 3
3. Ibid, 13.
4. Curzon, Susan C., "Coming Back From Major Disaster: Month One." In *Dealing with Natural Disasters in Libraries.* William Miller and Rita M. Pellen, eds. (Binghamton, NY: Hayworth Press, Inc., 2006), 27.
5. Alire, Camila. ed., *Library Disaster Planning and Recovery Handbook.* (New York: Neal-Schuman Publishers, Inc., 2000), 14.
6. Curzon, Coming Back From Major Disaster, 19.
7. Ibid, 20.
8. Ibid, 19-20.

9. Drabek, Thomas E., *The Professional Emergency Manager,* (Boulder, CO: University of Colorado, Institute of Behavioral Sciences, 1987): 239.

10. Quarantelli, E.L., "Ten Criteria for Evaluating the Management of Community Disasters." *Disasters* 21, no. 7 (1997): 4.

11. Alire, *Library Disaster Planning and Recovery Handbook,* 9.

12. Miller, William, "Natural Disasters in the Academic Library," *Library Issues* 28, no 3 (2008): 2.

13. Quarantelli, Ten Criteria for Evaluating the Management, 46.

14. Curzon, Coming Back From Major Disaster, 25.

15. Quarantelli, Ten Criteria for Evaluating the Management, 46-47.

16. Alire, *Library Disaster Planning and Recovery Handbook,* 16.

17. Ibid, 11.

18. Ibid, 35.

19. Thomas, Marcia, ed., *ClipNote #40 Emergency Response Planning in College Libraries* (Chicago: American Library Association, 2009), 7.

20. Ibid, 7.

21. Heritage Preservation, *Field Guide to Emergency Response* (Heritage Preservation, Inc., 2006), 44-45.

22. Ibid, 47.

23. Thomas, *Emergency Response Planning in College Libraries,* 7.

PART III: DISASTER RECOVERY

Chapter 6

COLLECTIONS RECOVERY: WORKING WITH RECOVERY TEAMS, VENDORS, AND INSURANCE PROVIDERS

"Books are the carriers of civilization. Without books, history is silent, literature dumb, science crippled, thought and speculation at a standstill." —Barbara Tuchman

When the initial response to the disaster has passed, and the early adrenaline and confusion have receded somewhat, the process of rebuilding the library begins. Emotions will still be very high, and those waves of anger and shock will return as the full extent of the loss is discovered; however, moving into an analytical phase of the process in order to restore the library's collections is necessary.

The process of rebuilding collections requires time and the application of organizational skills, patience, and great attention to detail. The initial goal is to document as precisely as possible what items were damaged or lost, what it would cost to repair or restore them, what is desirable to be replaced with an exact duplicate, or what is acceptable to replace in alternative formats or editions, and what will not be replaced. The building may still be damaged, which will limit access to the surviving collections, records, and work areas, creating difficult conditions in which to work on reviewing damaged materials. Concentrate on the goal of rebuilding a collection that will meet the needs of today's and future library users. While disasters are always horrible, they may also provide an opportunity to enhance collections by, for example, acquiring complete backfiles of journals that replace the partial set that was lost or helping libraries make significant progress towards the move from a primarily print-based journal collection to offering more electronic or digital collections.

The recovery process does have a logical flow, even if at times it seems random. Identify what was lost; decide on whether to repair, replace or discard; negotiate with the insurance company(ies) covering the loss; identify the companies that will help replace and repair materials; order and receive materials; and communicate with donors and users. The overarching flow does have a pattern; however, events may not happen in that logical sequence. Offers of materials will come before the losses are completely identified. Additional losses will be discovered after the negotiations with the insurance company for the value of the original loss were initiated. Making a decision not to replace a title may be followed by the discovery that it is a critically important title to some users. A title previously thought lost is found to be salvageable. Continue forward progress while being flexible in dealing with the exceptions and surprises. Try to stay organized, patient, and calm, even when presented with the unanticipated events that are an inevitable part of disaster recovery.

Recovery from a major disaster takes time. A flood may take only a few minutes to destroy a large part of the collection, while the recovery may take years. After the flood at Colorado State University, almost 8 years passed before librarians felt that they had completed the rebuilding process.[1] While the recovery time for many disasters will be far shorter, be aware that rebuilding takes a commitment of time, staff and money. Do not assume it can be accomplished while maintaining regular pre-disaster services and keeping all library staff in their pre-disaster roles.

Alternative Access to Collections During Recovery

Depending upon the nature of the disaster, access to the surviving collections may be limited for some time. During this initial period, try to provide alternative resources while losses are being documented and access to collections is being restored. Many producers of electronic databases will be willing to help during the recovery process. If a collection of materials related to social sciences is lost, for example, companies that have resources in that area may be willing to arrange extended trial access to their databases. Use such trials to identify potential replacements for areas that were lost. New resources may be discovered that would improve and expand collections.

Notify area libraries and regional consortia of the disaster. Other libraries may be able to help your users, and consortia may be able to designate interlibrary loan requests from your library as a priority. Depending upon the nature of the disaster, some areas of the collections may be unharmed; if so, paging or retrieving materials from those sections may be possible. The library may even consider opening portions of the building to the public while work continues in the damaged areas.

Documenting the Losses

The first step in rebuilding lost collections is to identify what was lost. Only extremely well organized and well-prepared librarians have complete online inventories with accurate information including the numbers, location, and value for all books, journals, manuscripts, and other collections as well as art work, equipment and furniture. More commonly, librarians attempting to recover from a disaster do not have such extensive information readily available. The initial priority is to develop a description of the estimated losses. Parent organizations, the insurance companies and the media will want immediate estimates on how many books, journals, maps, videos, etc., were lost or damaged in various subject areas. As work continues on the assessment of the loss and the documentation, refine the numbers and identify exact titles. In order to obtain an initial estimate, use a combination of records from the library online catalog and diagrams of the building to determine an estimate of the number of items lost.[2] If the catalog did not have records for all volumes, or if losses were in an area that had not been included in the online catalog, the extent of the damage can only be estimated.

Determining the specific losses from the collection requires time, careful review of the damaged collections, patience and persistence. Sadly, circumstances usually will not permit much time, and may render a thorough review of the damaged materials difficult or impossible. Providing the most complete information as can be reasonably gathered is very desirable. However, at some point one must accept the current reality that information may not be complete. Use the online catalog, shelflists, building diagrams and any other documentation available to identify what materials were damaged or lost. Consult with subject specialists who can provide more information about notable materials that were lost or damaged. Some materials in the damaged area may have been checked-out before the disaster. While the numbers of circulating materials may be too small to influence the size of an insurance settlement, that information will be needed when the process of replacing items is begun.

Reviewing Collections

Once collections can be physically examined, take extensive notes and photographs to document the damage. Begin the process of identifying what can be salvaged and what is a complete loss. Many materials that have been damaged by water can be air-dried or freeze-dried and returned to the collection; items receiving minor smoke damage can be easily cleaned. When first viewing the aftermath of a disaster, it is easy to be overwhelmed by the extent of the damage. Try to cope with that response and move towards a critical analysis of the situation. Begin by identifying what types of materials were involved (paper, photographs, microforms, etc.); what caused the damage (water, smoke, etc.); and whether any of the materials were unique or extremely valuable. If the damage did not involve a large number of materials and did not involve any special collections, the library staff may be able to use basic preservation techniques to salvage some materials. If the disaster was extensive, if formats such as microfilm were damaged, or if unique collections were involved, and depending on the level of in-house conservation expertise, the library probably needs assistance from professional salvage companies and conservators.

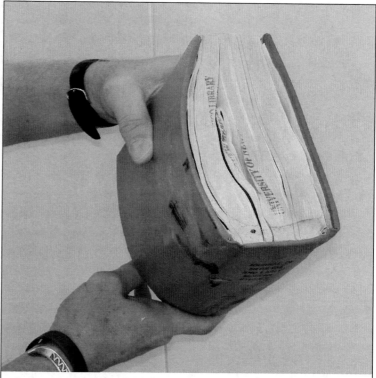

Figure 13: Water Swollen Damaged Book

Paper Collections Damaged by Water

Paper materials that have been damaged by water will swell; the paper will ripple; the inks may run; and coated, slick pages will begin to adhere to adjacent pages. (See Figure 13.)

If only a few items are involved, library personnel can dry the outside covers with ink-free paper towels or cloths. Then blotting paper can be placed between the damp pages to absorb the moisture. The materials can then be air-dried. This technique must be done as quickly as possible before mold develops. It requires space for the items to be spread out and time for staff to insert the paper. Materials damaged by water may still be swollen when they are dry. If so, they will require additional shelf space.[3]

If large numbers of print materials are damaged and the library has no capacity to move or treat the materials, the library may hire recovery vendors to freeze-dry the wet, damaged collections. Materials must be frozen as quickly as possible. The drying process can take several weeks, depending upon the extent of the damage. Moisture is removed, and the items do not swell as much as they would if they were air-dried.[4]

Paper Collections Damaged by Smoke

Much of the damage from a fire is caused by the smoke and soot that spreads through an area. Review the affected items to determine whether the damage is only to the exterior binding or if the interior contents of the books have been damaged. (See Figure 14.)

If the bindings have received minor smoke or soot residue, they may be vacuumed or wiped clean. Vacuums should be the types that are designed to

Figure 14: Smoke and Soot Damaged Books

minimize the amount of dust that could be re-circulated, such as those using a HEPA (high-efficiency particulate air) filter. Microfiber or magnetic wiping cloths, which attract dust with an electrostatic charge rather than with chemicals, should be used to clean books.[5] If the damage to the bindings is more extensive, items should be rebound.

Photographs, Film, or Microforms Damaged by Water

Some photographs can be destroyed very quickly, while others can survive water damage more easily, depending upon the nature of the paper and the photographic process. Generally, wet photographs must be air-dried or freeze-dried as quickly as possible. Remove the photographs from their frames or enclosures and drain off any excess water. Spread

them out to dry face up on absorbent materials such as blotters or paper towels. After they have been stabilized, consult with the library's conservator or archivist to determine possible treatment.[6] If film, microfilm, or microfiche were completely soaked, they must be handled carefully. Unrolling reels or separating individual microfiche can damage them; consult with salvage experts about the options. If the materials have received considerable damage, replacement may be more efficient than restoration.

Mold

Mold and mildew will develop quickly, generally within hours of coming in contact with water if the area is warm with poor air circulation. If mold forms on exposed items, contain and remove those materials very quickly, handling them as little as possible.

Use gloves, respirators and protective clothing when handling any moldy materials. If these items are very valuable, arrange with a trained conservator to deal with these materials. If the damaged materials will not require such extensive conservation, the materials should be disposed of quickly. Take photographs to document the damage, inventory the items, and dispose of them appropriately to prevent the spread of mold to other items. Consult the parent organization for instructions about the proper handling of hazardous materials.[7]

Removing Damaged Collections from the Library

If damaged collections are removed from the building by a company that will clean and restore them, create an inventory of what leaves the building. If the company discovers some materials that cannot be salvaged during the process of cleaning them, it will consult with library staff regarding the disposition of those items. When the materials do return and are unpacked, employees may determine that some materials should be replaced rather than be retained. This review process is extremely time-consuming because each piece must be evaluated. If the amount of materials being returned is large, employees may simply decide to accept the items and re-shelve them

without careful review, hoping to continue the process of evaluating these items at a future date. Time constraints may force such decisions; just be aware that postponing such a review to the future will be equally difficult. In addition, these decisions on disposition must be included in the documentation of the disaster recovery, now rather than years later.

Tracking the Losses

The importance of creating a system to track losses and decisions about replacements of collections cannot be over estimated. Depending upon the nature and extent of the disaster, a spreadsheet program may be a useful tool to record the titles lost, the recommendation for replacement, the estimated cost and the final result. If additional information is needed, such as bibliographic information, the consolidated final total cost for replacing a journal title that was purchased from multiple vendors, the rationale for not replacing an item, or the various vendors that could supply alternative formats, a more useful tool such as a relational database program may be chosen. In cases of very large disasters, a database created for a specific recovery project should be developed. (See Figure 15.)

In such cases, work closely with information technology personnel to identify all the factors that need to be included. Be sure to inquire whether the insurance company will cover the costs of the time taken to create the tool. If a large number of titles and subject areas are involved, a database that can be used by several different people may be justified. If that is the situation, a password-protected database hosted on a shared drive with both in-library and remote access capabilities will be very valuable.

Anticipate being asked for status reports and information frequently, and design the database so that it

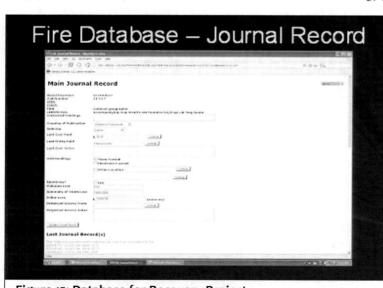

Figure 15: Database for Recovery Project

can be easily used to retrieve information. The questions will seem endless and will amplify an already frustrating situation. In order to reduce the level of frustration, create a brief summary of the losses and progress that can be updated easily and distributed widely. Depending upon the nature of the loss, consider creating a list of lost materials that can be shared with library users on the institutional Web site. Such a list may need to be an edited version of the internal documentation as the complete records with full bibliographic information may not be useful for most users. Remember that the list will need to be updated as new information becomes available.

Identify which materials are to be replaced in the original format and which ones are to be replaced in alternative formats. For example, if losses were in print journals, federal documents, or microform collections, consider replacing some of the items with digital resources. Identify what options are available and request pricing from vendors. Many digital collections of archival journals or newspapers require the initial cost plus an annual maintenance fee. Be certain that the operational budget of the library can cover these ongoing expenses since the insurance money will not cover those future costs.

Determining the Value of Lost Collections

Determining the actual value of lost materials can be complicated, but in the early stages average costs can be calculated to estimate the losses. Statistics on the average costs of academic books and journals are available from professional sources such as *The Library and Book Trade Annual* published by Information Today, Inc., and the annual survey of periodicals pricing published in *Library Journal* each spring. Publishers and vendors specializing in academic books, out-of-print books and journals, microforms or journal subscriptions can also provide information about prices for materials. Establishing

the value of unique and rare materials is more difficult, and may require assistance of appraisers with specialized knowledge in the areas where materials were lost. Library inventories should have included detailed descriptions of the condition and features of the most valuable rare books. That information will enable the specialists to determine the replacement value. Estimates of the original costs of materials may be required if the parent organization needs to deduct the amount of the loss from its overall valuation for risk management purposes. In such cases, work with the average costs for materials for historical pricing information and the statistics for the growth of the library in order to establish approximate values.

Budgeting and Financial Accounts

To facilitate timely and potentially large purchases, insurance company(ies) may advance a portion of the full amount after they have reviewed the initial report on the lost and damaged collections. Arrangements can be made with the parent institution to identify where the money will be kept and how access will be managed. In most cases, insurance payments are held in special accounts that are separate from the regular allocations to the library. This practice enables the funds to be tracked more readily. If the library maintains an accounting system that is separate from that of the parent organization, an additional category for the insurance funds will be needed. Be prepared to track diligently what is spent and report on the progress regularly. If the institution's financial system cannot generate the types of reports that are required by the insurance company, find alternative methods of documenting expenditures. Some insurance companies may want copies of the invoices for all purchases made. Such documentation is time-consuming to create late in the process, so be certain to understand and negotiate the requirements at the beginning of the replacement process.

If the insurance company does not advance a portion of the claim, work with the parent institution to identify sources of funds to begin recovery purchases. Some organizations will provide funding and then restore those funds when the insurance money arrives. In all cases, work closely with colleagues in the parent organization and be sure to document all expenses thoroughly.

Most insurance companies set a time limit for the completion of a claim. In many cases, they want to settle the claim within two years, an insurance industry standard. In the case of a major disaster, such a deadline may not be practical. If portions of the collection were removed for cleaning and were stored while the building was being renovated, the full extent of the damage may not be known for an extended time. Keep the insurance carrier/adjuster informed and negotiate with the companies to identify a time line that works for all concerned.

Even when arrangements for companies to do most of the cleaning and repairing of materials have been made, additional supplies for mending, rebinding and preservation may be necessary. These costs should be documented and charged to the insurance funds as well.

If losses were extensive, an RFP (Request for Proposal) may be required in order to select a new vendor or to increase the amount of business with current vendors. Many states require RFPs if an organization plans to do more that a specified amount of business with a company. Ask your organization about the requirements governing such circumstances.[8]

Insurance Negotiations and Reporting

Librarians must work closely with their parent organization and their insurance companies to provide information about the losses. When representatives from the insurance companies arrive, they will ask for specific information about what was lost and what it will cost to replace those materials. This initial estimate is important to help the companies grasp the extent of the damage and begin planning for the reimbursement. Identify the procedures that are required to inform the companies about the losses.

Some insurance adjusters have no experience working on a claim for library materials, so be prepared to provide extensive background on how library collections are acquired, processed and described. The reverse is also true. Most librarians have never been involved in large insurance claims, so use this opportunity to understand the major players in this situation, the business of commercial insurance coverage, and to ask for clarification on the definition of terms. The more precise information that can be provided, the more responsive the insurance companies can be to the claim. Show them the types of information available that describes the collection (such as descriptive cataloging, item and order records), and discuss how the value of what was lost and damaged will be estimated. Provide a preliminary estimate, and inform them that more detailed information will be forthcoming as the extent of the damage unfolds. Identify the people within the library, its parent organization, and within the insurance company who will be working together on the claim. Determine whether the insurance company will accept the methods described to identify the value of the lost materials. Be sure to include information about any rare or unique materials lost. Some companies may require appraisals by authorized individuals, especially if rare materials were lost. Remember, the more rapidly the data is provided, the sooner a partial payment will be authorized and received from the insurance company(ies). Identifying every lost or damaged item is almost impossible; however, the more complete the documentation, the better the claim to the insurance company(ies) will be. "Identifying materials destroyed, using bibliographic and item records can result in higher replacement payments than estimates."[9]

After the insurance company has been given the documentation of the losses, identify the next steps to be taken by the library and the parent organization. Determine what will be required in order to receive payments and how those payments will be processed. Will the funds be deposited directly in the accounts of the parent institution or handled by a state agency that is involved in the insurance process? Some companies may want copies of every invoice for every replacement item. Others may accept spreadsheets that list the titles and amounts spent. In all cases, be prepared to provide regular status reports to both the parent organization and the insurance companies that document the current status and progress in spending the money.

The insurance company may require replacement of items with materials that are an exact match or they may allow replacement of lost items with similar, but not exact, titles. Inevitably, some lost materials cannot be replaced because items will be out-of-print. The library may want to replace print journals with digital versions. Work with the insurance company to establish guidelines and the rationale upon which decisions are based. In some cases the digital replacement may be more cost effective as there are no physical pieces to be shipped, received, bound and processed. If the loss involved a print collection of materials about U. S. history, can the library acquire an online database that covers the same topic even if it does not include the exact titles that were lost?

Although not customary, insurance funds may cover the cost of staff time to identify and document the losses and to replace the materials. Ordering, receiving, and preparing materials for the shelves takes time. If insurance funds will cover such work, establish a process to document the time spent.

As the recovery process continues, unanticipated circumstances will be discovered that will require ongoing discussions with the insurance company. For example, if materials were damaged by water and were sent to a specialist for restoration, the items will probably be returned slightly swollen. These items will then require more space on book shelves. If additional shelving is required, will the insurance cover those costs?[10] Be prepared to negotiate for unexpected circumstances throughout the process.

Insurance policies can be complicated. Some general policies will not cover losses of art or exceptionally rare materials; those must be covered by special policies or amendments to the basic policy with separate deductibles. Policies can be very specific about the type and cause of damage that is covered. The insurance company may want to establish the original source of a flood or the cause of a fire. Such procedures usually involve the parent organization and its legal representatives. Some policies may insure rare books only while they are in secure locations within insured library buildings. Insurance policies may not cover books that were damaged in the process of being moved in order to save them. Negotiations can be very time-consuming; Tulane University was in litigation for years after the flood caused by Hurricane Katrina.[11]

Insurance almost never covers the personal property that employees have in their work areas. While such losses are very unfortunate, most organizations cannot attempt to reimburse the employees for such losses.

While every librarian who goes through a disaster wishes that they could just be handed a check for all recovery and replacement costs and forget all the requirements for documentation and accounting, that never happens. Be prepared to provide painstaking documentation, often repeatedly. Expect to deal with delays and bureaucratic red tape. Monitor the status and transfer of funds in both the institutional accounts and the library's accounts.

Negotiations within the library over the amounts that are spent to rebuild collections and those needed to restore the physical facility may also occur. The process will be much smoother if a good inventory of the collection exists, but even with extremely good information, the process will be frustrating and time-consuming.

Replacing and Restoring Collections

Despite the frustrations in dealing with the process of inventory and replacement, one of the few positive aspects of a major disaster is that insurance money and donations can contribute to improving the collection. Among the lost materials may be items that are no longer vitally important to the curriculum or institutional mission, and those replacement funds may be applied to the acquisition of more recent and relevant material. Where digital versions were previously unaffordable, replacing lost print materials with them may now be possible. Some of the materials that were lost might have been good candidates for withdrawal at some point. The collections may have been somewhat incomplete and the insurance funds will cover the cost to acquire complete backfiles of periodicals in the subject areas that were lost. Use this opportunity to evaluate the collections and end-user needs to identify options for replacement. "In the aftermath of a major hurricane, fire, or flood, much of the 'legacy' collection of paper-based materials will be lost forever, and the possibility of reconstituting the collection as it formerly existed is doubtful… Insurance companies and FEMA, which sometimes predicate reimbursement on replacement of identical items, will need to understand that such replacement would be a practical impossibility, and not even always desirable in the 21st century."[12] Identify what materials support the institution's core mission and priorities and target those areas for immediate replacement. Regardless of how thoroughly the losses are documented, only rarely can the insurance payments can cover the replacement of everything. Thus, librarians will need to identify the priorities for materials that will and will not be replaced.

Replacing Lost Materials

Involve library users in the discussions of what areas or items are targets for immediate replacement. Faculty can help identify the most important journals in their areas, which can be one of the factors in the evaluation process. However, once that process is begun, be prepared to research individual titles and to meet with users who are deeply concerned about the losses in their areas.

Some parent institutions may require that an RFP be issued to select vendors for the replacement of materials. Consult with the purchasing department within the parent organization to determine their requirements.

Once the priorities for areas and titles of replacement are identified, begin working with publishers and vendors to supply the materials. Some publishers, especially those who handle expensive print reference tools or microform sets, may supply replacements for lost or damaged materials without charge or with only minimal costs. Ask the sales representatives if that is a possibility. The nature of the lost material will determine the likely vendors with which the library will work. For example, companies specialize in formats such as journals, books, microforms, and digital resources or formats such as photographs. See the Appendix for lists of some of the major companies.

When vendors are given a list of items to be replaced, set guidelines with a range of the dollar amount the library is willing to spend for each item as well as informing the vendor of the total amount available. Stress the importance and methods of communication with vendors as they identify items that exceed the price guidelines. Some vendors can supply items with shelf-ready processing (cataloging, labeling etc.) for an additional cost, but verify that the insurance company will cover those costs before agreeing to the purchase.

Local and regional materials are usually difficult for national vendors to obtain. A more efficient and effective method may be to ask local library, historical and literary societies for assistance in procuring such specialized materials.

Establish a time line with vendors for purchasing materials. Once the insurance companies determine when the final documentation from the library or parent organization is due, schedule the date for the last payment to all vendors. That date will determine when the vendor must stop sending invoices. In some cases, a deposit account with a vendor can be established so that materials can be processed and sent after the final billing date. However, such arrangements must be negotiated very carefully and well in advance with all concerned parties.

Repairing Damaged Materials

Damaged materials should be carefully reviewed to determine how they should be handled and what type of treatment they should receive. Depending upon the materials and the damage, items may be discarded, cleaned, repaired, rebound, boxed, or carefully conserved. If the item has minimal damage to the spine or edges, simply and carefully wipe the item and return it to the collection. Some materials may need very minimal attention, such as replacing labels, date-due slips, and other markings that have been damaged or lost. Damaged spines can be removed and items rebound. If extensive repairs are needed, decide whether it will be less expensive to replace the item. Repurchasing a book may be easier and far less expensive than it would be to have a damaged copy dried, cleaned and rebound. Unique and rare materials and special formats such as photographs or microfilm may require specialized treatment by a conservator or specialist. Identify the personnel within the library who will conduct the review, make the decisions, do the repair work or work with companies specializing in restoration of materials. For work to be done by outside conservators, consult with and negotiate pricing with experts on the type and extent of the treatment in advance of signing agreements or shipping materials. See the Appendix C for information about resources concerning conservation and preservation assistance.

If the amount of damaged materials is significant, it may be more efficient and cost-effective to hire a company to handle the basic cleaning or rebinding. Consider using the library's current binder if only a few thousand volumes require rebinding. As with other aspects of the recovery effort, negotiate a price and schedule shipments over a prescribed period of time. If the costs exceed the amount of mon-

ey that was set in your original binding contract, an exception may need to be negotiated through the parent organization, or perhaps a new RFP may be required.

Carefully document the decisions and track the time spent. Some insurance policies may cover the costs of the time and the supplies used to repair materials. This documentation of decisions will also contribute to the necessary updates to the catalog records and holdings statements.

Donations and Public Relations

As people learn about the disaster, many will want to help with the recovery. Some people will send money while others will offer to help replace the lost materials. While the support is heart-warming, handle the offers of materials very carefully. During the early part of the recovery operations, storage of donated materials may be problematic which will limit the acceptance of immediate gifts. This limitation can be very discouraging to donors who may never return with the materials. Try to arrange for temporary storage space for the items truly needed. When talking with media, stress that the library cannot deal with the unexpected arrival of donations that have not been negotiated and authorized.

Even with good media coverage indicating the inability of the library to accept book donations, many offers of materials that are not needed will be made. In some cases, the potential donors will have misunderstood what was lost. In other cases, they will believe that since some materials were lost, certainly the library would like their donation even if it is not in the same subject area of the damage. The challenge is to respond graciously while refusing the materials that are not needed. Suggest other potential places that might be interested in accepting the materials. Other donations may be offered with the condition that the library pays for the shipping and packing costs. Evaluate such offers very carefully to identify the costs involved. Such offers may be bargains, but some can be more expensive than purchasing the materials from a vendor. And again, check with the insurance company to determine if they will reimburse the library for postage or shipping costs.

Development officers and fund-raising campaigns organized by parent organizations can be very effective at publicizing the damage and generating donations. Work with them to explain some of the constraints in accepting unsolicited donations and to encourage cash donations. Do not be surprised at the number of people who will rally to support the recovery efforts.

Conclusion

Rebuilding collections that were damaged or destroyed is painstaking and detailed. Complete, current inventories make the work easier, but the process is never going to be simple. Documenting the losses, negotiating with insurance companies and working with vendors are frequently complicated tasks. As progress from the initial estimates towards the specific documentation is made, be prepared for many of the early emotions to resurface. As it is learned which exact materials were lost, the impact of the disaster can become even more intense for library staff and the community. Be prepared to deal with reactions from users and librarians when they learn of the extent of the loss in their subject areas. The emotional reactions are normal; seek help to work through the ups and downs of the recovery. Although difficult to see at times, the process of rebuilding the lost collections can often result in a stronger, more cohesive collection and a more accurate inventory of holdings; however, the process is time-consuming. The goal is to restore and improve the collections as much as possible, while acknowledging that some materials are irreplaceable.

Notes

1.   Beth Oehlerts, "Inventory: Risk Identification and More." *Library & Archival Security* 22, no. 2 (2009): 73-83.

2.   Diane B. Lunde and Patricia A. Smith, "Disaster and Security: Colorado State Style," *Library & Archival Security* 22, no. 2 (2009): 99-114.

3.   Northeast Document Conservation Center. Preservation Leaflet 3.6. Emergency Salvage of Wet Books and Records http://www.nedcc.org/resources/leaflets/3Emergency_Management/06SalvageWetBooks.php (December 14, 2009).

4.   Ibid.

5.   Northeast Document Conservation Center. Preservation Leaflet 4.3. Cleaning Books and Shelves http://www.nedcc.org/resources/leaflets/4Storage_and_Handling/03CleaningBooksAndShelves.php (December 14, 2009).

6.   Northeast Document Conservation Center. Preservation Leaflet 3.7. Emergency Salvage of Wet Photographs http://www.nedcc.org/resources/leaflets/3Emergency_Management/07SalvageWetPhotos.php (December 14, 2009).

7.   Northeast Document Conservation Center. Preservation Leaflet 3.8. Emergency Salvage of Moldy Books and Paper. http://www.nedcc.org/resources/leaflets/3Emergency_Management/08SalvageMoldyBooks.php (December 14, 2009).

8.   Frances C. Wilkinson and Linda K. Lewis, *Writing RFPs for Acquisitions: A Guide to the Request for Proposal* (Chicago, American Library Association, Association of Library Collections and Technical Services, 2008), 3-6.

9.   Oehlerts, Inventory, 73.

10.   Lunde and Smith, Disaster and Security, 107.

11.   Andy Corrigan, "Tulane University: Hurricane Katrina," (case study in Part IV of this book).

12.   William Miller, "Natural Disasters in the Academic Library," *Library Issues* 28, no. 3 (2008): 2.

Chapter 7

FACILITIES RECOVERY: WORKING WITH ARCHITECTS, CONTRACTORS, AND OTHERS

"Barn's burned down, now I can see the moon." —Masahide

The activities between emergency response and recovery will often overlap obscuring the distinction between the two phases. In a few cases the response may be an organized linear sequence of events. Emergency response and recovery activities during large-scale disasters most often will be fast-paced and underway simultaneously. In such situations, the urgency to protect people, collections, and facilities will dictate priorities.

Assessing the Damage

Access to buildings to assess damage will depend on the extent and nature of the disaster. Facilities managers are often involved in the immediate emergency response to an event and will quickly begin to make note of the damage. Who better knows the layout of a building or locations of utility turn-off valves and mechanical rooms to assist emergency personnel, than the facilities staff who work in that building every day? Some damage will be obvious: burned or water-damaged walls and ceilings, buckled floors due to heat or movement due to earthquakes, collapsed roofs from fallen trees or heavy snow. Some parts of buildings may be a total loss; in other instances, only some portions of the structure and furnishings may be damaged or destroyed. In many cases, the full extent of the damage may not be revealed until the conclusion of the emergency response phase. On-site assessments by experienced experts will be followed by careful evaluations to determine the full loss. For example, damage due to smoke or soot can be particularly difficult to assess. Did the smoke cause only surface damage, or has it infiltrated the wall board and ceiling tiles? How extensive is the damage to electrical wiring or mechanical systems?

As the buildings and surrounding areas are stabilized, consider how collections, furniture, and equipment will be removed from damaged buildings. In order to prevent mold growth, wet objects should be moved to freezers within 48 hours of being damaged. This time frame is extremely short when dealing with the urgency of a disaster.[1] Elevators or escalators may be unavailable and stairwells blocked. It becomes a numbers game. What is the cost of paying laborers to carry out single boxes of books up or down several flights of stairs for several days or weeks? Alternatively, what is the cost of a mechanical conveyor with the capacity to move hundreds of boxes an hour when placed within a service entrance or window opening to a landing where an awaiting high-capacity construction bucket or pallet can be loaded and then be lowered or lifted by a crane to ground level? (Figure 16)

Obviously, solutions will vary by location and situation. This is the time to encourage and support creative problem solving. Personnel that work for disaster recovery companies and construction contractors have extensive experience finding new solutions to these kinds of situations. The best companies are always looking for the most efficient ways of dealing with these practical challenges. Being prepared with a pre-negotiated contract with a disaster recovery firm is highly recommended. The sooner their experience and expertise is contributing to

Figure 16: Conveyor for Removing Materials through Library Skylight

solving problems, the better. See Appendix for a sample request for proposal (RFP) for contracting with such companies.

Important partners in any recovery process are the representatives from the organizations that will be authorizing and/or funding the activities. In some cases, a parent organization (or governmental entity) may be self-insured for incidents with limited damage or where the cost for repair is below the deductible amount included in a commercial insurance policy. Where damage is extensive, institutional risk management professionals and insurance adjusters will be active participants in all phases of the recovery process. State and federal government personnel may also be involved when there is a widespread disaster due to natural causes. The business of risk management and insurance cover-

age are complicated issues. Exploring the details of institutional coverage is nearly impossible to accomplish in the middle of responding to a disaster. Instead, while drafting the disaster plan investigate the applicable institutional insurance coverage and review the risk management process.[2] Full replacement cost value for collections and facilities plus code upgrades for buildings are generally accepted and highly recommended as part of insurance coverage.[3] Additional policies providing extra coverage for fine art or objects in special collections should be in place as well. Working with insurance companies may be extremely complicated or comparatively straightforward. In cases of major disasters, satisfactory settlements of insurance claims can take years and may even require litigation. The best way to avoid, or at least minimize, such complications is through regular communication throughout the disaster recovery process.

As the recovery efforts quickly advance to repair and renovation, understand what sources of funding are available to cover business continuity costs in the event a library must be relocated and establish an operation in a new building while the damaged structure is being renovated.[4]

Restoration: Remodeling, Rebuilding, Renovating or Replacing

Contemplating the future rebuilding or renovation of damaged library structures while in the midst of reacting to the initial emergency may seem a distant concern. However, addressing that stage of the recovery will become a reality very soon with high expectations for timely resolution. Parent institutions, library patrons, university students, faculty and staff and library employees will all be anxious to have their library back—be it that favorite study table in a quiet corner, access to a body of literature a faculty member was using to research her latest book, dedicated library employees eager to return to their work areas, or the media clamoring for information on when the library will be reopened.

No matter how small the event or disaster, some damage to the physical environment of the library will result. It is never too early to begin assessing the damage done to facilities and begin planning for the recovery. Even relatively minor events such as water damage from small water pipe breaks or roof leaks will result in some repair and/or restoration of buildings, furnishings, equipment. Planning is essential to the successful recovery project.

If minimal damage is sustained, the services of an architect or contractor may not be required, and the repairs can be accomplished within the familiar routine of regular maintenance procedures and personnel. In the event of a major disaster experienced by a large public or academic library, it is highly recommended that a project restoration team be assembled. Members of that team will likely include represen-

tatives from the parent institution responsible for safety and risk management, facilities maintenance and capital building project management. Insurance adjusters, disaster recovery personnel, architects, engineers, contractors and planners may also be included. Library representatives must be included in the membership of this team. The library dean or director and facilities managers should attend the initial meetings where the overall assessments will be discussed and decisions made as to scope of work and overall timelines. Many of the same players involved in the emergency response and recovery activities may find themselves active members of this team reporting on the current status of the recovery efforts; assessment of the damage; and condition of collections, furnishings and equipment. This group, in cooperation with the funding body, will determine the level of restoration that will be required, estimate the cost of that work, and make recommendations for the compilation and issuance of contracts or RFPs.

In the ebb and flow of national recessions and economic downturns, funding to remodel or renovate libraries may be very difficult to acquire. While no one would ever wish for a disaster to strike their library, it might offer a silver lining peeking through the heavy clouds of damage and destruction. Instead of rebuilding the damaged area as it was, take a moment to consider how the space could be reconfigured. Refer to the latest customer satisfaction survey, review current trends in library services and buildings, and share those ideas with the recovery team. Discuss all reasonable options. For example, insurance funding might provide the opportunity to build a learning commons or install efficient compact shelving, making room for inviting public spaces, group study rooms, or a digital learning lab. Creating new, enlivened library spaces may lift everyone's spirits and inspire creative ideas, giving the team new energy before they must take on yet another fast-paced and demanding phase of the recovery.

Once the decision is made to remodel, renovate or rebuild a library, the steps to manage a building program will be set in motion. Many of the same members of the project restoration team will remain on the building project team. Leadership of the building team can vary by organization and experience. One of the strengths of personnel from capital projects departments often includes project management. If architects or architectural and/or planning firms are brought into the project, that leadership role may be included in their scope of work and contract. Consistent and accurate documentation is essential throughout the design and construction of the building. A series of meetings will be required, more frequently at the onset of the project and tapering off as the project winds down.

Establishing how knowledgeable or experienced the major players are with restoring and building libraries as structures is crucial. Restoring existing libraries or planning new ones may be new experiences for many on the project team. Library representation in this project group is imperative as they are responsible for continually defining and clarifying library needs and terms. In many instances the library and the parent organization are the owners of the project. The library representative must be actively engaged with the project, be prepared to meet deadlines, respond to requests in a timely fashion, devote the time to attend meetings, read and understand memos, review architectural plans, speak up when proposed plans do not meet the needs of the library, and communicate with the project team as well as internally with library administration or functional units to understand the requirements of their physical space. The library representative may also be leading the program planning efforts within the library to gather information that will determine the workspace needs of the functional units and then taking that information back to the planning team.

Some characteristics of office buildings or schools have elements in common with library structures; however, libraries present some unique challenges to planners and designers. Library building codes are typically included in building specifications for educational institutions and these codes require some interpretation when applying them to libraries. The physical buildings can be quite complex and require an understanding of the current and future functions or activities that are being planned for the new space. "The library building is recognized more than ever as a locus for educational effort in a social setting. The building must meet the need for the "library as place" within academe…This intangible characteristic is often a major force in shaping the academic objective of the library building to meet the institutional goals for years ahead."[5]

Building Program

Building projects are commonly organized in the following stages: programming, site analysis, schematic design review, design development, construction documents, bidding process, building construction, and occupancy. Project managers, consultants, or architects may organize their projects with some variations of these stages depending on requirements of the parent institution or governing body. Depending on the extent of the post-disaster rebuilding or renovation, some steps may not apply, such as exterior site analysis would not be required if all renovation is limited to interior portions of a building. Librarians are now stepping firmly in the world of architects and planners.

If the funding has been identified and immediately available, the planning and construction of this new space may be on an accelerated pace. The library user community is eager to have their library restored to them, insurance carriers are interested in limiting the business continuity costs (storage of materials, rental of alternative library space, 24/7 security services, etc.), and library administrators are anxious to get employees back on the job and restore services.

Programming

During this phase, architects and planners will gather information by survey or interviews on how the space being renovated will be used. They will seek input from the library to identify any special requirements of the space such as room adjacencies or proximities; mechanical, electrical and plumbing replacements and upgrades; interior design elements, furnishings and equipment; and exterior site development including parking and landscaping.[6] Sannwald's *Checklist of Library Building Design Considerations* provides an excellent and comprehensive overview of the variety of spaces and functions that should be considered when programming a renovation or rebuilding project.[7] Employee input to the project is especially important when rebuilding workspaces. A series of meetings involving the planners and library employees should be conducted at an accelerated pace and recommendations documented.

Discussions and agreement on building efficiencies may be recommended, especially if the space is being completely replaced or repurposed. Building efficiency is defined as the net square footage (space described by the program) divided by the gross square footage of the building.[8] McCarthy offers the following as a guide: generally, the higher the ratio, the less open user space is available for seating, aisles, lobbies and entrances.[9]

Building Efficiency	Description
50 percent	Opulent, grand
60 percent	Monumental public building
65 percent	Comfortable
75 percent	Economical
80 percent	Spartan
85 percent or higher	Difficult to attain

Some important questions will need to be addressed and understood to inform the post- disaster planning process and define the scope of work. For example:

- If power was severed from the building, determine the time line when utilities will be restored.

- Will portions of the library remain open and functioning throughout the rebuilding process? If so, determine unacceptable levels of noise and air quality (including odors) and plan accordingly.

- Will safety officers permit the disabling of fire detection devices in areas under construction to reduce the number of false alarms ringing throughout the building during regular business hours? If so, require contractors to supply manual fire watch personnel during construction.

- Will collections remain in the building in some proximity to the construction? If so, will they require protection and security?

- What are the access points into the library? Are loading docks available, are service elevators functioning, and is parking available for contractors and their employees?

- Will work outside the scope of the construction be underway that may intersect or interfere with contractor work, such as installing shelving or moving collections or employee offices?

- Identify code compliance issues—does the building have historical significance or is it protected by the National Register of Historic Buildings? If so, the costs may be higher and design elements may be prescribed. Make sure the planners and designers understand the implications of compliance with provisions of the Americans with Disabilities Act for large public buildings.

- Will the renovation/rebuild require Leadership in Energy and Environmental Design (LEED) certification? A LEED-certified building will require green, sustainable design and construction processes that could increase the cost of the construction and extend the design and building timelines. Some states and governmental agencies are requiring some level of LEED certification for public buildings. "New Mexico is one of over 20 states in the U.S. to adopt LEED Silver certification (or LEED standards) for the greening of public buildings."[10]

Site Analysis

The need for a site analysis will depend on the extent of the renovation or rebuild. If a totally new building will be constructed, an extension is being added or if the damage to the building was a result of flooding due to an existing poor site location, this phase will be essential. The site analysis is the process that determines the placement of the structure on the building site in relationship to topography, adjacent buildings, zoning restrictions, street access, utility easements and setbacks, orientation to the sun, location of the parking lot and walkways, and outbuildings if any.

Schematic Design Review

Leighton describes the schematic design phase as the "process that translates the written facilities program into a graphic representation of the architectural concept."[11] The architect takes the information gathered from the programming phase and begins to create the basic floor plans and elevation drawings of the building. This step provides the architects, engineers, librarians and physical plant personnel an opportunity to visualize and virtually walk through the new space. Many questions will arise about space allocations by function, such as are the adjacencies workable, is the service elevator located on the opposite side of the building to the shipping and receiving function, are the doors to public bathrooms obscured by runs of tall shelving, is the circulation service desk located near public entrances, or is there adequate space for the number of employee workstations indicated in the plan? Descriptions of the mechanical, plumbing and electrical systems will be provided and locations identified. Estimates of the reconstruction costs will also start to emerge suggesting that the design should either be scaled back or enhanced.

Design Development

After the set of schematic design documents are approved by the owner and funding authorities, the architects, designers and engineers will start creating detailed floor plans to scale; specify construction techniques and materials; and provide specifications on moldings, casework, finishes, and lighting. Mechanical, electrical, and plumbing systems will be refined and described in greater detail. Security, alarm and fire suppression systems will be described and located within the building. Proposed interior arrangement of furniture will be represented in interior elevation drawings. Cost estimates will be recalculated and presented to the owner. Architects and owners will once again review the set of design drawings, make revisions and ultimately agree to proceed to the next step in the process.

Construction Documents

This phase of the project will result in the production of detailed or working drawings upon which the bids for the construction of the project will be based. All parties should be comfortable with the design drawings and decisions at the beginning of this phase as any modifications other than change-orders typical in any construction project will be expensive and delay the work of architects and engineers. McCarthy suggests that this phase is the most time-consuming for the project architect, representing approximately 40% of the architect's time.[12]

The construction drawings and accompanying text provide in precise detail descriptions of the building design and structure; building materials and construction methods; specifications on doors and windows including hardware; conveying systems such as elevators, escalators, book delivery systems; security, alarm, and suppression systems; finishes on floors, walls and ceilings; mechanical HVAC systems; electrical design and fixture details; and automated control systems. These drawings and documents will require detailed scrutiny by mechanical and electrical engineers, plumbers and construction experts representing the owner.

Bidding Process

Working closely with the purchasing department of the parent organization, bid documents will be compiled according to the rules and regulations of the institution. Depending on the size of the project, the bid documents will include instruction to bidders, bid forms, specifications on required performance bonds, liability insurance, and conditions of the contract. Once the set of construction drawings are approved and the bid documents are compiled, the project will be advertised requesting bids from qualified contractors.

In large public institutions, on-call or pre-approved contractors may be identified. These contractors may have already proven their financial capacity to complete the project successfully and have a track record with the parent organization. The rules governing the certification of contractors will vary by organization.

Large construction projects will often require a pre-bid meeting and walk through of the work site. The library representatives on the project team should attend this meeting to hear the questions from the potential bidders. A list of attendees should be compiled and minutes of the meeting should be kept that include questions and answers. Changes to the drawings or construction documents may result from this meeting which then become part of the total bid package. Clear and complete communication is imperative at this stage. Any contractor that feels they have been treated unfairly can later challenge the award of the bid which can delay the start of the project. The opening of the bids will take place on a predetermined date and time. As the library expert, the library representative on the project team should be an official member of the review committee. Precise rules from the parent organization will dictate the review, selection and award of the contract. Once the contractor is selected, the owners and their rep-

resentatives will negotiate and sign a contract, and a notice to proceed will be issued to the contractor. The contractor will begin to assemble the sub-contractors needed for the project and the library will prepare for the next stage of the recovery.

Building Construction

Typically, the management of the construction process will fall to the lead architect or parent organization's construction project manager. Project meetings will be scheduled frequently at the beginning of the project, perhaps daily, and taper off once the project is established, perhaps meeting weekly to biweekly. Several excellent sources exist that describe library construction projects.[13,14,15]

A project team will be formed which should include representatives from the library. Ideally, library representation should include the facilities or building manager and/or a library administrator who has been involved in the previous recovery process and who understands many functional areas of the library. Clear internal communication and a defined chain of command within library management should be established. Library deans or directors should be kept informed of building progress including problems and successes as they are encountered. Employees, students, faculty, and the media will all be very interested in knowing the current status of the project.

Be prepared for surprises daily. Unexpected noises; odors; and temporary loss of power, heating, or air conditioning will undoubtedly occur. If portions of the building remain occupied during the construction, try to anticipate the surprises and forewarn library staff and customers of these circumstances. The library or parent institution's marketing or public affairs units may want to consider creating blogs, installing webcams, bulletin boards, or posting photos on the library Web site to document the construction progress.

One of the final and important steps as the completion of the construction project approaches is to walk through the building to determine if work is not completed or repairs are needed. A formal meeting or series of meetings will eventually be called to create the punch list of remaining work. At a minimum, representatives for the contractor, architect, and library will systematically review all areas of the construction. This review is the opportunity to test all aspects of the rebuilt library, for example, test all HVAC and security systems; turn on lights; confirm water faucets, toilets and drains are working; inspect for missed or sloppy painting; and insure all carpet is properly installed. If furniture is part of the construction contract, try it out. Visiting the site after hours may prove valuable to inspect effectiveness and placement of lights. The contractors can now repair work that was previously completed but was damaged along the way. Problems that are not identified and placed on the punch list at this juncture may become the responsibility of the owner to complete at their own expense. Fire, safety and building inspectors will also schedule their assessments in preparation for the certificates of occupancy. Their findings may also contribute to the punch list. The urgency to occupy the space will be most evident when the construction activity begins to subside and only the last details remain. The library representative should not feel pressured by the contractor, architect or parent organization to sign off on the punch list until they are confident the final construction product has been tested and checked and the punch list is accurate and complete.

When the architect, contractor, and owner are all satisfied with the accuracy of the punch list, a certificate of substantial completion may be issued by the architect. This is a milestone to be celebrated and one of significance in the shift of responsibility for the building. This date will determine the beginning of the building warranties; insurance, utilities and building security will become the responsibility of the owner; and the remaining substantial payment to the contractor will be transferred. The owner and parent organization will have to weigh the benefits of taking advantage of this option, such as moving in sooner, against the risks of potential damage to the building when responsibility for the repairs may be murky. Know and understand the risks.[16]

Occupancy

When all inspections are complete and the final certificate of occupancy has been issued by the local building authority, the construction project is officially closed and all responsibilities for the building are transferred to the owner. Although some work will remain to be done from the punch list, library collections can be returned and employees can begin moving back into the building in preparation for opening day. Library personnel and the contractors are now gearing-up for some of the hardest work of the project. Depending on the circumstances in which collections were removed, the order and organization of the collections could be in complete disarray. Staging areas to sort returning collections must be identified and outside labor and expertise may be necessary to facilitate the pack-back. See the "Zimmerman Library Fire: A Case Study in Recovery and Return of Library Collections" in Part IV of this book for more details about the pack-back process. Library staff begin to occupy the building, discovering all the great new features, such as furniture, equipment, and space; and some of the shortcomings. No matter how diligent the inspections to create the punch list were, the need for some changes and warranty work will be revealed. Negotiations among the architect, contractor and owner may continue for several months to sort out solutions, responsibilities and payment for previously undiscovered work.

Conclusion

From the first moment a disaster strikes the library, the goal of returning library collections and services to the university community of students, faculty and staff and library employees should be ever present in the minds and hearts of the many people involved in the emergency response and recovery activities. Depending on the circumstances and extent of the damage, recovery can be quick or can extend for years. Recovery and rebuilding are significant team efforts involving disaster recovery experts, contractors, insurance adjusters, physical plant personnel and library representatives. Planning new library spaces will be demanding but inspiring when unforeseen opportunities are seized. Librarians witness the restoration of not just a building, but the transformation of a disaster site to an attractive, lively center of a campus.

At last, celebration day has arrived! All the appropriate dignitaries will be in attendance, expressing their gratitude for all the hard work that was accomplished to restore the library to its new and better condition. The process has been long and exhausting for the facility managers, contractors, and library employees, but rewarding beyond anyone's expectations. No one is the same person they were moments before receiving that fateful call informing them that the library was at risk and help was needed.

Notes

1.   Heritage Preservation, *Field Guide to Emergency Response* (Heritage Preservation, Inc., 2006), 36.

2.   Mary Breighner, William Payton, and Jeanne M. Drewes, *Risk and Insurance Management Manual for Libraries* (Chicago: American Library Association: Library Administration & Management Association, 2005), 3.

3.   Halcyon Enssle and Cathy Tweedie, "Why Can't Facilities Fix This." In *Library Disaster Planning and Recovery Handbook*. Camila Alire, ed., (New York: Neal-Schuman, 2000), 101.

4.   U. S. Library of Congress. U. S. Library of Congress Preservation: Emergency Preparedness: Insurance/Risk Management http://www.loc.gov/preserv/emergprep/insurancemain.html (December 22, 2009).

5.   Philip D. Leighton and David C. Weber, *Planning Academic and Research Library Buildings* (Chicago: American Library Association, 1999), 25.

6.   Richard C. McCarthy, *Managing Your Library Construction Project: A Step-by-Step Guide* (Chicago: American Library Association, 2007), 17.

7.   William W. Sannwald, *Checklist of Library Building Design Considerations*. (Chicago: American Library Association, 2009).

8.   McCarthy, *Managing Your Library Construction Project*, 23.

9.   Ibid, 24.

10.   LEED Management Services. How-To Guide to LEED® Certification for New Mexico Buildings (Lafayette, CO: LEED Management Services, 2007), 4.

11.   Leighton and Weber, *Planning Academic and Research Library Buildings*, 419.

12.   McCarthy, *Managing Your Library Construction Project*, 50.

13.   McCarthy, *Managing Your Library Construction Project*.

14.   Leighton and Weber, *Planning Academic and Research Library Buildings*.

15.   Sannwald, *Checklist of Library Building Design Considerations*.

16.   McCarthy, *Managing Your Library Construction Project*, 77.

Chapter 8

LESSONS LEARNED

*"Believe that problems do have answers, that they can be overcome,
and that you can solve them."* —*Norman Vincent Peale*

The University of New Mexico, University Libraries, experienced two floods and a major fire within three years. Those experiences and the lessons shared by colleagues who also experienced disasters taught us more than we ever would have thought possible about the library, its employees, the University, the disaster response community, and ourselves. This chapter is a departure in style from the previous seven chapters. In this chapter, we, the authors, are taking a more informal, personal tone as we share with you some of our painfully gained knowledge.

The lessons are arranged in six broad categories, including preparation, communication, leadership, taking care of people, documentation, and evaluation. Like the response and recovery stages, many of the lessons overlap and could fit into multiple categories. Also, the lessons listed below are not in order of importance because what was most important for our library may not be the most important lessons for your specific situation.

Preparation
- Preparation can save you by preventing some disasters or at least reducing the damage, costs, losses, and recovery time.
- Have an updated disaster preparedness, response, and recovery plan. All managers must have copies at home and at work and possibly in their car as well. If you have an intranet, put a copy there. Have copies on a flash drive that can be given to police and fire departments responding to the disaster.

- Have a well trained disaster response assistance team appointed and ready to do what is needed.
- Know where controls for the utilities and alarms are located. Be able to show them to the rescue workers responding to the disaster. If your parent organization will permit it, train staff to shut off utilities.
- Know the location of air handling units, and familiarize yourself with how they operate.
- Have current building plans in multiple locations because they may be needed by fire fighters and/or police.
- Periodically review your emergency evacuation procedures, and be sure all staff are familiar with these procedures and emergency exits near their work areas. This is particularly important for night and weekend personnel.
- Establish and maintain good relationships with all other campus departments. You never know when you may need their assistance, and during emergencies it is very helpful to have positive relationships to call upon for assistance.
- Do an environmental scan of your library. Correct vulnerabilities when possible. Document what problems require attention and share that information with the parent institution.
- Be sure all library emergency responders and facilities personnel have cell phones.
- Protect art and artifacts as much as possible.

- Be sure that fire doors are rated and located properly at electrical closets and fire separation points in the building. Check with campus safety personnel for assistance.
- Have physical plant check to be sure all fire penetrations in slabs are properly filled to help prevent spread of fire. Fire penetrations are any holes in the slab, or open spaces around conduit or pipes running through a slab.
- Confirm with library IT personnel that all server and essential desktop PC files are properly backed-up with copies stored offsite.
- Have disaster supplies and make sure that they are kept current.
- Have additional batteries and chargers available to recharge cell phones and laptop computers.
- Have a complete inventory of your collections, furnishings, and equipment. The inventory needs to be backed-up with copies in multiple locations.
- Having pre-disaster contracts with recovery companies can save time, money, and collections. If you do not have them, try to get them.
- Know your insurance coverage, requirements, and exclusions.

Communication

- Know who to call: police and fire departments as well as parent organization's administration, physical plant maintenance staff, and insurance company representatives. Have all available contact information: home and cell phone numbers and all e-mail addresses; be sure that they are current.
- Have a current contact list for all library employees that includes all home and cell phone numbers, all e-mail addresses and any other means of contact. Department heads should have that information for all their student employees.
- Have a spokesperson and an alternate available for interviews and to communicate with the media. Arrange training on how to respond to the media for them in advance.
- Use technology to keep in touch: cell phones, e-mail, text messaging, instant messaging, Twitter, Facebook, blogs, and other social networking tools.
- Communicate continuously with employees. Have staff meetings in addition to posting information on the library's Web site and e-mail. Face-to-face meetings are especially crucial when staff are scattered and working in different locations. Technology-enabled virtual meetings are an alternative when face-to-face meetings are not practical.

Leadership

- Deploy only trained, capable staff in the response and recovery stages. Individuals must maintain composure and common sense throughout intensified physical and emotional circumstances. Staff must be able to follow directions carefully and completely, and also be able to think and act constructively on their own without ego issues.
- Know that some decisions will have to be made quickly. Know that some decisions will be second-guessed and others will be changed. Do the best you can, and keep moving forward. Document and share those decisions with the recovery team.
- Know that some decisions will not be up to the library administration to make. Depending on the nature of the disaster the building may be under the control of another entity such as the police department, the fire marshal, Homeland Security, FEMA, or other agency.
- Patience is imperative. Know that some things will seem to take forever. While some things do take a long time, such as investigations of what caused the disaster, others just seem to take longer because it is a crisis situation.

- Fight for insurance payments and additional support from the parent institution.
- You cannot do it alone—either as a dean or director, a disaster response team leader, an individual administrator, even library (if it is a major disaster). It takes a team effort to recover, and that team will include the entire library, campus, disaster recovery companies, architects, construction companies, and materials vendors if the disaster is extensive.
- Realize that recovery takes time and attention. Your existing staff cannot attend to the disaster recovery and their former jobs equally well. Reassign responsibilities officially and announce the changes to the organization.
- Be aware that the process of recovery circles; it is rarely a linear process. Just when you think everything is complete, you will discover one more thing—a title you had missed, a donor that just learned about the disaster and wants to help, or a physical area or piece of equipment that suddenly fails as a result of undiscovered damage. Recovery is a cyclical process.
- Stay flexible. Situations change by the moment. You cannot anticipate everything. You often must react and decide quickly.
- Seek help: from disaster recovery companies, from colleagues, and from your community.
- When you have recovered from a disaster, help others to prevent, plan for, and recover from disasters. Share your knowledge.

Taking Care of People

- Accept the emotional aftershocks. Some people will go through many of the seven stages of grief (shock, denial, bargaining, guilt, anger, depression, and acceptance). Others may have some post-traumatic stress reactions. Respect that, and do not dismiss it. Patience, empathy and support are vitally important.
- Depending upon the person and the situation, counseling referral services may be helpful.

Emotions may resurface strongly at anniversaries of the disaster.
- Celebrate the steps in the recovery and publicize them. Staff can be submerged in the details of recovery and not see how far things have come. The public can assume everything is fine long before the recovery is done.
- Provide snacks, pizza, and beverages throughout the disaster response and recovery phases.
- Say thank you often and mean it.

Documentation

- Document the disaster thoroughly, as it is happening. You will need the information both in the short range for insurance and rebuilding the facilities and collections, as well as for the long range documentation of the history of the building, the collections and the organization.

Evaluation

- Silver linings can happen. That will not seem believable when the disaster first strikes, but you may have the opportunity to improve some things. Depending upon the circumstances, you may be able to renovate the area physically, introduce new methods of working, acquire new collections, build increased support from community, or expand your fundraising. Do not assume that you have to replace everything exactly the way it was. Can you combine insurance and other funds to renovate the building in a more up to date, student friendly design? Can you shift from print to digitized collections for some materials? Plan your recovery. Use it to do things you had wanted to do, but did not think were possible or affordable.
- After a disaster, evaluate the disaster plan, debrief, and revise the plan.
- Evaluate the training program, what helped and what did not.

- Ask the first responders and the library staff what would have made things better. What parts of the plan worked well and what did not?
- Use the knowledge you get from surviving a disaster to prepare for another disaster, which you hope will never happen.

We could have benefitted from these lessons before our disasters struck, but we learned more with each new emergency. The compelling case studies in Part IV of this book offer many more valuable lessons shared by staff in five other libraries who experienced different types of disasters. Their challenges and successes can assist you if a disaster strikes your library. We hope that the lessons shared in this chapter ease your work to develop a plan and respond to a disaster should the need arise.

PART IV: CASE STUDIES

CASE STUDIES

California State University, Northridge: Sustained Upheaval: Rebuilding the Oviatt Library after the Northridge Earthquake
Susan E. Parker, Ph.D., Deputy University Librarian
University of California at Los Angeles Library
(Associate Dean, Oviatt Library at California State University Northridge from 1997-2005)

Colorado State University: 500 Year Flood
Diane B. Lunde, Coordinator of Metadata and Preservation Services and
Patricia A. Smith, Coordinator of Collections & Contracts, Colorado State University Libraries, Fort Collins, CO

Tulane University: Hurricane Katrina
Andy Corrigan, Association Dean for Collections at Tulane University, Howard-Tilton Memorial Library, New Orleans, LA

University of Hawaii at Mānoa: Flood
Paula T. Mochida, Interim University Librarian, University of Hawaii at Mānoa, Hamilton Library, Honolulu, Hawaii

University of Iowa: Flood
Nancy L. Baker, University Librarian, University of Iowa, Iowa City, IA

University of New Mexico: The Zimmerman Library 2006 Fire That Led to the 2007 Library Flood: An Overview
Edward Castillo Padilla, Library Facilities Manager,
Nancy Dennis, Associate Dean of Facilities and Access Services,
Linda K. Lewis, Collection Management Coordinator, and
Frances C. Wilkinson, Deputy Dean of University Libraries
University of New Mexico Libraries, Albuquerque, NM

University of New Mexico: Zimmerman Library Fire: A Case Study in Recovery and Return of Library Collections
Anne D. Schultz, Training Specialist, and
Teresa Y. Neely, Director of Access Services
University of New Mexico Libraries, Albuquerque, NM

Sustained Upheaval: Rebuilding the Oviatt Library after the Northridge Earthquake

Susan E. Parker

The Oviatt Library at California State University, Northridge recovered from devastating damage inflicted by a major earthquake in 1994. This is a story of the library's renewal, marked by episodes of bravery, tenacity, service, knowledge, and determination.

Northridge, California is a community of about 61,000 people living in approximately 11 square miles in the San Fernando Valley (SFV), within the city of Los Angeles. It is situated about 25 miles northwest of downtown Los Angeles. Serving 36,000 students and employing more than 4,000 faculty and staff, California State University, Northridge occupies 356 acres bounded by Devonshire Avenue, Reseda Boulevard, Zelzah Avenue, and Nordhoff Street. Originally a satellite campus of Los Angeles State University, in 1958 it became San Fernando Valley State College, a 4-year college meant to serve the quickly growing population in the area. Valley State in 1972 was renamed California State University Northridge, popularly known as CSUN. It is one of the largest of the 23 campuses in the state university system of California. A major regional comprehensive university, it offers bachelors and masters degrees and teaching credentials in 116 fields.[1]

At Impact

January 17, 1994 was a holiday, and it was also an intersession period at CSUN. Students were completing registration activities in preparation for the semester about to begin within a week or two. Faculty were planning their courses, and staff were catching up on tasks that are easier to complete when classes are not in full swing. At 4:31 a.m., the 6.7 magnitude Northridge earthquake hit, shaking citizens from San Diego all the way up north to Santa Barbara. People could feel the earthquake throughout an area of more than 200,000 square kilometers in the United States and Mexico, as far away as 400 kilometers from the epicenter.[2]

The earthquake lasted for 8 seconds, but most who lived through it say that it felt much longer, and there were dozens of strong, frightening aftershocks that went on for days and weeks after the quake. The earthquake was the result of the rupture of a blind thrust fault under the mountains north of CSUN. It came up to a depth of within 5 kilometers of the surface of the earth, and the epicenter was the northeastern San Fernando Valley, near the intersection of Wilbur and Arminta Avenues.[3] This location lies within two miles of the CSUN campus. Many awakened this morning had vivid and horrible flashbacks of the February 9, 1971 Sylmar Earthquake, which had a devastating magnitude of 6.6 and had struck early in the morning, also damaging some of the same parts of the San Fernando Valley area.

Damage

So intense was the devastation in and around Northridge that residents, most of whom were fast asleep at that early hour, were thrown from their beds or injured when furniture, ceiling fans, and mirrors fell on them. Books and other objects launched from their shelves and became projectiles; glassware and crockery emptied onto kitchen and dining room floors and created jagged obstacle courses. Electricity was knocked out, and people had to cope with the chaos and the frightening shaking in the dark. Telephone service was also unavailable. The Northridge Meadows apartment building a few blocks from the CSUN campus completely collapsed; three stories were pancaked on top of one another into the basement garage, resulting in fatalities. Gas mains broke, and fires erupted in the hilly, gated suburban neighborhoods north of the campus. At the Northridge Fashion Center shopping mall close by the CSUN campus, a vast parking structure collapsed. A total of 50 people died in the Los Angeles area as a result of the earthquake, most of them in Northridge. Approximately $15-20 billion worth of damage resulted. Homes were cracked open; residents in the SFV camped out in parks and back yards for weeks while inspectors checked on the safety of residential structures.[4]

On the east side of campus, a four-level parking garage sagged under the weight of its partial collapse.[5,6] The concrete parking structure was only 18 months old and had conformed to the existing building code specifications for earthquake safety. While the exterior columns were built to carry all earthquake stress, the interior support columns were designed to carry only the structural weight load and not earthquake stressors.[7] Building codes in place at the time had treated this design as adequate, but this and other building failures on campus gave evidence that proved otherwise. Information gathered from the study of the building failures at CSUN was later utilized to alter and update local building codes to require all structural columns in a building to be designed and equipped to resist the horizontal and vertical shaking and lift forces of earthquakes.

Classroom, office, and student housing buildings were shaken open: a high-rise dormitory, the old South Library building, and the Fine Arts building, designed by famed architect Richard Neutra, were so badly damaged that they were eventually razed.[8,9,10] Black, acrid smoke poured from the up-

per floors of two of the science buildings. Firefighters had to allow the fires to burn until they could learn what compounds were involved to handle them properly. Researchers were finally able to get word to the first responders that the noxious odors were from toxic fires consuming lithium bromide.[11]

In the center of the campus, the Delmar T. Oviatt Library suffered dramatic damage. The library, a five-story structure, is comprised of a core building built in 1973 with east and west wings originally added in 1991. Its signature look comes from the 45 columns that surround the building, each 55 feet high and weighing 40 tons. Many of the columns came loose at their footings when the bolts and four-inch thick steel base plates holding them in place snapped from the force of the earthquake and its up and down, side to side shaking motion.[12] In addition, the cantilever roof over the front and back entrances collapsed.[13,14,15]

The core of the building, fronted by glass on each of the four stories above ground level, was penetrated by some of the columns after they became loosened.[16,17] Interior library offices were overthrown and contents of bookcases emptied onto the floor. Dust covered everything; broken glass was strewn throughout offices along with computers, books, papers, and other objects on the floor. In some areas, filing cabinets that had been anchored in one corner of a room were found upside down in the opposite corner. Had library staff been at work at their desks at the moment of the earthquake, most would likely have been hit by these flying objects and glass, possibly even by the toppling columns themselves.

The 600,000 books sitting on shelves in the library's core were shaken out of the stacks onto the floor and would have to be reshelved.[18] Books were piled as high as three feet between ranges of shelving. The library's shelving, heavily bolted and braced, remained in place. Microfilm cabinets, situated in the basement level and buffeted by the earthquake's force, suffered the failure of their locking mechanisms. In cabinet after cabinet, drawers filled with heavy microfilm and microfiche had flown open, pulling the cabinets themselves into the aisles.[19] Some microfilm cabinets, known as "piggybacks," had been properly stacked and bolted on top of others, but the power and torque of the earthquake had wrenched them off and flung them into other areas of the room.[20] Legs collapsed on one end, study tables and index tables in the first floor reading room tilted haphazardly. The Automated Storage and Retrieval System (ASRS) in the lower levels of the east wing of the building remained stable, protecting approximately 700,000 books and periodicals, or about half the library's collection.

Decisions

That morning, campus officials, including the dean of the library, Dr. Susan Curzon, made their way cautiously to campus, driving on streets without benefit of the traffic signals that are essential to Southern Californians' daily commutes. The university president, who had been vacationing north of the city, flew in by helicopter because a key freeway overpass leading to the San Fernando Valley from the north had collapsed. Immediate concerns were for life safety, but then minds turned to the business of the university. Faculty members needed to retrieve their things from broken buildings—in some cases, their life's work was in peril. The library's books had survived, but they needed protection from the rain, dust, and debris damage. The decision was made to reopen the university for the spring semester, so that students would not lose their academic footing and staff would not lose their jobs. "CSUN Stands" was a slogan on billboards around campus, trumpeting the university's refusal to die.[21]

If the new semester was going to begin more or less on schedule—within two weeks—the library staff had much to do and little time in which to accomplish it. Initial efforts were devoted to locating faculty, staff, and students and helping them find family and loved ones. In the first days following the earthquake, the entire university operated in

an open, muddy field in the center of campus with a small core of volunteers, including the dean of the library. Most of the staff had to stay away on administrative leave for the first few weeks following the disaster. It was simply too dangerous an environment, with hazardous materials, asbestos, loose pillars and mortar, glass and debris, and unstable buildings.[22] Next, military tents arrived, and then some 300 trailers were set up for campus operations, including as classrooms. Library service started at the beginning of the new semester in FEMA trailers near the library building.[23] Library Dean Sue Curzon recalled, "We offered interlibrary loan and reference and were able to circulate some classroom media which we had rescued. We also activated our electronic resources."[24] At the dawn of the electronic era, however, thousands of periodicals were still delivered by mail, and a manual check-in system was devised.[25] Because library operations were quite limited, some library staff members were reassigned to other tasks essential to support the operation of a major university from a temporary field office setting. Primarily, people answered the phones, gave out the latest information to students, families, and the media, reassuring callers and one another.

Along with most of the buildings on campus, the Oviatt Library was deemed unsafe because of visible and suspected structural damage. The library was closed indefinitely, and it was not possible to retrieve many materials. Gradually this situation improved, and finally it was possible to page items from the library. Meanwhile, the library staff arranged for CSUN students and faculty to use the libraries at UCLA. The campus operated an hourly round trip bus service for students and faculty to the UCLA campus, 10 miles to the south. In exchange, CSUN librarians worked at UCLA libraries' reference desks.[26]

Students and faculty voted for the library to be the first and most important building that needed to be restored.[27] The damage in the library's core building included exposed asbestos; cleaning this hazard and refurbishing the different areas became a priority. After 68 days, the Oviatt Library core building was restored to service in August, 1994.[28] Marked by a campus-wide celebration honoring the return of the landmark building, the Library's services and collections had to be redistributed to fit a significantly smaller footprint than the Library had occupied before the earthquake. Decisions were needed about what services and collections would be available in the newly opened library core and what services and collections would be rearranged and placed into different accommodations. Books and book stacks, reference, periodicals, course reserves, computing servers, a computer lab, the ASRS, and offices for reference staff and administration would remain in the Oviatt core building.

Reconfiguration and Relocation; Re-reconfiguration and Re-relocation

Temporary housing was needed for Technical Services staff and their operations. This included book and periodical acquisitions, cataloging, binding, and special collections and archival processing. In May, 1994, they were located into a 16,000 foot renovated goat barn on the north end of campus well known to Valley residents as Devonshire Downs, a former racetrack that was home to regional agricultural fairs and the infamous Newport Pop Festival of 1969, featuring Jimi Hendrix.[29] Also offered in this location, which became known as the North Library Annex, was a vast area of study space for students, and banks of computers for accessing licensed electronic resources.[30]

The staff and collections for arts and music, microfilm and microfiche, and the Instructional Media Lab (IML) were situated in the 10,000 square foot Lindley Avenue Library Annex (LALA), or dome, an aluminum-ribbed Sprung Instant Structure, whose roof and sides were protected by a silver-colored polyurethane coated membrane.[31] A smaller 5,000 square foot "Study Hall Dome" sat nearby, while another library operated study space for

students. Many of these domes housed office workers, including the campus provost, for the duration of the campus recovery. When the campus sold the lot on which the North Library Annex sat, the Library's Technical Services units had to relocate again in late 1997, this time to a clutch of FEMA trailers set together on the east side of the campus in the middle of what was at the time designated as student parking lot C, near Prairie Street.[32] Not only were the Technical Services trailers now closer to the core library building than they had been at the North Library Annex, but they also offered their staff denizens a highly prized perk among college and university workers: parking right next to one's office door.

The difficult efforts of reconfiguring collections and operations, offering high quality services, relocating staff and work areas, transporting materials between facilities, planning and building new east and west wings, and coping with the vast challenges of temporary facilities, went on during all seven years of recovery between January, 1994 and the reopening of the renovated Oviatt Library in June, 2000. Service, staff, and collection reconfigurations had to be reinvented over and over again. The physical environment was challenging, and sometimes unsafe. Immediately following the earthquake, staff first worked outdoors, and even though the typical January in Southern California is relatively warm, in 1994 it was sometimes rainy and muddy, and uncomfortably cool. Dust from collapsed concrete structures sifted everywhere, especially in the first months, and repeated strong aftershocks made most buildings and their environs a hazard. The aftershocks were also scary and afflicted many with disturbing flashbacks of the 6.7 magnitude temblor. The various temporary facilities were prone to water leaks and incursions of ants and rodents. The North Library Annex had numerous roof leaks during the rainy winters of the early recovery years. The LALA dome, sitting next to athletic fields, suffered more than one tear in its fabric roof from stray softballs, tennis balls, and golf balls. The Study Dome sheltered tennis instruction and equipment in foul weather. The trailers housing Technical Services during the last years of recovery separated staff from one another and required them to go outdoors to make use of sanitary facilities in a restroom trailer. This trailer often heated up to 120 degrees or more when its cranky air conditioner failed. Visitors to the restroom trailer could hear student athletes training with weights in the exercise dome adjacent to it. The trailers smelled of animals and mold.[33] They leaked at the roof and in some cases, through the windows, and the walkways and ramps connecting them were in constant need of repair.

From 1994 until 2004/2005, the rest of the campus, too, was hard to negotiate because of the massive construction projects as almost every existing building was under construction or being torn down, and new buildings and pathways also were under being built during most of this time.

A Study for Earthquake Engineering

The Oviatt Library was built in two stages, comprising three separate buildings linked together as one. The core building, opened in 1973, was a concrete and rebar reinforced structure. The symmetrical east and west wings opened in 1993.[34] The east and west wings were steel frame concrete structures erected in conformance with existing building codes and thought at the time to be more earthquake resistant than other types of concrete buildings. However, the Northridge earthquake demonstrated that this was a faulty premise. Although it was not visible to inspectors at first, the east and west wings suffered severe structural damage during the earthquake. Engineers had declared the library to be safe, but it took significant effort on the part of the library administration to assert the need to study the wings' structure more carefully. This was based on the staff's familiarity with the building prior to the earthquake. Something was wrong, in fact: the floors were "slowly collapsing downward."[35] Their structural integrity had been compromised.

Engineers who studied the damaged wings noted two significant findings. First, the two wings and the central core structure had rocked and crashed against one another with significant lateral force during the earthquake, rather than performing as one structure.[36,37,38] Second, "dramatic failures were observed in the x-braced perimeter frames... and many of the heavy baseplates fractured across the width and through the thickness [and] horizontal cracks were also observed along the welds connecting column flanges to the baseplates."[39] This finding necessitated the demolition of the wings, which began in late 1997.[40] Campus foot traffic was rerouted for most of a year while wire fences surrounding the Oviatt Library's wings rose out of the muddy flows that were characteristic of the rainy winter of 1997-98. The rebuilding of the Oviatt Library's east and west wings would occupy the next three years.

Technology played a significant role in the immediate and long term recovery of the Oviatt Library and its operations. Because the online catalog could be made available, along with interlibrary loan and a very powerful suite of licensed electronic resources, this was one of the first major library disasters whose impact on student and faculty work was mitigated by the availability of ubiquitous digital resources. It was also easier for library staff to perform their duties of ordering and receiving print materials, providing reference services and document delivery. After the earthquake, networked staff computer workstations became the norm.[41] Because half of the library's book collections were housed in the ASRS, computer aided retrieval and electronic inventory lessened the impact on library users compared to what it would have been had this disaster occurred in a previous decade.

Mold Remediation: Automated Storage and Retrieval Facility (ASRS)

In a memorable example of a disaster within a disaster, the ASRS became the focus of a massive recovery effort that was necessitated by an accident that occurred during the renovation of the wings. The west wing of the Oviatt Library was razed to the ground, but the east wing housed the ASRS. The ASRS itself sits inside its own concrete bunker within the wing, occupying the level below grade and the main floor. The installation contains 13,260 steel bins coated with enamel paint, each measuring 2' x 4', mounted on a rack structure that occupies an 8000 square foot room that is forty feet high.[42] The ceiling of the room is at the level of the ceiling of the main floor of the Library. The bins are arranged on both sides of six aisles, each of which is served by a "mini-load crane," guided by rails at top and bottom.

During the first phase of the renovation project, the top levels of the east wing had been torn away, down to the ceiling level of the ASRS. A temporary roof was to be placed to protect the ASRS, but before it was built, the vulnerable roof could not adequately protect the ASRS when an unexpected rainstorm in January 1998 poured water into the facility. Water flowed straight down through empty bins, headed for the bins containing books, which absorbed it like a sponge. It was impossible to retrieve and empty more than 13,000 bins within the 24 to 48-hour window before mold could be expected to grow. The ASRS water breach and the resulting massive mold outbreak was declared an occupational safety emergency; the campus Environmental and Occupational Health and Safety office supervised the closing down of the area and hired environmental consultants who tested for mold, mold growth, and damage, and moisture content in books.[43] A disaster remediation company was hired to begin immediate remediation;[44] a second contractor completed the task after learning how to operate the ASRS to assure every item was removed, inspected, and treated and to make sure that people requesting the books could receive them. A protocol of standards and procedures was developed, along with a separate inventory database for tracking. Salvaged materials were wiped with disinfectant. Especially hard hit were the top tiers and eastern two aisles of the

two story tall array, in which were stored the bound periodicals. Many bins were crammed with bound volumes so swollen with water that they were difficult to remove. Also damaged were monographs and archival materials, including photos. Five thousand books were discarded because they could not be salvaged (4000 of these were bound periodicals dating prior to 1990).[45] Cleanup continued for about almost four years, especially since archival material that was affected required specialized conservation treatment. A vendor was hired to replace lost material, identified using the online catalog as an inventory record. The catalog as inventory was central to obtaining insurance payout funds to pay for the lost material.

The vast amount of documentation that was required was a heavy demand during the initial earthquake recovery, through the ASRS mold disaster, all the way to the end of earthquake recovery. The effort required staff to work with multiple vendors, with campus engineers and architects, and with other engineers hired to manage the multiple building projects on campus. Although the total damage to the university amounted to somewhere between $350 million and $380 million, CSUN's recovery efforts were funded by what was at the time the largest amount of money FEMA had awarded to a disaster in an American university: $40 million. The Oviatt Library restoration was funded using a little more than half of those FEMA funds.

Persistence and Resilience Required

The strain of working so hard, so long, and under such demanding conditions cannot be underestimated. As Associate Dean, I arrived at the Oviatt Library in 1997. Among my responsibilities, I was to support and configure temporary operations; relocate staff, furniture, books, files, and computers; undertake the rebuilding of the wings; and help plan the library's return to physical and operational wholeness. I joined a staff that was already weary from more than three and a half years of working through the trauma that was post-earthquake life in Northridge. By day they negotiated and rebuilt our damaged workplace, but when they went home in the evening, they faced further physical, environmental, financial, and psychic undertakings. Some people had suffered personal disasters and either had to manage the rebuilding of their homes or give up homes as total losses. It takes much hard work, trust, and will to sustain the hope and participation of people who work during a long term recovery following a library disaster of this magnitude. This is true even when the recovery is a successful one.[46] If your library suffers a major disaster, Dean Curzon advises, "Prepare yourself for almost a decade of recovery."[47] It took the Oviatt Library seven years and the CSUN campus about 11 years to recover and return to something like business as usual.

All the effort and labor that was wrapped into those days, weeks, months, and years of labor gradually became momentum. Over a three day period in July, 2000, the library staff, faculty, services, and collections that had been displaced in 1994 moved back into the newly renovated building with its wings and left behind them for good the Prairie Street trailers and the Lindley Avenue Library Dome. The rededication and reopening ceremony for the Oviatt Library was held on September 26, 2000.[48]

Aftermath

Many of us associated with the Oviatt Library's recovery have made it a point to document our efforts and experiences in writing and through presentations to professional associations. We know that it is important to help educate library professionals about disaster before it comes, and to reach out with help to any library staff that has suffered a disaster and faces that long recovery ahead. The ruined Oviatt Library wings served as a learning laboratory for earthquake engineers from around the world, and the study of their failure contributed to new and better understanding of earthquake forces, which has translated into improved building codes for earthquake prone areas. The long period of redeployment of collections and services in different combinations and locations served as a confidence builder for the library faculty and staff, who, regardless of their physical location, harnessed library tools and technology to enable their consistently high quality delivery of library services, to order, check in and catalog materials, and to provide information access via in-person and electronic means. The Northridge Earthquake may have arrived in a time before widespread use of cell phones, e-mail, and the internet, but in additional to traditional means of working with print vendors, tools like OCLC and many electronic databases were fundamental to the Oviatt Library's recovery. Technology, data networking, and physical disruptions made possible changes in processing workflows and responsibilities behind the scenes, accelerating the nascent trend of blurring boundaries between librarian catalogers and staff catalogers.[49]

Many of the lessons from the Oviatt Library's successful recovery are ones that have been repeated in the library disasters that have occurred in the years since the Northridge earthquake. Among these, of course, is disaster planning and preparation. A significant takeaway, however, is the choice of university and library leadership to fight to recover, to operate while recovery took place, and to use recovery as an engine of development and a vehicle for deploying best practices in higher education and academic libraries. CSUN undertook a decade of struggle in its determination to recover from what well could have been a mortal blow. The university community chose its library as the emblem of that struggle and made it a priority for the library to receive the support and funding it needed to be the symbol and engine of recovery and progress. "Not just back... better" was a fitting slogan for the University during its early recovery, and it has proved to be true now as well, 15 years beyond the Northridge Earthquake.

Notes

1. "About CSUN" (California State University, Northridge, 2009). http://www.csun.edu/aboutCSUN (November 27, 2009).

2. United States Geological Survey. *USGS Response to an Urban Earthquake: Northridge '94.* Prepared by the U.S. Geological Survey for the Federal Emergency Management Agency (FEMA). Open File Report 96-263. (1996).http://pubs.usgs.gov/of/1996/ofr-96-0263 (November 11, 2009).

3. Ibid.

4. "The Great Quake of '94." January 17, 1994. Narrated by Tom Brokaw, Larry Carroll, and Roger O'Neill. *NBC Nightly News, Special Report.* http://www.youtube.com/watch?v=1xV1xRP7XQI&NR=1&feature=fvwp (November 28, 2009).

5. Photographer Unknown. (1994a). *Earthquake-damaged Parking Structure at Zelzah Avenue and Plummer Street, California State University, Northridge (CSUN).* From the University Archives Photograph Collection, Delmar T. Oviatt Library University Archives. Digitally reproduced by the California State University Northridge Digital Library. http://digital-library.csun.edu/cdm4/item_viewer.php?CISOROOT=%2FUniversityArchives&CISOPTR=139&DMSCALE=50&DMWIDTH=600&DMHEIGHT=600&DMMODE=viewer&DMFULL=0&DMX=176&DMY=30&DMTEXT=&DMTHUMB=1&REC=3&DMROTATE=0&x=513&y=107 (November 28, 2009).

6. Photographer Unknown. (1994b). *Parking Structure Earthquake Damage.* From the Delmar T. Oviatt Library University Archives Collection. Digitally reproduced by the California State University Northridge Digital Library. http://digital-library.csun.edu/cdm4/item_viewer.php?CISOROOT=/SFVH&CISOPTR=1647&CISOBOX=1&REC=13 (November 28, 2009).

7. United States Geological Survey, http://pubs.usgs.gov/of/1996/ofr-96-0263

8. "CSUN at Forty: Growth Amid Upheaval: Cal State Northridge." (1998, Sept. 21). *Los Angeles Times.* Valley Edition. Special Section, page 5. http://pqasb.pqarchiver.com/latimes/access/34503589.html?FMT=ABS&FMTS=ABS:FT&type=current&date=Sep+21%2C+1998&author=&pub=Los+Angeles+Times&edition=&startpage=5&desc=CSUN+at+40%3B+Growth+Amid+Upheaval%3A+Cal+State+Northridge (November 28, 2009).

9. "Earthquake: The Road to Recovery: Picking Up the Pieces; Cal State Northridge Struggles to Reopen and Rebuild." *Los Angeles Times.* Home Edition. Metro Section, Part B, page 5 (February 13, 1994). http://pqasb.pqarchiver.com/latimes/access/59311958.html?FMT=ABS&FMTS=ABS:FT&type=current&date=Feb+13%2C+1994&author=&pub=Los+Angeles+Times+(pre-1997+Fulltext)&edition=&startpage=5&desc=EARTHQUAKE%3A+THE+ROAD+TO+RECOVERY+Picking+Up+the+Pieces+CAL+STATE+NORTHRIDGE+STRUGGLES+TO+REOPEN+AND+REBUILD (November 28, 2009)

10. B. Wyler, *Fine Arts Building. San Fernando Valley State College.* [1960]. Delmar T. Oviatt Library University Archives Photograph Collection. Digitized by the California State University Northridge Digital Library. http://digital-library.csun.edu/cdm4/item_viewer.php?CISOROOT=/UniversityArchives&CISOPTR=2&CISOBOX=1&REC=16 (November 28, 2009).

11. "Northridge Earthquake." (January 17, 1994). Narrated by Harvey Levin. *Action News*, CBS2, Los Angeles. http://www.youtube.com/watch?v=J02N_qD9n6c (November 28, 2009).

12. Photographer Unknown. (1994c). *Cracked 4-inch Steel Baseplate.* (1994). Delmar T. Oviatt Library, University Archives. http://library.csun.edu/mfinley/quake/eqsteel.html (November 28, 2009).

13. Susan C. Curzon, "When Disaster Strikes: The Fall and Rise of a Library," *American Libraries* 31, no.5 (2000): 64-69.

14. "Oviatt Library Quake Damage" (Delmar T. Oviatt Library, California State University Northridge, 2005). http://library.csun.edu/mfinley/quake.html#photolist (November 28, 2009).

15. "Library History" (Delmar T. Oviatt Library, California State University Northridge, 2006). http://library.csun.edu/About_the_Library/ovbldghs.html (November 28, 2009).

16. Photographer Unknown. (1994d). *Oviatt Library Earthquake Damage*. From the Delmar T. Oviatt Library University Archives Collection. Digitally reproduced by the California State University Northridge Digital Library. http://digital-library.csun.edu/cdm4/item_viewer.php?CISOROOT=/SFVH&CISOPTR=1643&CISOBOX=1&REC=10 (November 28, 2009).

17. Photographer Unknown. (1994e). *Exterior Damage Photo 2*, Delmar T. Oviatt Library, University Archives. http://library.csun.edu/mfinley/quake/eqexdam2.html (November 11, 2009).

18. Photographer Unknown. (1994f). *Books on Floor after Northridge Earthquake*. Delmar T. Oviatt Library, University Archives. http://library.csun.edu/mfinley/quake/eqbooks.html (November 4, 2009).

19. Photographer Unknown. (1994g). *Microform Room Damage Photo 1*. Delmar T. Oviatt Library, University Archives. http://library.csun.edu/mfinley/quake/eqmicro1.html (November 11, 2009).

20. Photographer Unknown. (1994h). *Microform Room Damage Photo 2*. Delmar T. Oviatt Library, University Archives. http://library.csun.edu/mfinley/quake/eqmicro2.html (November 11, 2009).

21. Photographer Unknown. (1994i). *CSUN Stands*. From the Delmar T. Oviatt Library University Archives Collection. Digitally reproduced by the California State University Northridge Library Digital Library. http://digital-library.csun.edu/cdm4/item_viewer.php?CISOROOT=/UniversityArchives&CISOPTR=271&CISOBOX=1&REC=3 (November 28, 2009).

22. National Library of Medicine. "Susan Curzon, Dean of the Oviatt Library at California State University, Northridge talks about the earthquake that affected the academic library in January, 1994." *NN/NLM Emergency Preparedness & Response Toolkit: Library Disaster Stories*. (2007). Blog archive: University Library for California State University, Northridge. http://nnlm.gov/ep/2007/06/27/library-disaster-stories-northridge-earthquake (October 15, 2009).

23. Photographer Unknown. (1994j). *Temporary quarters (tents)*. From the Delmar T. Oviatt Library University Archives Collection. Digitally reproduced by the California State University Northridge Digital Library. http://digital-library.csun.edu/cdm4/item_viewer.php?CISOROOT=/SFVH&CISOPTR=1651&CISOBOX=1&REC=15 (November 28, 2009).

24. C. Mediavilla, "Surviving the Northridge Earthquake: Cindy Mediavilla Interviews Susan Carol Curzon." *Clarion: A Publication of the California Library Association* 4, no.1 (2008): 13-17.

25. J. C. Wakimoto and G. R. Hsiung, "Blurring the boundaries between professional and paraprofessional catalogers at California State University, Northridge," *Library Collections, Acquisitions, & Technical Services*, 24 (2000): 171–188.

26. Curzon, "When Disaster Strikes," 64-69.

27. National Library of Medicine, http://nnlm.gov/ep/2007/06/27/library-disaster-stories-northridge-earthquake

28. "Library History," http://library.csun.edu/About_the_Library/ovbldghs.html

29. K. Roderick, "Hendrix at Devonshire Downs" *L.A. Observed: Los Angeles Media, Politics, and Sense of Place Since 2003* (June 21, 2007). http://images.google.com/imgres?imgurl=http://www.laobserved.com/images/hendrix69.jpg&imgrefurl=http://www.laobserved.com/archive/2007/06/hendrix_at_devonshire_dow.php&usg=__FR4dqfwqSY6La__wI1v1fivuHro=&h=127&w=200&sz=10&hl=en&start=16&um=1&tbnid=QJGq-lpf0b1giM:&tbnh=66&tbnw=104&prev=/images%3Fq%3Ddevonshire%2Bdowns%26hl%3Den%26sa%3DX%26um%3D1 (November 28, 2009).

30. "Library History," http://library.csun.edu/About_the_Library/ovbldghs.html

31. James, Moore, *Lindley Library Dome at California State University, Northridge*. From the University Archives Collection, California State University Northridge . (1994). Digitally reproduced by the California State University Northridge

Digital Library. http://digital-library.csun.edu/cdm4/item_viewer.php?CISOROOT=/UniversityArchives&CISO PTR=267&CISOBOX=1&REC=1. (November 11, 2009).

32. "Library History," http://library.csun.edu/About_the_Library/ovbldghs.html

33. Curzon, "When Disaster Strikes," 64-69.

34. Library History," http://library.csun.edu/About_the_Library/ovbldghs.html

35. Mediavilla, "Surviving the Northridge Earthquake," 13-17.

36. J. Chandler, "Design of CSUN's Library Blamed for Quake Losses Aftermath: Consultant Says Facility's Two New Wings Lacked Sufficient Bracing to Resist Forces Unleashed by the 6.7-Magnitude Temblor." *Los Angeles Times*, Valley Edition. (April 24, 1995). Metro Section B, p. 1. http://pqasb.pqarchiver.com/latimes/access/21402634.html?FMT =ABS&FMTS=ABS:FT&type=current&date=Apr+24%2C+1995&author=JOHN+CHANDLER&pub=Los+Ang eles+Times+(pre-1997+Fulltext)&edition=&startpage=1&desc=Design+of+CSUN%27s+Library+Blamed+for+Q uake+Losses+Aftermath%3A+Consultant+says+the+facility%27s+two+new+wings+lacked+sufficient+bracing+to +resist+forces+unleashed+by+the+6.7-magnitude+temblor (November 28, 2009).

37. Wenshui, Gan, Earthquake Response of Steel Braces and Braced Steel Frames: A report on Research Supported in Part by Grants from CUREe (California Universities for Research in Earthquake Engineering) and the Earthquake Research Affiliates program at Caltech. Pasadena, CA: Caltech Earthquake Engineering Research Laboratory. Report No. EERL 96-06. (1996). http://caltecheerl.library.caltech.edu/109/00/9606.pdf (November 11, 2009).

38. J. Reese, "Bringing it home: Indian earthquake proves Suzzallo renovation needed," *The Daily of the University of Washington*. (February 1, 2001). http://archives.dailyuw.com/2001/020101/N4.BIH.html (November 28, 2009).

39. Gan, http://caltecheerl.library.caltech.edu/109/00/9606.pdf

40. Photographer Unknown. [1997]. *Oviatt Library Demolition, West Wing*. From the Delmar T. Oviatt Library University Archives Collection. Digitally reproduced by the California State University Northridge Digital Library. http:// digital-library.csun.edu/cdm4/item_viewer.php?CISOROOT=/SFVH&CISOPTR=1653&CISOBOX=1&REC=6 (November 28, 2009).

41. Wakimoto and Hsiung, "Blurring the boundaries," 171–188.

42. Library History," http://library.csun.edu/About_the_Library/ovbldghs.html

43. Susan E. Parker, Don Jaeger, and Kristen Kern, "What to Do When Disaster Strikes." *The Serials Librarian* 44, no.3/4 (2003): 237-432. Co-published simultaneously in *Transforming Serials: The Revolution Continues*. Proceedings of the NASIG 17th Annual Conference, The College of William and Mary, Williamsburg, Virginia, June, 20-23, 2002. Susan L. Scheiberg and Shelley Neville. Binghamton, NY: The Haworth Information Press, 2003.

44. "Success Stories: Library - Earthquake: California" (BMS CAT, 2009). http://www.bmscat.com/services/success- stories (November 28, 2009).

45. Parker, Jaeger, and Kern, "What to Do When Disaster Strikes," 237-432.

46. Susan E. Parker, "Organizational Learning, Motivation, and Employees' Mental Models Following a Disaster: A Case Study of the Morgan Library at Colorado State University." (Doctoral Dissertation, Capella University, 2007).

47. Mediavilla, "Surviving the Northridge Earthquake," 13-17.

48. Library History," http://library.csun.edu/About_the_Library/ovbldghs.html

49. Wakimoto and Hsiung, "Blurring the boundaries," 171–188.

RESPONSE AND RECOVERY FROM A 500-YEAR WATER DISASTER

Diane B. Lunde and Patricia A. Smith

On the night of July 28, 1997, run-off water from a heavy rain deluged the streets west of Colorado State University Libraries (CSUL), broke through a wall in the basement and plunged over 500,000 volumes, including twenty years worth of bound journal volumes and substantial portions of the social science and humanities books, into eight feet of muddy, debris filled water. Colorado State University (CSU), located in Fort Collins, Colorado, is the land-grant university for Colorado. As such, it not only provides an agricultural and scientific education for around 25,000 students, but also has strengths in the liberal arts and business. Its veterinary school is one of the top-ranked in the country. CSU is classified as a Carnegie Doctorate/Research-Extensive University and is a member of the Association of Research Libraries. At the time of the disaster, the library collections numbered just under two million volumes, so almost 25 percent of the collection was damaged in the water disaster, making this one of the most devastating disasters ever to hit an academic library. This case study will present an overview of the July 28, 1997, disaster. Camila Alire's book, *Library Disaster Planning and Recovery Handbook* describes the disaster in detail.[1]

Description of the Disaster

Fort Collins is a city of around 125,000 and is frequently ranked by various polls as one of the choice places to live in the country for its cultural advantages and weather. Sitting at the foot of the Rocky Mountains, it has a semi-arid climate with an average annual precipitation of 15 inches. The last thing anyone expected was massive flooding in the streets, but that night, overflowing streets and creeks damaged numerous homes and buildings. Witnesses reported cars floating and power lines discharging in the water. Just south of the University, a railroad car derailed and blocked a tunnel through a railroad dike turning a trailer court into an instant lake trapping inhabitants in their trailers. Unfortunately, five people in Fort Collins died.

Fortunately, in Morgan Library, the bell had just sounded for closing time and most patrons had left the building before waters hit the basement. Staff on hand were warned to leave and were able to call the Assistant Dean for Technical Services, who in turn roused the network administrator, who braved the weather to come in to turn off the power to the computers but found that the water filling the basement had already cut off power to the building. While staff were told to stay home, library administrators and the Library Disaster Recovery Team (LDRT) arrived to review the damage the next morning. The daylight view of the disaster was via the west side into lower level in which water covered all book stacks and went up past the ceiling tiles. The book stacks nearest to the hole in the west wall were tipped over with most of the volumes off the shelves. Besides the collection, other damaged contents in the lower level included two staff offices, one computer lab, multiple facilities rooms and tables and chairs for patrons.

The CSUL Disaster Plan in 1997

The 1996 version of the disaster manual was very similar to recommended manuals presented in various disaster books with sections on the disaster team and their responsibilities; campus administration for disasters, including reference to the university disaster manual; response procedures for various natural and man-made disasters; and priority lists for materials recovery. From the detailed response procedures, the CSUL had developed a *Disaster Plan Quick Reference Guide* to be used by all staff members.

The CSUL Disaster Recovery Team, chaired by the Preservation Librarian, included the Assistant Dean for Technical Services, Assistant Dean for Public Services, Assistant Dean for Administration, the Collections Coordinator, the Computer Recovery Coordinator, and the Building Proctor. The team members had various levels of training, including table top exercises, and had held fire drills, although they had never held a full scale disaster drill. During the building construction in the mid-1990s, CSUL staff had responded to numerous small disasters, most of them localized with little permanent damage to materials. In addition, Preservation Services operated the Wei T'o Book Dryer which had processed various types of paper materials for clients. While staff could handle small and medium disasters quickly and decisively, they were not ready for the disaster of the magnitude of the 1997 water event.

Although the CSUL Dean was not a stated member of the LDRT, in 1997 she immediately assumed its leadership. Because of the campus-wide scope of the disaster, CSU Administration quickly took control of all disaster recovery efforts with the library being only one of 34 damaged buildings, albeit, with the largest monetary loss. The Dean oversaw coordination with the University, work with vendors, and public relations efforts while the disaster team concentrated on their respective response and recovery responsibilities.

When the disaster manual was revised between 2003 and 2006, three major changes were made. Although the Preservation Librarian remained the chair of the Disaster Preparedness Team, the Dean now headed a separate Disaster Response and Recovery Team. While the Dean would assume leadership in the event of a major disaster similar to 1997, the Building Proctor would handle most other emergencies. Second, responsibilities were split between the Preservation Librarian and Building Proctor, with the Preservation Librarian only involved in emergencies that affected the print collections. The Building Proctor assumed all other disaster response and recovery responsibilities. Third, access replaced ownership as the key to collection recovery, with reliance on electronic resources and interlibrary loan for patron access. A "Do-Not-Recover" list was created for types of materials that would not be recovered; for example, the newspaper collection.

Disaster Response

The response of the CSUL was intertwined with the response efforts of the University. One of the first acts by the University Administration was to hire an outside contractor to handle the recovery efforts for the campus. The contractor had experience with physical disasters such as the World Trade Center bombing, but had no experience with restoring a library collection. The difference in types of recoveries quickly became apparent and led to some interesting tensions throughout the recovery effort between the for-profit contractor and the non-profit, service-oriented staff.

With activation of the disaster plan that first morning, LDRT members met in the main foyer of the library and reviewed what needed to be done. The immediate concern related to the building and its contents:

- *Stabilization of the environment of the building.* Since the electrical and HVAC systems were not functional, a major concern was the possibility of sauna-like conditions which might affect the collections on the first to fourth floors A disaster response vendor was hired the first day to run drying tubes working off external generators throughout the building.

- *Removal of the water from the lower level.* Nothing could be done for the collection until CSU facilities staff pumped out approximately 4.9 million gallons of water from the lower level.
- *Security of the building.* Because the campus-wide disaster security forces were stretched thin, staff covered the front door, monitoring staff and others seeking entrance. Once the water was removed, the large hole was visible in the west wall; even boarded up it was a security concern.
- *Assessment of the damages.* The first staff members were allowed into the lower level to make initial assessments on the third day. While we knew what was in the basement in terms of collections and offices, we needed to know the scope of the damage. While all materials had been completely under water, had the volumes remained on the shelves? Were the materials still recognizable as books? How did the damage differ from nearest the water impact point versus the farthest corners? How would we stage the removal of the materials up and out of the lower level? Photographs were taken to record the damage for insurance purposes later.
- *Removal of the damage materials.* Common practice says that it takes 48 to 72 hours before a mold outbreak under the favorable temperature and humidity conditions. With an estimate of approximately 500,000 volumes to be removed, it was going to be a mammoth undertaking. The "pack-out" began on the fourth day and continued until the eighteenth day, or 2.6 weeks after the disaster occurred, and resulted in over 7,000 pallets of materials. Mold was definitely a major concern for the restoration of the materials.
- *Removal of the main computer out of the building.* Although the computer network equipment was on the first floor and undamaged, it was moved for its own protection and access.

- *Restoration of the building.* Since the HVAC system and electricity were not working, the elevators and the fire alarm system were not operational. With the expectation of an open and functional library when school started at the end of the August, restoration of the HVAC and electricity were top priorities.

At the same time, the disaster team dealt with response issues related to human resources and communication.

- *Public relations* efforts focused on three levels: information to staff affected; information to the University, and information to the external community, including faculty, staff and students, contractors, the news media, and the general public. While the University Administration was responsible for most external public relations, the news media also focused on the CSUL. In fact, the media was one of the first non-campus groups to arrive at the CSUL with television broadcast trucks parked in the plaza. The Dean, as designated spokesperson for the CSUL, was featured in numerous newspaper articles and television reports.
- *Staff Communication.* The importance of good communication cannot be underestimated. During the first night supervisors activated the phone tree, instructing staff not to come to work the first morning. Communication during the first month was a challenge with staff at many different locations around Fort Collins. On the third day, the Dean held an all-staff meeting in the CSUL courtyard to brief staff on the progress of the recovery. To boost morale, the Dean planned several informal get-togethers at a local pub which allowed staff to unwind and socialize in a non-library environment.
- *Human resources.* Because staff were out of the building for the first month, one of the

first questions involved pay and leave. The status of permanent staff remained the same, but hourly students could not be paid unless they worked. Of particular concern was the seemingly unequal activities during the hiatus—technical services staff worked on a bar coding project in the Lake Street book storage facilities, some staff worked on regular activities in other locations while others were told to stay home until called. In addition many staff members were affected both at work and at home; and the staff in two units lost personal items when their lower level library offices were destroyed. The Personnel Librarian arranged for the CSU Employee Assistance Program psychologist and student psychology staff to meet with classified staff, faculty and students as individuals and as work units or departments.

Restoring Libraries Services

Restoring library services was a challenge during the first month, although reference, interlibrary loan, circulation, and the online catalog became functional in a short amount of time. The challenge accepted by the staff was to provide services to patrons in new, innovative and user-friendly ways.

- *Reference* librarians established services in the Veterinary Teaching Hospital Branch Library (approximately 1 mile from the main campus) and transferred all service desk phone lines to that location. No reference materials were damaged, and once the computers were operational, patrons had access to electronic databases and other resources. However, staff rewrote handouts and guides, created a *Library Locator* to update patrons on damaged materials returned to the shelves, and adjusted instruction lectures. Staff also increased one-on-one assistance to help patrons find alternate resources to the missing part of the collection.

- *Interlibrary Loan (ILL).* Since the bound journals were the major loss, ILL focused on finding resources to fill the huge void with the goal of 24 to 48 hour turnaround time. Fortunately, neither the ILL equipment or server were damaged in the disaster, and the department had already automated most procedures. Within six hours of the disaster, ILL could send requests from staff homes. Within two days, ILL had set up operations at the Fort Collins campus of the Front Range Community College (approximately three miles from the main campus). ILL developed a new FastFlood program that fully-automated ILL requests, streamlined fulfillment of requests with six partner academic libraries and provided direct delivery of materials to the patrons. Also, over sixty additional academic institutions provided CSU patrons with free and expedited ILL service. These new ILL services evolved into the international RAPID interlibrary loan system.[2]

- *Circulation and reserve.* With the suspension of regular service for most of August, circulation staff divided into two teams with the first team functioning as part of Morgan Library security team as the front door "greeters," while the second team operated as the renewal/telephone receipt team at the Engineering Branch Library. CSUL suspended bills and fines and automatically renewed all checked-out items. While patrons were urged to keep the books they had checked out, they could drop them off at the front door, where staff placed any wet books in plastic totes to be routed for drying. In order to be ready for fall semester, a reserve drop off site was established for faculty at the nearby Physics Building; staff transported the processed materials to the library on the first day of class.

- *Access to the circulating collection.* With the loss of such a high percentage of its prime collection, the CSUL focused on alternate access options. Even with expanded ILL service and electronic resources, library staff felt that it was necessary to provide patrons direct access to other libraries' collections. For the first semester, the CSUL provided shuttle services to regional academic libraries, but that service was suspended after the spring semester when some volumes were returned to the shelves.

Recovery of the Collections

Almost immediately several overriding questions related to recovery efforts were asked.

- *How many volumes were damaged?* Theoretically every volume should have an item record in the online database, except for older volumes that had been added to the collection before bar coding was instituted. The total volume count increased continuously as restored volumes were processed back into the collection.

- *Would insurance cover the damage and for how much?* The University was self-insured under Colorado law, however University Administration had to establish that the damage to the CSUL was not from a flood but from water runoff from the streets as insurance coverage for a water runoff disaster was higher than from a flood from an existing body of water.

- *What percentage of damaged volumes could be salvaged?* Initial estimates from consultants ranged from ten to twenty percent, although the CSUL administration was not so optimistic and estimated approximately twice as many volumes would be "total loss."

- *Did CSUL want to restore the collection?* The answer was a resounding "Yes" from CSUL staff, University Administration, and the insurance representatives. There were enough unique and specialized materials to make wholesale disposal of the damaged collection out of the question; any other option would not attain the goal of making the libraries "whole."

- *Who would do the work?* University Administration clearly established that the response vendor would also be the recovery contractor. However, CSUL staff were heavily involved in the planning, provided all early training for vendor staff, wrote detailed procedures, designed special databases, and provided continuous quality review of vendor work. The Preservation Librarian was the general liaison between the CSUL and the contractor's processing plant.

- *How long would it take?* Although we initially estimated that at least two years would be required to return or replace the materials damaged in the disaster, the overall recovery effort took seven years from 1998 to 2004 and had three phases.

Phase One: Gift Project, 1997-1998

Almost immediately the CSUL received offers of gift volumes to replace the damaged volumes. However, insurance representatives indicated that they would only pay for processing gift volumes that were exact matches to individual damaged volumes. In approximately eight months, the contractor's processing plant staff returned to the shelves nearly 100,000 replacement volumes from faculty, private donors, publishers and other libraries; the majority were journal volumes.

Phase Two: Salvage of Damaged Materials, 1998-2002

In the summer of 1998, the processing plant changed gears from handling gifts to restoring the water damaged volumes. At a freeze drying facility in Texas, the vendor thawed the frozen materials, cleaned them and removed the covers, and then refroze the volumes before putting them in the freeze drying chambers. After drying, materials were treated with ozone for odors and with gamma radiation to kill the mold on the volumes. The mold stains would remain but the volumes would be safe to handle and read.

The salvage work at the contractor's processing plant in Fort Collins matched the volume against the CSUL online catalog item record, creating a record if there was none found, assessed the damage to the volume, determined if the volume would be salvaged or was a total loss, provided conservation treatment for all damages, made replacement pages as needed, and sent volumes to the commercial binder. The CSUL established an acceptance review process in which a percentage of the completed volumes went through quality control before they were returned to the shelves. Although the CSUL established an acceptable error rate, the contractor's error rate was usually higher than this benchmark.

Work in the online catalog was an important aspect of the recovery project. Shortly after the disaster, CSUL staff coded all item records for volumes known to be in the damaged area with a status of FLOOD. During processing of the gifts and recovered volumes, processing plant staff coded each action taken with notes such as "Salvaged," "Replacement pages," "Item record created" and "Gift in process." These codes were very useful in statistical reports and evaluations of the recovery process. When the volumes were ready to be reshelved in Morgan Library, staff updated each online record to let patrons know that the volume was available for use.

Phase Three: Repurchasing, 2002-2004

In the final phase, the University Administration allowed the CSUL to use funds received from insurance to repurchase 25% of the remaining damaged materials. The CSUL and campus faculty determined which of these materials were core to the mission of the university. The contractor was not involved in this operation; instead, the CSUL hired temporary staff and worked with a monograph vendor and back order journal dealer to purchase and process these materials. Priority was given to electronic copies if possible. In other projects, staff replaced all lost CSU theses and dissertations, repurchased the most heav-

ily used 5,000 titles for patron use in late 1997, and added selected new-to-the-library volumes from the initial Gifts Inventory.

Statistics

As mentioned previously the official final count of the damaged volumes changed constantly during the recovery project. In summary, the CSUL replaced almost 100,000 volumes through gifts, repaired and salvaged over 163,000 volumes, repurchased over 45,000 volumes, and augmented the collection from gifts with over 27,000 volumes for a total of approximately 271,000 volumes. The number of total loss volumes will never be known, but is over 200,000 volumes.

Redesign/Mitigation/Renovation

After the demolition of the lower level, reconstruction began on the damaged sections of the building and renovation continued for the construction project. Very little was changed in the design and function of the lower level; the weight load for movable shelves required the lower level location. Outside the building, Federal Emergency Management Agency (FEMA) paid for the creation of a retaining wall on the west side of the lower level slope, and other entrances were rebuilt so that waters from another 500-year flood could not penetrate the building.

Conclusion

In looking back, there was nothing that the CSUL staff could have done to prevent the disaster. Disaster preparedness, response and recovery plans were in place and staff were trained for handling small disasters; however, the magnitude of the 1997 disaster was many times beyond the level of disaster for which staff trained and planned.

The Alire book provides key recommendations for handling each aspect of the CSUL disaster.[3] Overall, staff who experienced the disaster are justifiably proud of the recovery effort and feel that strong, positive and innovative leadership was key to the success. The Dean of Libraries, who had only been on the job two weeks when the disaster hit, knew she quickly had to establish effective communication with the University, with the staff and with the public. The Assistant Deans and others found ways to stretch scarce resources using outsourcing, vendor services, and automation.

The CSUL would have preferred to have supervised the recovery and salvage operations, or at least, the external contractor the university hired to handle the recovery and salvage operations. Because staff were grounded in conservation treat-

ment techniques and were experts in the online catalog, their leadership would have greatly enhanced operations of the contracted processing plant where the staff had minimal experience working in libraries or other similar organizations. However, when the CSUL recovery and response effort came to completion, it had made a substantial leap into new endeavors, including the RAPID interlibrary loan system and access to electronic resources, and was well positioned for the future. CSUL staff have used this experience in two much smaller sprinkler disasters and are now interested in a recent regional initiative toward shared disaster response.

Notes

1.   Camila A. Alire, *Library Disaster Planning and Recovery Handbook* (New York, Neal-Schuman, 2000).

2.   RapidILL http://rapid2.library.colostate.edu (September 28, 2009).

3.   Alire, *Library Disaster Planning and Recovery Handbook*.

Bibliography of Articles/Books Written on the 1997 CSU Libraries Disaster by CSUL Staff

Alire, Camila A. "And on the 8th Day ... Managing During the First Week of Library Disaster Recovery." *Colorado Libraries* 24 (Fall 1998): 10-12.

———, ed., *Library Disaster Planning and Recovery Handbook*. New York, Neal-Schuman, 2000.

———. "The Silver Lining: Recovering from the Shambles of a Disaster." *Journal of Library Administration* 38 (2003): 101-107.

Carpenter, Kathryn H. "Dealing with Disaster: An Interview with Camila Alire." *Library Administration & Management* 14 (Fall 2000): 188-190.

Delaney, Thomas G. "The Day It Rained in Fort Collins, Colorado." *Journal of Interlibrary Loan, Document Delivery & Information Supply* 8 (1998): 59-70.

———. "Necessity is the Mother of Virtuality." *Colorado Libraries* 24 (Fall 1998): 13-15.

Enssle, Halcyon. "Security Following a Disaster: The Experience at Colorado State University." *Colorado Libraries* 24 (Fall 1998): 16-18.

Lederer, Naomi and Douglas J. Ernest. "Managing the Media During a Library Crisis." *American Libraries* 33 (Dec. 2002): 32-33.

Lunde, Diane B. "Aftermath of a Disaster: Establishing a Rebinding Program." *New Library Scene* 17 (June 1998): 10-13, 19, 22-23.

———. "The Disaster at Colorado State University Libraries: Recovery and Restoration of the Collection." *Colorado Libraries* 24 (Fall 1998): 22-26.

————. "What Do You Do with 426,500 Wet Books: Or, Options for Restoring a Water-damaged Collection." *Library Journal* 124 (Dec. 1999 supplement): 6-7.

————. "When Disaster Strikes: A Case Study: Colorado State University Libraries, July 28, 1997." *Serials Librarian* 26 (1999): 363-382.

Lunde, Diane B. and Patricia A. Smith. "Disaster and Security: Colorado State Style." *Library & Archival Security* 22 (2009): 1-16.

Moothart, Tom. "Muddy Waters Bring the Library Blues and Enhanced Electronic Access to Journals." *Serials Review* 23 (Winter 1997): 79-82.

Schmidt, Fred C. "Disasters: Plans, Clean-up, and Recovery—The Colorado State Experience." FDLP Desktop: Proceedings of the 8th Annual Federal Depository Library Conference, article # 31) http://www.access.gpo.gov/su_docs/fdlp/pubs/proceedings/99pro31.html (September 28, 2009).

Smith, Patricia, Beth Oehlerts, Glenn Jaeger, and Sandy Belskis. "Repurchasing Journals Lost in a Major Disaster: Library and Vendor Perspectives." *Serials Review* 32 (2006): 26-34.

Switzer, Teri R. "The Crisis was Bad, but the Stress is Killing Me!" *Colorado Libraries* 24 (Fall 1998): 19-21.

Wessling, Julie and Thomas Delaney. "After the Flood, Colorado State Reaps a Harvest of Invention." *American Libraries* 31 (Nov. 2000): 36-37.

HURRICANE KATRINA

Andy Corrigan

Tulane University is in New Orleans. Its large main campus is located in a tree-shaded section of the city uptown, separated from the giant live oaks, waterways, and lawns of Audubon Park by an historic streetcar line. It has a second campus downtown for its health sciences divisions and hospital. It is among the top research institutions in North America[1] as well as the largest private academic institution in New Orleans and the central Gulf Coast. Its schools and colleges offer undergraduate, graduate and professional degrees in the liberal arts, science and engineering, architecture, business, law, social work, medicine and public health and tropical medicine. The university is ranked by the Carnegie Foundation for the Advancement of Teaching as a university with "very high research activity," a prestigious category that includes only 2 percent of the more than 4,300 higher educational institutions rated by the foundation. With about 4,400 employees, Tulane is the largest private employer in New Orleans.

Tulane's libraries generally stand in the lower middle tier among members of the Association of Research Libraries (ARL), a group recognized as the top 123 research libraries in North America.[2] Its general collections serve as a major cultural resource for researchers and scholars from throughout the region and its special collections often draw researchers internationally, especially in the areas of Latin American studies, jazz, and New Orleans history.

The Disaster

On August 29, 2005 Hurricane Katrina made landfall near the Louisiana and Mississippi border and set in motion a series of catastrophic events that stunned the nation and much of the world. From the coastal parishes south of New Orleans to its urban center and then east to the coastal communities of Mississippi and Alabama, the storm cut a huge swath of physical destruction, environmental devastation, and human suffering. Not only would Katrina become the most expensive natural disaster in U.S. history, the storm and levee system failures in New Orleans would also make this disaster one of the deadliest. At least 1,100 in the New Orleans area alone would lose their lives during the storm and its chaotic aftermath.[3] The year following Katrina saw a 47% increase in the proportion of deaths among those slowly returning to the city at the time, likely due to stress combined with exacerbated public health issues.[4]

In a paper published not long after the storm a group of experts reviewed the research from previous disasters to produce a calendar of historical experience against which to gauge progress in reconstruction. It concluded that Katrina would produce a post disaster period likely to be longer in duration than that of any other studied and that rebuilding might take eight to 11 years.[5] At the time of this writing, four years after the storm, this predicted time frame seems to have been fairly accurate, although substantial progress has been made. In the downtown business district and the French Quarter of New Orleans, heavily dependent on visitors, little evidence of the storm is still visible. In many residential areas that flooded in the city and especially in the coastal areas to the south and east, much work remains.

After the hurricane, approximately 80 percent of New Orleans[6] became a vast urban lake that encompassed the lower-lying two thirds of Tulane University's uptown campus. Broad levees protecting the perimeter of the city bordering Lake Pontchartrain and along its crescent-shaped southern edge bordering the Mississippi River held through the storm. But smaller drainage canals on its eastern and western sides collapsed in several places when filled by the hurricane's storm surge. This caused most of the city to fill like a bowl, including areas above sea level such as Tulane's uptown campus.

In an early chapter of Dave Eggers' nonfiction book *Zeitoun*, its subject silently paddles his canoe through neighborhoods uptown a few days after the storm—looking through dark green water at the tops of cars submerged several feet below. In this accurately illustrative scene he surmises correctly that the water must have come from the lake, fully six miles away to the north. Then he wonders what the city will look like when all this rancid water recedes. How will so many hundreds of thousands of cars, uprooted trees, and downed power lines be cleared? What of these hundreds of thousands of flooded homes and their contents? How will people return? To what will they return?[7]

At the same moment and a few blocks away the basement of Tulane's main Howard-Tilton Memorial Library had filled with more than eight feet of water. Roughly the size of a football field, this area housed the highly-regarded Maxwell Music Library as well as very large collections of government documents, newspapers, microforms, valuable books in "protected storage," books waiting to be cataloged, and other general collections in storage. Jones Hall across the parking lot houses the library's Special Collections. Its basement was filled with about four feet of water, inundating a large volume of historical political papers and ephemera.

Deep lower-level lagoons in both buildings produced rapidly growing humidity while the loss of power shut off any circulating air. In the late summer heat, interior temperatures quickly began to climb. These buildings, especially the larger Howard-Tilton building, were about to bloom with mold. Mold is considered an environmental hazard, especially on this scale. Millions of print volumes and documents for research were in serious danger.

The Disaster Plan

The Howard-Tilton Memorial Library had maintained a detailed disaster plan, a 28-page document updated less than two months before Katrina struck. The plan had identified a Library Emergency Response Team management group as well as a separate onsite disaster response group with a chain of command and emergency contact numbers. It outlined specific action steps to prepare for a storm event. It included post event procedures for staff to follow in returning to a damaged building and even for the packing and removal of wet materials. It discussed recovery methods in detail. It prioritized collections for recovery and separately for each stack floor and collections area. It included a phone tree with emergency contact numbers for all library department heads plus fire evacuation procedures, maps, and floor plans. The plan was physically accompanied by a dozen or so "disaster trunks" with mops, sponges, flashlights, and the like that were strategically located throughout the library's buildings.

Very little in the plan could be used for Katrina. Specifically, none of the post event portions of the plan proved applicable. For months after the storm, library personnel were scattered throughout the county. Regular phone and power lines had been downed, twisted, and snapped across a storm path at least 90 miles wide. With Tulane's servers and network systems out of commission, university e-mail and web pages were no longer available. Cell phone towers in the area had been wrecked by the storm. Even if the library's planned response teams had been able to quickly return to the city, the plan had not anticipated the level of building remediation and climate stabilization that a real disaster can require.

Nor did it anticipate the huge scale and the logistical complexity of the response that would really be needed. It did not recognize the scale or specialization of the equipment that would be needed as well. Missing too, understandably, was any real in-house experience or expertise in handling what would lie ahead.

The Response

The library's practical role became one of advice and assistance. As part of the university's campus-wide emergency plan, BELFOR, an international disaster management company with offices across the globe, was called almost immediately by university officials who had quickly established emergency headquarters in Houston.

Meanwhile a handful of key library personnel informally established contact with each other within a week or so after the storm from their various locations in exile. Under a federally-enforced mandatory evacuation order, joining the salvage effort in New Orleans early on could require sneaking past military check points and then past private security crews marshaled to guard Tulane's campus from potential looting. The library's actual disaster response emerged ad hoc, in direct response to actual conditions and the circumstances of those involved.

On September 9 BELFOR headed for the library and Tulane's other facilities needing remediation in New Orleans. The city was closed off by then and the military had established a 4 pm city wide curfew for authorized private emergency crews, only then just beginning to move into the area. Initially BELFOR crews needed to clear debris from roadways on their own in order to move in their trucks, workers, and supplies. The closest place that BELFOR could find housing for its personnel was in Lafayette, Louisiana, more than 100 miles west of New Orleans. The following day on the 10th, crews first began pumping water from the Howard-Tilton building. On that first day there was standing water still outside the building and water seeping back into the building would be a continuing problem. On September

12 the water outside had finally receded and debris was cleared from around the library buildings and on adjacent Freret Street to allow for large truck access. Generators and other large equipment were quickly staged both outside the Howard-Tilton building and Jones Hall.[8]

To stabilize the climate in the Howard-Tilton building, BELFOR trucked in and set up two large 300 kilowatt generators. These powered four desiccant dry air machines together capable of pushing 30,000 cubic feet of dry air per minute into the building. Also set up were four additional cool air units capable of pumping some 40,000 cubic feet of air per minute into the building as well. In Jones Hall, two more 300 kilowatt generators were set up to power two desiccant dry air machines together capable of pushing 20,000 cubic feet of dry air per minute and two cool air units capable of pumping some 20,000 cubic feet of air per minute into this building. The desiccant dry air and the cool air were blended to gain control of the humidity and temperatures and avoid huge mold outbreaks on the upper floors. In the lower reaches of both buildings this created a reasonable work environment for teams packing out wet materials.[9]

BELFOR's army of emergency workers fitted in white coveralls and filtered masks, installed several thousand of feet of big inflated tubes to circulate pumped treated air throughout each floor in library danger. By September 16, water from both buildings had largely been pumped out, although these basements were still very wet from seepage. The next day crews began the first pack-out of materials selected for salvage.[10]

All salvaged collections were carefully packed at the disaster site in waterproof bags placed into marked boxes. The boxes were then placed in freezer truck trailers lined up outside and then trucked away to be retained in frozen storage. The first material hauled out to frozen truck trailers was a small portion of the microfilm collection comprised of critically important older Louisiana newspapers and Latin American titles. Only about 5 percent of the microfilm collection would eventually be salvaged because printed materials were thought to have a greater chance for restoration and the film had spent so much time underwater. With wet printed materials now exposed to open air, time was a factor to be weighed against the huge task at hand and priorities had to be set.[11]

BELFOR was careful to let the library determine these priorities, a task handled by a small group of key library personnel that included in the main Howard-Tilton building the chief bibliographer for social sciences and government publications normally on site; the interim head of the music library during the early stages in the salvage of music materials; and the associate dean for collections at points regularly throughout. The library's assistant dean for special collections oversaw the initial salvage work in Jones Hall. All general salvage priorities were affirmed by the associate dean for collections.

These decisions were necessarily very broad because of the scope of the materials affected and restricted only by practical and logical factors that included: the obvious condition of different formats of materials after spending so much time under dirty water, time, and the availability of frozen truck trailers.

First priorities for higher volume salvage were: (a) all materials damaged in Jones Hall since these were inherently irreplaceable and (b) the music scores, books, and journals from the music library, which had been collecting valuable printed musical works for the past 100 years. Pack-out for materials in Jones Hall began on September 18 and in the music library the following day. The salvage operation in the music library was hampered by the collapse of a portion of the shelving there, which caused some of the materials from those shelves to be lost in the soup, but it was also helped greatly by the proximity of this area to the large stairwell at the front of the building. About 70 percent of the music print collection was salvaged.[12]

Less than a week later, the salvage operation and New Orleans suffered a major setback with the news that another large storm, Hurricane Rita, was on the way. All emergency crews in the city, including BELFOR's, were ordered to evacuate on September 23. This second storm would send to the west many of the military personnel that had been working in the city, as well as much of their equipment. During the next week or so the city was in disarray once more, but BELFOR was able to remobilize and re-enter the city on September 28. The salvage of priority microfilm and printed music materials in the Howard-Tilton building was completed by October 1 and the salvage of wet documents in Jones Hall finished on October 5.[13]

Drained of water, the basement spaces of the Howard-Tilton building had become a foul, dank 40,000 square foot cave whose pathways amidst the dark debris were lit only by the occasional bare bulb from utility lamps strung along yellow extension cords. The last stage of the salvage operation in the Howard-Tilton building, the rescue of mostly older uncataloged government documents and a cataloging backlog, was difficult since these materials had been shelved in compact, high-density shelving that no longer moved on its runners. Most of these shelving units had to be demolished to get at the materials inside. This was soggy and messy work that was finally completed on October 15, after which BELFOR crews removed all wrecked equipment and any speck of debris from these lower reaches, which were then gutted and any mold scraped away.[14]

Perhaps as many as 700,000 print volumes were underwater in the main Howard-Tilton building; about 480,000 or so were lost. In addition to all 12,435 recorded audio materials in the music library and its substantial audio-visual media collection, about 1.4 million pieces of microform were lost. In Jones Hall the area that flooded housed archival collections comprised largely of historical manuscripts but also other primary source archival materials for research that included registration cards, film reels, magnetic tape (recordings,) newspapers, books, posters, matted prints and other art work, cartoons, photographs, lithographs, ledgers, diaries, journals, scrapbooks, and miscellaneous ephemera. This included 218,760 manuscript folders and easily more than 300,000 other archival items. At this stage it appears that a sizeable portion of the nonprint materials in these archival collections were effectively lost. But some 209,894 important printed volumes, about 4,800 linear feet of manuscripts, perhaps nearly as many linear of other archival materials, and 18,269 reels of microfilm were salvaged and frozen for transfer to BELFOR's restoration facility in Fort Worth, Texas.

The Recovery

The library's recovery four years later is not complete. Steady progress has been made in some areas and setbacks have occurred in others. The recovery can be described as taking place along three basic tracks: (a) one dealing with temporary and longer term measures that address severe damages to the library's buildings; (b) another dealing with the restoration of salvaged materials and rebuilding library collections; and (c) a third related to library personnel—both those who came back from the storm and its long evacuation period and those who came later to join a library environment far from typical.

Buildings

Tulane University could not have effectively reopened without the library, so as the collections salvage work wound down in the fall of 2005 a temporary strategy was developed to leave the Howard-Tilton basement as a vast empty cavern, gutted and scraped, and to reroute the building's power and data lines to restore service to the upper floors. Eight large temporary HVAC units were installed along the rear of the building connecting through windows to each floor. Air was circulated through plastic inflatable tubes again, but this time the tubes were mounted from the ceiling to allow library users to walk freely

through the building. This temporary HVAC system was supposed to last six months. It is still being relied upon today in 2009, and is expected to be needed through 2012.

Soon after reopening its campus for spring 2006 the university began to plan to address the library's rebuilding issues through a build-back and hazard mitigation program offered by the Federal Emergency Management Agency (FEMA) and through a long and heavily regulated process guided by FEMA representatives.

Eventually a plan was agreed upon that would reconstruct the library's mechanical systems and flooded basement spaces in additional floors to be constructed atop the main building. But at the point at which the project was to be put out to bid for actual construction, FEMA's promise of funding was rescinded. Not until August 2009 was FEMA funding for the project finally reinstated[15] through appeal but 3 years were lost in the effort. Meanwhile, the library in partnership with the university's Technology Services division, built a temporary Learning Commons space, complete with new coffee shop, on the first entrance level of the main building, above its gutted basement. That space was officially opened in September 2009.

With the total loss of some 40,000 square of space to house collections, open user spaces on the upper floors of the main library were filled in with shelving. The library's offsite storage facility, brand new before the storm and originally projected to provide for many years of extra space, by 2009 was completely full.

FEMA funded renovation will address only the parts of the library's buildings that were effectively destroyed. So the university will need a separate architectural program to address and rebuild library spaces as a whole while providing for collections growth. Longer term planning, fundraising, and construction will need to proceed independently from the FEMA funded remedial renovation.

Collections

Immediately following collections salvage, BELFOR began to thaw and restore the library's salvaged materials at its recovery headquarters in Fort Worth, TX. For printed material the remediation process involved unfreezing each salvaged item, washing its pages, drying to remove moisture, and radiation treatment to eliminate any residual mold.

Once the materials were individually allowed to thaw, they were identified and moved to a washing table. Each print volume or document was carefully washed, page by page, with a gentle stream of filtered water and with a soft bristle brush or a foam brush if required. It was placed on the table in its natural shape and the excess water allowed to drain off. Then it was placed on a drying cart, care taken to support all the item's edges.[16]

Carts full of washed materials were then refrozen and later placed into a vacuum freeze-dry chamber, which uses vacuum pumps to remove 99 percent of the air that is normally present in the atmosphere. The very low pressure level makes sure that all drying takes place by sublimation (ice changing to vapor without passing through the liquid phase) and that nothing will dry by evaporation (liquid changing to vapor). This reduces the degradation of the materials during the drying process. It also seems to negate the waving and expansion that normally occurs when wet paper dries.[17]

Microfilm was also packed and frozen at the salvage stage. But once at the restoration facility, the film was inspected and set up for processing on a 35 mm microfilm processor using multiple rinse tanks. The film was carefully monitored as it was cleaned by hand and dried since sticking or breaks may occur during this procedure. After reprocessing the film was placed on new spools, inspected, and then placed in light resistant black plastic boxes with new labels using information from the original.[18]

With a reduction in staff overall after the return to campus, the library was stretched thin to handle its normal workload, too thin for any hope of handling on its own handle the extra work of physically processing several hundred thousand recovered materials and of cataloging donations. So plans were laid for an idea called the Recovery Center, with which the library would stage its multi-faceted collections recovery. Physical space for the Recovery Center was found in an unleased corner of the same large warehouse building that houses the library's off site library storage facility, located about two miles from Tulane's uptown campus and where recovered and donated materials could be received, processed and stored.[19]

The Recovery Center would provide the staff necessary to manage and process materials so that they could be identified in the library's catalog and eventually placed on the shelves. Its eventual task would be to process more than 800,000 items from restoration, donations, and replacement. The library at first sought private funding for the Recovery Center but by meeting directly with FEMA early on, it secured promised funding via 16 interconnected FEMA project work sheets that address many of the Recovery Center's major goals.

Library Associates Companies (LAC), based in California, was the contractor that the library hired for its Recovery Center processing and cataloging operations through a competitive bidding process completed in spring 2007. Work began within the Recovery Center in February 2008. In an important milestone, the first initial batch of restored music books was delivered to the library from the Recovery Center in a small ceremony on Friday, March 14, 2008. Most of the library's restored printed music books and scores—a top recovery priority—were back on the library's shelves, on schedule, by the end of that summer. The other tasks of the Recovery Center were projected to take about 24 to 36 months overall. Most aspects of the Center's work have proceeded on schedule.

Recovery Center operations are determined and coordinated through weekly meetings with LAC's project manager and project team leaders at which the library is primarily represented by its associate dean and its director of technical services, usually a representative from its special collections division, and others brought in as projects require. Then progress is reviewed by a larger Recovered Materials Group back at the library after each weekly meeting with LAC.

The largest and perhaps most critical phase of the Recovery Center's overall task has been the processing of restored materials. This has also been the important process through which the library has been able to determine which of the materials formerly housed in its storm-affected areas were lost and which were saved. It involves the physical handling of each item and two basic categories of work: (a) checking returned items against the library's holdings to reactivate online catalog records while updating holdings information where needed and (b) basic sorting of restored uncataloged material such as manuscripts from Special Collections.[20]

Many of the books restored were next shipped to a separate bindery company for rebinding and then returned to Fort Worth for quality control review. All restored materials were returned to the new Recovery Center site in boxes shipped on pallets, generally 32 boxes per pallet and more than 400 pallets in all. It was estimated that 111,975 of these returning items needed to be checked against the library's holdings to reactivate their online catalog records and the rest of the items will need basic sorting, reboxing, and inventory.[21]

The processing of donations requires the items handled to be cataloged, including some original cataloging for items such as music scores and foreign language materials. This has required a much higher level of expertise different from the basic processing of materials returning from restoration so, while copy cataloging has been handled by LAC staff onsite, items requiring more complex cataloging are generally shipped out to LAC's cataloging specialists based around the country. More than a hundred libraries and individuals across North America donated materials and especially music books, scores and CDs— some 20,000 titles in all.

The scale of the cataloging phase has grown to include replacement purchases in addition to donations. Once all the restored items from the music library were compared against and reinstated in the catalog, lost lists were generated for music books, scores, and recordings. These became the basis for a new Recovery Center acquisitions project in which the LAC staff was tasked to begin automatic ordering, receipt, and cataloging of lost list items using a set of general parameters. Replacement purchases of large-expense microform collections or digital versions of these are ordered directly through the library's regular acquisitions process, although all physical replacements are processed and cataloged through the Recovery Center.

The processing of restored special collections material from Jones Hall turned out to be a much larger undertaking than initially foreseen. The initial estimated scale of project was based on very early Jones Hall box count estimates provided by BELFOR in the fall of 2005, shortly after the company had salvaged materials onsite and had just begun the restoration process. It was based on a simple count of boxes into which salvaged materials had been placed to next be frozen. For unit estimation a rough average number of books that would normally have been placed in a box was used for all print materials salvaged. Thus as the library began to plan for materials recovery overall the number of units salvaged for restoration from Jones Hall was estimated at a very low 64,260. But for manuscripts the actual unit handled is a folder and unit definitions for the other archival materials also needed to correspond to similar levels of actual items being handled and inventoried.

Once the boxes of special collections material were loaded off of pallets and sorted onto shelves, folder counts from the first manuscripts collections processed and additional sample counts from other boxes determined that the initial project estimate had been undercounted by a factor of eight. There were really some 515,186 restored special collections units to be processed.

This project requires examining all boxes returned from restoration to determine whether box labels match box contents and relabeling the temporary BELFOR boxes when necessary; ordering the boxes in relation to the specific collections in which they belong; checking individual folders in each box to determine if folder labels match folder contents and rectifying when necessary; and reboxing the collections into new archival boxes (since the old archival boxes were destroyed) and labeling them. The project also includes creating an inventory that compares the materials restored against previous collection finding aids to determine which materials have been lost. This involves identifying collection contents at the series, sub series, box, and folder levels and the LAC special collections project team is entering inventory data into Archon so that the inventory can serve as a base for the new electronic finding aids. Archon is a software program that provides both a way to record in easy templates descriptive information about archival collections and a means to view, search, and browse that information in a public web site.[22]

Personnel

One critically important measure that allowed the university to reopen after having been closed for entire fall 2005 semester was keeping its faculty and staff on the payroll throughout the long four and a half-month evacuation period. But with severe revenue losses and hundreds of millions of dollars in physical damages to address quickly, staff reductions were inevitable.

In early spring 2006 the library was asked to reduce the number of positions in its overall workforce by 15 percent. At the same time, some employees whose homes were destroyed or otherwise given up simply could not muster a return to

New Orleans. Some who initially returned found their circumstances in that first difficult post-Katrina year in New Orleans too difficult and decided to leave the city. Thus by the end of that year the library was left with a significant loss of personnel both in positions that had initially been designated as "noncritical" but also in many key positions, including some at the senior level.

By the close of 2006 the library found itself with the need to recruit nationally to fill eight professional vacancies while news filtering out of New Orleans about conditions in the city continued to be overwhelming negative. Meanwhile, it became common for supervisors throughout the library to report that some staff members were suffering through difficult periods of post-storm stress or grief. Tulane's Human Resources Department began to organize small group meetings throughout the university, including meetings for library personnel, to talk about post-Katrina experiences in an attempt to manage stress. The meetings were met with mixed reviews. But for those experiencing more serious problems the university offered individual counseling sessions with mental healthcare providers through United Healthcare and Cigna Behavioral Health.[23]

The library reorganized to adjust for some lost positions and, eventually, it was the city's recovery progress that overcame the library's recruiting challenges. Indeed most potential candidates came for interviews citing a desire to help New Orleans rebuild as an important factor, if not the most important factor, in deciding to apply for a job at Tulane's library. In the end each professional vacancy was filled by a highly qualified, highly motivated candidate. But even four years after the storm, some storm-related personnel problems persist. "There is a level of stress and fragility that you see in some staff who are still rebuilding or still dealing with Katrina-related problems that you wouldn't see in other places," according to one supervisor who joined the library after the storm. "In most workplaces there is a real separation between one's work life and home life. There is less of that separation here. You just have to be understanding."

And then there are said to be some in the library who quietly wonder if Katrina might on occasion be used among some of their colleagues today as a handy, all-purpose excuse. But new recruits generally settled into areas revitalized by renovation and the storm itself was uneven in its personal impact. Among those library personnel who went through Katrina, some were living at the time in housing that did not flood or did not otherwise experience major property losses or damages, while some lost homes completely or faced long rebuilding projects often hampered by problems with insurance, recovery assistance, unreliable post-Katrina contractors, permits, or stamina. Very few librarians had school age children at the time of the storm or after; members of the support staff were much more likely to have had this difficult layer added to their experience, as they were much more likely to have had extended family members who were also affected. Unlike librarians, support staff members were forced to use up their cumulated leave while the university had been closed, and some went into a deficit that prevented them from using personal leave days for many months after returning. The subtle effects of these differing experiences deserve watching in the future, and perhaps point to a need for further examination of the effect of major disasters on workforce issues or organizational climate.

Lessons Learned

The scale of the disaster that engulfed New Orleans and the surrounding area in the wake of Katrina precludes a lot of practical second guessing. And while disaster planning was a standard practice and almost everyone in the region had a general sense of vulnerability to hurricanes, the general public could not have predicted the collapse of the canal flood walls that tragically flooded New Orleans after the hurricane had passed.

Plan to Communicate

Our experience shows that the most important aspect of a disaster plan is very likely an effective strategy for communication after an event. This should include planning for effective communication among members of a Library Emergency Response Team, the core group of decision makers who will need to formulate an event-specific response, but also among library staff, especially displaced library staff after an event. Katrina caused library staff to be dispersed throughout the United States for months. In many if not most cases, alternate contact info dutifully collected on lists before the storm turned out not to be reliable. Staff eventually regrouped remotely by means of a Yahoo e-mail news group established ad hoc after the storm and that was maintained over the long evacuation period unevenly. Today the library maintains a special emergency blog on a third party host server that easily allows for both official news posts from library administrators and comments from all staff who can access the site.

In 2008, Hurricane Gustav also prompted a large-scale evacuation of the city and uncovered still more challenges in maintaining effective communication after a storm. Gustav skirted New Orleans but caused heavy damage not far to the west and through much of the lower central portion of Louisiana, an area, especially around Baton Rouge, that serves as a traditional evacuation destination for large numbers of New Orleans area residents. As a result, Gustav disrupted power, cable, land line phone, and cell phone service outside the city and thousands of evacuees scrambled for temporary lodging alongside the highways while they waited for the city, largely undamaged, to reopen. Hence even Internet access to the library or university emergence information proved problematic for some during the short term. Luckily, Gustav did not require a long term evacuation; most library staff evacuees were able to return to work within a week.

Rely on Qualified Disaster Management

Clearly, for a large scale disaster Tulane's library was best served by the university's overall reliance on a highly qualified, well-prepared disaster management firm than it would have been in relying on its own resources and disaster planning. The library simply could not have mustered an effective response on its own or by additionally relying largely on assistance from within the university.

Establish Liability Beforehand

One of the most difficult aspects of the recovery process has been continuing litigation over insurance coverage of destroyed or damaged library collections, and which is still affecting the library's collections rebuilding efforts and draining valuable time and energy four years after Katrina. University risk management officers must ensure that insurance liability, as well as the processes for covering losses and damages, is clear and agreed upon by all parties before a disaster occurs.

Separate Recovery Work from Normal Work

A strategy that has generally worked well has been to try, whenever possible, to separate recovery work from the regular work of running the library. It was decided at the start that the large scale aspects of collections recovery and rebuilding could not be done unless a means could be found to accomplish the work as an add-on, using out-sourced labor and expertise. The scale of the recovery work was simply too big; with staff reductions the library was already challenged to process more annual acquisitions than pre-Katrina due to more efficient buying and other factors and it needed to make up lost ground in areas such as information technology to be competitive with Tulane's peer institutions. By diverting by far the most labor intensive aspects of the recovery to BELFOR and the Recovery Center the library successfully shielded many of its personnel from this work.

The initial decision to separate recovery work from the routine work that occupies other librar-

ies was made largely out of necessity and it forced the library to be creative. It forced planners to risk spending a lot of time on big ideas with little if any precedent and no firm funding commitments. But this resulted in the plan to first build a large processing and temporary storage infrastructure (our Recovery Center) that would later allow the library to really rebuild. The means were there; they just were not obvious and required extra steps to discover and acquire them. This discovery phase was enhanced early on when the library was able to meet and plan its options directly with FEMA and state recovery authority representatives. It would have been far more difficult later when the university necessarily needed to centralize contact with FEMA, the state, and its insurers as the number of Tulane's recovery projects grew and as some aspects of the recovery came under litigation. Therefore to move quickly early on is important.

Time Heals

One more lesson is the importance of context; that our library recovery has been inextricably linked to the recovery of the region as a whole, to that of New Orleans, to the rebuilding of our neighborhoods, our schools, often our own homes, sometimes ourselves. In a disaster such as one wreaked by Hurricane Katrina, recovery is a long process, full of setbacks and successes, and interwoven into a much broader framework than one library or one campus.

Despite the continuing work to be done at its libraries, the progress made by Tulane University has been remarkable. Aside from repairing more than $600 million in damages thus far, Tulane has renewed its campus, raised its academic stature, ensured its financial stability, and increased its role in the New Orleans community after the storm. Undergraduate applications have increased from around 18,000 the year before Katrina to 40,000 in 2009. Today Tulane's first-year undergraduate classes are among the most selective and academically qualified in its 175-year history. Its retention rate that reflects the percentage of first-year students who return to complete their degree has risen to more than 90 percent. There have been increases in enrollment and academic quality in nearly all of the university's graduate and professional programs.[24]

Tulane is today a better university. Its library will be a better library too.

Notes

1. "AAU 2009 Facts and Figures" (Association of American Universities). http://www.aau.edu/workarea/showcontent.aspx?id=9990 (October 10, 2009).

2. "ARL Statistics" (Association of Research Libraries). http://www.arl.org/stats/annualsurveys/arlstats/preveds.shtml (October 10, 2009).

3. United States. Congress. *A Failure of Initiative: Final Report of the Select Bipartisan Committee to Investigate the Preparation for and Response to Hurricane Katrina.* Washington, DC: Government Printing Office. (February 19, 2006): 7. http://www.gpoaccess.gov/katrinareport/fullreport.pdf (October 10, 2009).

4. Kevin U. Stephens Sr., David Grew, Karen Chin, Paul Kadetz, P. Gregg Greenough, Frederick M. Burkle Jr., Sandra L. Robinson, and Evangeline R. Franklin, "Excess Mortality in the Aftermath of Hurricane Katrina: A Preliminary Report," *Disaster Medicine and Public Health Preparedness* 1, (2007): 14-20.

5. R. W. Kates, C. E. Colten, S. Laska, and S. P. Leatherman, "Reconstruction of New Orleans after Hurricane Katrina: A Research Perspective," *Proceedings of the National Academy of Sciences* 103, no. 40 (2006): 14656.

6. Times-Picayune Publishing Co., *The Times-Picayune Katrina: The Ruin and Recovery of New Orleans* (New Orleans, LA: Times-Picayune, LLC; Spotlight Press distributor, Champaign, IL, 2006): 23.

7. Dave Eggers, *Zeitoun* (San Francisco: McSweeney's Books, 2009): 104-106.

8. Andy Corrigan, "Disaster: Response and recovery at a major research library in New Orleans," *Library Management* 29, no. 4/5 (2008): 297.

9. Ibid, 297.

10. Ibid, 297.

11. Ibid, 297.

12. Ibid, 298.

13. Ibid, 298.

14. Ibid, 298.

15. John Pope, "Tulane library getting FEMA aid; $16 million to help replace machinery," *Times-Picayune (New Orleans)*, Metro Section, September 3, 2009, 1.

16. Corrigan, Disaster, 299.

17. Ibid, 299.

18. Ibid, 299.

19. Ibid, 302-303.

20. Ibid, 303.

21. Ibid, 303.

22. "Archon's Key Features" (Archon). http://www.archon.org/features.php (October 10, 2009).

23. Madeline Vann, "Tulane Offers Help for Lingering Post-K Stress," *New Wave.* October 12, 2006. http://tulane.edu/news/newwave/101206_tulane_offers_help_for_lingering_postk_stress.cfm (October 10, 2009).

24. Scott Cowen, "Tulane Talk," August 28, 2009. http://tulane.edu/administration/president/tulane_talk/tt_083109.cfm (October 10, 2009).

LIBRARY FLOOD

Paula Mochida

"Water!"

At 7:30 p.m. on October 30, 2004 Andrew Wertheimer and his class of twenty-four graduate students in Library Information Sciences heard the fire alarm go off. The LIS program was located on the ground floor of the Thomas Hale Hamilton Library, the research library, at the University of Hawaii at Mānoa. It was a Saturday evening. The Library had closed to the public at 6 p.m., but the LIS class was in the last two hours of a week-end intensive course.

Wertheimer and the students paused to look outside at the heavy rain and thought the alarms were probably a malfunction due to the rain. At about 7:45 p.m. the power suddenly went out plunging the class into darkness. Even the emergency safety lights went out. As the class adjusted their eyes to the darkness, and wondered if they should wait a while to see if the power returned or if they should end the class, someone yelled, "Water!"

Within minutes water burst through doors into the LIS lounge and reading room and began flooding the classroom occupied by the LIS students. The group began making their way through shin-deep water to a bank of six-foot high vertical windows that opened onto the campus Mall. A few of the students called 911 on their cell phones, but only got busy-signals. No one panicked, but one young woman began shouting, "Break the windows! Break the windows!" Another student picked up a round, library step-stool and "attacked" one of the tall vertical windows breaking the glass to clear a way out. By that time the water was knee deep and a river of water was filling up the entire ground floor of

Hamilton Library. As Wertheimer and the last student scrambled out of the window they looked back and could make out the walls of the LIS faculty offices collapsing under the pressure of the water. The group held hands as they made their way to safety across campus through two-foot deep water in the dark and in the rain.[1]

The University of Hawaii at Mānoa is located at the mouth of Mānoa Valley. The ridges that form the valley walls can be seen when you look towards the mountains from Waikiki. On this particular night, an accumulation of over ten inches of rain during a 12-hour period came out of the back of the valley. The Mānoa stream began to fill rapidly with torrential waters that gathered up debris along its banks. Mid-way through the valley are two (man-made) right angle turns in the river's bend, one on each of two streets that border a small shopping center. The tidal wave of debris-filled water overflowed onto the road at the first right angle, but then jumped the banks of the second turn. The huge wave of water lifted several cars into trees and submerged cars parked on the street. The flood washed through an elementary school and through quiet Mānoa neighborhoods before arriving on the University campus. Its path took it through the first floor of the former medical school and its adjacent parking lot and then through a narrow driveway and across the street to Hamilton Library.

The water might have gone around the building were it not for a dry land moat around three sides of the building that provided natural lighting to some of the departments on the ground floor below. The moat immediately began filling with the flood of water, eventually bursting through a fire door and windows. The water never stopped until it drained out the broken window through which the LIS students and professor had escaped, moving or taking down everything in its path. The watermark along the 324 feet length of the floor—and throughout the 61,000 square feet of the entire floor—ranged between eight to 12 feet high.

University of Hawaii Background

The University of Hawaii main Web page describes the university as "UH Mānoa is one of only 13 institutions to hold the distinction of being a land-, sea-, and space-grant research institution. Classified by the Carnegie Foundation as having "very high research activity," UH Mānoa is known for its pioneering research in such fields as oceanography, astronomy, Pacific Islands and Asian area studies, linguistics, cancer research, and genetics. The National Science Foundation ranks UH Mānoa in the top 30 public universities in federal research funding for engineering and science and 49th overall. In 2008, UH Mānoa received $273 million in awards, with research grants reaching $173 million and non-research awards reaching $100 million.

The first UH Mānoa library opened in February 1908 with three titles—a dictionary, an atlas, and a 16-volume set of the *Encyclopedia of Americana*.[3] The Library joined the ARL membership in 1976, and by 2004 had over 3.3 million volumes with collections and services centralized in two buildings, the Thomas Hale Hamilton Library and the Gregg M. Sinclair Library. The Sinclair Library houses the Music collection, Audiovisual Center, Reserve Materials Collection, and the Student Success Center which was established in 2007. It is located on the opposite side of campus from Hamilton Library and had no flood-related damage. The UH Mānoa Library is the only major research library in the 10-campus system, and in the State of Hawaii. There is a separate Law Library and a separate Health Sciences Library that work closely with the UH Mānoa Library, but have different reporting lines.

Hamilton Library was built in three phases. Phase I was completed in 1967, phase II in 1976, and phase III in 2001. Phases I (four floors including the ground floor) and II (six floors including the ground floor) are joined and phase III is a separate seven- floor "tower" connected to the original two phases by a "bridge" on the first and second floors. The ground floor of phases I and II was destroyed, and there was some water damage to the ground and first floors of phase III.

Response to the Flood

The first responders started to arrive by 8:30 p.m., including then University Librarian Diane Perushek and Network Specialist Tom Ishimitsu.[4] They were followed by then Assistant University Librarian Bob Schwarzwalder, Head of Preservation Lynn Davis, Building Manager Steve Pickering, then Head of Government Documents and Maps Gwen Sinclair, Documents Librarian Mabel Suzuki, and Preservation Assistant Kyle Hamada. The Library has an emergency flowchart of contacts and cell/home phone numbers. The University Librarian, the Associate and Assistant University Librarians, the Head of Preservation, and the Building Manager are always the first to be notified.

They made independent checks on various parts of the Library from the roof on down. It was pitch black as they tried to make their way through the building with flashlights. Water was still at least six feet high as they looked down the stairwells to the ground floor below. In fact Steve and Gwen came across Diane and Tom in a stairwell. Tom had slipped on the wet stairs, falling into the muddy and stench-smelling water and twisting his ankle.

It did not take long for them to realize that the entire LIS program had been destroyed, including their computer lab, student lounge, classrooms, and faculty offices containing student records and faculty research. The Library's entire Collection

Services division—Acquisitions, Serials, and Cataloging departments; 95% of the Regional Federal Depository Library and the Maps Collection; the Staff Room; the primary utility room; and the main server room—were also destroyed.

Perushek invited the first responders to reconvene at her house, which was about a five minute drive away. There, in the middle of the night, Perushek, Bob Schwarzwalder, Lynn Davis, Gwen Sinclair, and Steve Pickering determined that the Maps and Aerial Photographs collections would be their first priority to find and try to salvage. By 1:00 am they had put an emergency call in to Hawaii Restorative, a Honolulu company equipped to handle environmental emergencies.

Most of the first responders were back on campus at daylight Sunday morning. They immediately realized that there were safety issues that had to be dealt with before entering the building. The UH facilities office had made arrangements for contractors to disable the basement toilets, but no one came to give the "all clear" for the electrical-clearance, though it was self-evident that there was no electrical power. They were concerned about the potential for *leptospirosis*, a life-threatening infection caused by parasites sometimes found in Hawaii's mountain streams and waters. They knew they would have to warn anyone with open wounds to stay away from the mud and water. (Luckily no one working in the Library contracted the disease, though one person cleaning up the biomedical building was eventually reported to have contracted a mild case.)

Disaster Recovery and Disaster Plans

Dozens of other buildings sustained water damage: among the more serious were the biomedical building which was eventually evacuated because of water damage to labs and the library and the one-story buildings of Krauss Hall, housing the offices of the Outreach College. The floodwaters made their way across the campus and eventually 'water-falled' over the walls of the lower campus quarry and 'pooled'

onto athletic fields. During the first several days, staff found remnants of the Library's collections all along the path of the water to the athletic field.

The Library did have a disaster plan that consisted of an *Emergency Handbook* that dealt with everything from *Alarms* to *Workplace Violence and Other Violations of Law*, and included *Water Leak or Flooding* and *Collection Emergency*. The latter included instructions under the headers:

- Observe Safety Rules
- Protect Library Materials
- Stabilize the Environment
- Mobilize the Collection Disaster Response Team (who were trained in basic collection emergency measures)

The Library administration knew it had to get equipment, refrigeration containers, commercial clean-up services, and a host of supplies in very large quantities as soon as possible in order to halt damage and start the recovery process. No one at the campus level seemed prepared to grant authorization for such extraordinary measures until David McClain, then President of the University of Hawaii System, stepped forward. Thanks go to the President, Lynn Davis, John Awakuni, the Library's superhero Fiscal Officer, and the University's Auxiliary Enterprise unit who all persisted to get the supplies and contracts needed to get the urgent jobs done.

It was extremely important that any materials that could be salvaged were refrigerated, freeze-dried, or cleaned and dried within the first 48 hours before mold set in. As library staff received word about the flood on Sunday, Lynn Davis and the Library's administrators surveyed the extent of damage. The ground floor of the building and everything in it was covered with a thick layer of wet mud. There was no electricity, therefore no lights. Stacks of collapsed shelving, mountains of muddy over-size map cases, unrecognizable materials in print and non-print formats, furniture and personal belongings tossed about, photocopier machines shoved across rooms, and even the walls of former departments barely standing and hanging onto frames made for a very dangerous environment. The campus facilities staff had their hands full with the rest of the campus and ended up handing over responsibility for the Library's initial recovery to the Library.

At first tentatively and then with all the strength and determination of a rescue team, library administrators, faculty, and staff, flashlights in hand, began to seek out the salvageable collections. Among the top priority items were 90,000 maps, including 300 year-old maps of Oceania drawn by early European explorers, and thousands of original historical aerial photographs of Pacific islands. Maps and photographs had to be rinsed, laid flat, and transferred to the freezer containers. Water-logged books had to be boxed and packed into the containers. Other materials were rinsed and hung on lines to dry.

On Monday morning, only about 36 hours after the flood, library administration gathered the dozens of library staff who had reported to work. They met on the library's first floor just beyond the main entrance. The only light came from a 50 feet long glass wall. Lynn Davis described the major assignments and "team" leaders and asked the staff to volunteer as they wished. Because the stairwells were still dangerously wet and blocked with debris, staff entered the ground floor from an outside entrance. Wearing rubber slippers, sneakers, and hand-held flashlights, they used book trucks as make-shift dollies and hand tools bought at a local hardware store to empty the floor of as much of the muddied collections and moveable furniture as possible. Although the Library has had an integrated library system since the 1980s, there were only paper shelf-lists for government documents, maps, and paper worksheets for thousands of items in process. Most of these paper records were lost in the flood. The replacement of materials without records became a huge challenge. A large percentage of the items had been purchased on acquisitions trips in Asia and the Pacific, areas of academic and collection strength,

and the records of those purchases were now gone.

Staff rescued thousands of pieces and, under the direction of Lynn Davis, prepared them for either freeze-drying or immediate washing and drying on makeshift lines strung up outside or in a room in Phase III. Others had jobs that varied from monitoring water pumping systems that had been brought in to guarding entrance points and interior stairwells to make sure that only authorized personnel had access.

Library administration triaged in the Administration Offices, also without electricity, but luckily the phone lines worked. University Librarian Diane Perushek was on the phone with library administrators at Colorado State University (CSU). They had survived a major flood in 1997 and reported that they were still dealing with ramifications from the flood. Camila Alire, then CSU University Librarian, is the co-author and editor of , *Library Disaster Planning and Recovery Handbook* (2000), a work that became Perushek's major reference during the recovery period.[5]

Attempts were made to document the rescue and recovery efforts. The following excerpt is from the Library's Science and Technology department history of the recovery:

"After several long days of concentrated recovery work in the dark, muddy basement by library staff, the ground floor was sealed off for health and safety reasons and to prevent humidity levels from rising in the rest of the Library. Two Texas-based disaster management companies were contracted: BMS CAT did cleanup and environmental maintenance work while Belfor USA worked on document recovery. In a few days BMS CAT installed several mechanical air handlers around Hamilton to pump fresh air into the dark, closed building through large yellow plastic caterpillar-like tubes that reached to Hamilton's upper floors. A maze of clear-plastic air ducts ran along the interior ceilings, supplying cool, dehumidified air to prevent an additional disaster of mold attacking and destroying the millions of other books in the Library."[6]

The response from volunteers from across the campus was heart-warming. Students and faculty volunteered to help with the salvage and assist with the cleaning of the materials. Lynn Davis realized that more refrigeration/freezer containers were needed and persisted with two local cargo companies, Horizon and Matson, until they managed to provide additional containers. Without her tenacity, thousands of documents would have been lost forever.

Auxiliary Enterprises brought a small generator to power temporary strings of light in early December. Library staff had to turn it on and off at the beginning and the end of the day. Large capacity generators arrived on December 27, 2004, and Phase II (only) was powered up on January 19, 2005. Because of submerged main breaker panels, Phase I needed a lot more electrical work, and did not power up until March 9, 2005.

Between January 26 and February 3, 2005, air conditioning was restored, in stages, to Phases I and II. The remaining temporary light strings were taken down on March 8, 2005. And all phases of the Library reopened to the public on March 28, 2005, five months after the flood.

A temporary power pole was installed on Maile Way on August 6, 2005, and the Library switched over from generator power to HECO power, the Hawaiian electric company, (via a line from an adjacent K-12 school) on September 17, 2005. The big generators were hauled off (to post-Katrina New Orleans) on September 26. The Library was on this temporary power configuration until August 15, 2009.

Of course no one ever expected a flood of this size, nor damage to collections of this magnitude.

The flood was called "The 100 year Flood". It definitely was not a situation that could be handled by the Library alone, and indeed the revised disaster plan procedures include contacting the Disaster Recovery Contractor.[7] Its list of procedures have the following headers:

- Safety First
- Halting Damage
- Document
- Stabilizing Environment
- Evaluating Extent of Damage
- Stabilizing Collections
- Collection Disaster Response Team
- Collection Disaster Recovery Procedures
- Follow-up After Recovery

In the midst of what felt like initial chaos - certainly stages of shock - there were a number of extremely important logistics that had to be coordinated. One was how to coordinate the large army of volunteers and how to feed a hundred people every day during the first weeks of cleanup. Individual donations of snacks and fruits were very much appreciated and luckily local eateries began to donate meals and cases of drinks.

Jean Ehrhorn, Associate University Librarian at the time, served as media spokesperson as the destruction of the ground floor was the largest loss on campus and was unprecedented in magnitude in the history of the University. In addition to media coordination, Ehrhorn immediately began to canvas other buildings and inquire with other departments for temporary workspaces for the 140+ staff. Because there was no electricity, and there would not be electricity capable of powering lights, air conditioning, elevators, etc. for five months, library staff that had not been flooded out, also needed temporary quarters. Susan Murata, head of a nearby community college library and a former Hamilton department head, was granted half-time leave from her campus in order to coordinate the details of the staff moves.

Another very important responsibility that required coordination was keeping staff informed. Especially after the first week of physical work to salvage and clean materials, communication became more and more important. Perushek held daily updates on the first floor. She used a portable loudspeaker and would bring in staff or campus experts to provide much needed information. The administration also wrote up a daily newsletter called *The Appriser*, which was distributed by e-mail and by print copy. Try, as the administration did, the staff never felt that there had been enough communication.[8]

The Library's Information Technology division knew it was extremely important to get the on-line catalog up and running as quickly as possible. Thanks to the generosity of vendors, help from campus personnel, and outstanding staff in both the Systems office and the Desktop Network Services office of the Library Information Technology division, the online catalog was available on November 3, 2004, just five days after the flood. Wing Leung, the IT Specialist for Server Support, was able to activate a replacement proxy server, and restore files from back-up tapes that had been located on a different floor. Much of the credit goes to Assistant University Librarian Bob Schwarzwalder and his staff who also spent days locating computers in the mud-filled graveyard and cleaned, revived, and saved files as best they could. More than $300,000 in hardware had been lost.

"By the middle of November a paging system was operational, allowing students and faculty to request library items and pick them up from the 1st floor Addition [phase III].... Limited library services continued to be offered from the SciTech 1st floor until 8 January 2005 when the first four floors of the Addition were opened again to library users. Paging of materials from the closed Phase I and II areas continued until 29 March 2005 when all of Hamilton Library—except the ground floor—opened to the public."[9]

The above description covered the immediate days and months of response and recovery. There is a much longer story after the first six months for which there is not enough space within this case study. It would have included a report on the rash of intentionally set fires that resulted in checking individual IDs and installing more security cameras. It would have included describing the lengthy process of redesigning the ground floor, because more square footage was added when the architects decided to cover the moat in order to mitigate future problems. It would have included the trials and tribulations of the actual construction. And it would have included the difficult change in library administration, and the recent successes and exciting prospects for the future.

In the end, the cost of reconstruction, which includes a separate utility building, a server room located on an upper floor, and the entire ground floor amounted to almost $26 million. Expenditures for the replacement of material, equipment, furniture, temporary personnel, and treatment contracts were almost $6 million. It is estimated that the Library received $8 million in donations of government documents.

Lessons Learned

One of the lessons learned is how valuable it would have been to have pre-qualified recovery companies in place. Hawaii has a tedious state procurement process that even in an emergency still requires hoops to jump through. Our goal is to have local companies that have been authorized to bring in refrigeration units; large size generators, fans, air scrubbers, and stocks of canopies as needed, and to have pre-qualified major international companies such as BMS CAT and Belfor USA already cleared to arrive on the scene as quickly as possible.

It would also be wise to have an integrated emergency and disaster recovery plan for the entire campus, and to even include the Honolulu Police Department and the neighboring community. The campus revised the *Mānoa Emergency Response Plan* in 2006, but it does not include a recovery plan.[10] That is still a serious gap and something that will hopefully be addressed in the near future.

As mentioned above, there were a number of activities that had to have coordinators. These included coordinators for:

- Volunteers (their assignments, their supplies, their meals)
- Staff counseling and guidance to deal with the traumatic and emotional impact of a disaster
- Staff relocations (short- and long-term temporary locations, furniture, equipment)
- Internal communication and external communication to the media, including television stations and newspapers.

Another challenging lesson was dealing with FEMA and the whole area of funding support. The Hawaii State Legislature made a special emergency appropriation in early 2005 to cover up front costs. These funds were coordinated at the campus level, and funneled through the State Civil Defense Office to FEMA which reviewed expenditures and then partially reimbursed the State. FEMA staff did not arrive until February 1, 2005, three months after the flood. In the midst of ongoing recovery, temporary/makeshift locations and services, and coping with post-traumatic syndromes, FEMA required the obligatory bureaucratic paperwork for documentation. A dedicated person was eventually hired in the Fiscal Office to assist John Awakuni, the Fiscal Officer, and his regular staff, with the tracking. The FEMA representatives were great people and pleasant to work with, but there was a lot of turnover because they move from one disaster to another. The Library, in fact, had to ask for several extensions to complete projected jobs that had met with unforeseen delays. FEMA approvals often came months after the request for extension had been submitted. Nonetheless, the Library was grateful for their aid. FEMA and State funding ended June 30, 2009. Temporary staff who had been hired between 2005 and 2008 to help in all departments impacted by the flood were terminated at that time.

Opportunities

As Rahm Emanuel has stated, "Never waste a good crisis." Seize strategic opportunities in response to any kind of crisis.

Build Long-Term Friendships and Development Opportunities with the many individuals, academic departments, organizations, and businesses that lend a helping hand. Let the media distribute your story, reach out to those who care about the library, and bring them back in to library events and activities. People will care for a long time. In 2008, for example, the Hawaii State Legislature came through with an unprecedented $2.4 million supplemental budget allocation based on our story of survival and vision for the future. Those who have resources to invest do not want to hear sob stories. They want to hear stories of survivors and heroes.

Build expertise and capacity. Share and teach others skills and methodologies that staff learn as they go through the response, salvage, and recovery periods. Lynn Davis, for example, assumed a major role in WESTPAS (Western States and Territories Preservation Assistance Service when it received a grant from the National Endowment for the Humanities. She has been conducting workshops in Hawaii and in U.S. territories in the Pacific, including Guam and American Samoa. She has trained workshop participants to take appropriate action in the event of an emergency, had them complete written disaster response and collection salvage plans, and had them develop mutual aid agreements to enable library and archives staff to work collaboratively to respond to disasters.

Lynn Davis has also organized week-long workshops for experts to share the latest techniques in conservation and preservation methodologies, the use of special equipment, and tools. There is a greater awareness of what can be done to repair and save precious materials, and a much greater appreciation and respect for the unique talent and skills of the Preservation Department and the Disaster Response Team. Kyle Hamada, one of the

Preservation technicians, received the Chancellor's award for outstanding work in 2008 for inventions he created to save flood-damaged materials and his repeated quick response to numerous other collection emergencies in the last years.

Look at new models. Do not, necessarily, go back to the same way of housing collections, offering services—public or technical services. Before you rebuild physical facilities or think about item for item replacements, think about different technologies, different infrastructure or delivery systems. This is probably the single most difficult thing to do in the midst of a disaster, but the long-term rewards can be transformative.

Although the regional Federal Depository Library was able to replace almost 75% of its print collection because of donations from other government documents libraries that were weeding their holdings, they also decided not to pursue a project to find comparable replacements for damaged aerial photographs at NARA. A larger percentage of photographs was deemed salvageable over time than expected. Instead a large room in the newly constructed Docs and Maps area that was destined to be a storage room will be a classroom/lab for the Library's new GIS program. A vacant government documents librarian position was re-described and filled with an energetic and visionary GIS librarian. The demand for this program has grown so much in the last two and a half years, that the Library must now seek ways to increase capacity. This is exciting and has given the Library a new arm to reach out to the campus and external communities to bring them back in.

There will surely be "temporary" kinds of services that are different from traditional services that can be considered for the longer term. Although the UH Mānoa Library reverted back to traditional reference services and delivery services, it is now talking about revisiting models used during the first year of the flood, such as embedded librarians, shared reference desks, and new delivery services.

Plan strategically. Although some may argue the timing of working through a new strategic plan, or looking at streamlining processing workflows, or changing the organizational culture while still "in recovery", the Interim University Librarian insisted that it was imperative that the UH Mānoa Library do this now. After an inclusive team-led strategic planning process in early 2008, she established eight strategic action teams in early summer 2008. One of the teams was to address the need to analyze the processing workflow in collection services. R2 Consulting LLC from New Hampshire was contracted through a RFP process and in early July 2009 presented their report and recommendations.

The collection services staff will have been in temporary locations in Hamilton and Sinclair libraries for over five years before their scheduled move to the reconstructed ground floor in early 2010. The Government Documents and Maps staff and collections are in three different buildings (Hamilton, Sinclair, and an off-site location.) The Cataloging librarians and staff have been in the Archives and Manuscripts processing area. Serials and Acquisitions are in different "phases" of Hamilton in large rooms intended for other purposes. The systems staff was split between Hamilton and Sinclair where the LMS server has been temporarily located. Nonetheless the staff are currently embarking on the implementation of almost 50 recommendations, some that will transform the culture, and they can hardly wait to get started.

Notes

1. Lori Ann Saeki. October 30, 2004. Unpublished account by a graduate student who was in the LIS 650 class that safely escaped the flood.
2. "University of Hawaii at Mānoa" http://hawaii.edu/about/ (October 1, 2009).

3. Paul Wermager and others, *SciTech: History and Recollections of the Science & Technology Reference Department, University of Hawaii at Mānoa Library, and the University of Hawaii* (Honolulu: University of Hawaii at Mānoa Library, 2008), 5.

4. The response to the flood and descriptions of the first days are based on personal recollections and interviews conducted with Lynn Davis, Jean Ehrhorn, Kyle Hamada, Tom Ishimitsu, Steve Pickering, and Lori Ann Saeki in April 2009.

5. Camila Alire, ed., *Library Disaster Planning and Recovery Handbook.* (New York: Neal Schuman Publishing Company, 2000).

6. *SciTech: History,* 61.

7. UH Mānoa Library, Preservation Department, http://library.manoa.hawaii.edu/departments/preservation/index.html (October 1, 2009).

8. From an interview with Jean Ehrhorn, April 2009.

9. *SciTech: History,* 62.

10. *Mānoa Emergency Response Plan, 2006.* Mānoa Campus Emergency Management Program, http://manoa.hawaii.edu/emergency (October 1, 2009).

Case 5: University of Iowa

FLOOD

Nancy L. Baker

Background

In June, 2008, much of the state of Iowa experienced severe flooding when nine rivers reached all-time record flood levels, resulting in billions of dollars in damage. Severe ice, snow, and rain throughout the previous winter and spring proved more than the local rivers and the regional reservoirs could manage. In the end, eighty-five of the state's ninety-nine counties were declared disaster areas. Iowa City, home of the University of Iowa, was among these communities. The Iowa River divides the university into east and west campuses. Most of the time, the university and the river live quite amicably together but in a little over a week that June, the University suffered an estimated damage of $743 million. Forty-two campus buildings were flooded to one extent or another.

The University of Iowa is a large research university, a member of the Committee on Institutional Cooperation (CIC) and the Big 10 NCAA conference, with over 30,000 students. The University Libraries house over five million volumes, in a wide range of formats, along with impressive collections of rare books, unique manuscripts, and other special collections. At the time of the flood, these collections, along with over one hundred and eighty professional and support staff, occupied twelve campus libraries. Three libraries were directly affected by the flood—the Main Library, the Rita Benton Music Library and the Art Library. Although the Fine Arts campus was especially hard hit by this flood, neither the Art nor Music Library collections were damaged since they were located on the second

floors of buildings that never flooded above their first floors.

Pre-Flood

All the University of Iowa Libraries had been very crowded at that time and the long overdue off-site collection storage facility, while planned, had not yet been built. Although the basement of the Main Library had served as collections storage for ten of the libraries, the basement had been full for several years, housing approximately 500,000 books, around 700 16mm and 35mm films, some collections of microfiche, and hundreds of boxes of manuscript collections. The Main Library is separated from the Iowa River by a large parking lot, a railroad track, and a bit of green space. No one initially thought this building would be flooded since it had not been damaged during the previous major flood in 1993. Earlier that week, Special Collections staff members had begun to move some of the manuscript collections from the lower shelves in the basement, mainly for their own peace of mind. The morning of Friday, June 13th, as images of the record-breaking flooding upriver in Cedar Rapids dominated the national media, it was apparent that this flood would be considerably more serious than the one fifteen years earlier. Library staff began to move some of the books from the lower shelves of the basement to the second floor. We issued a call for volunteers, using the campus and local media, which quickly brought about two hundred people to the library. As volunteers poured into the building, it was immediately apparent that we needed to have someone just to coordinate the volunteers as they arrived. One of the staff supervisors in Access Services assumed this role and made sure volunteers were sent where most needed.

The basement storage area is full of compact shelving, so the aisles are very narrow, making it especially difficult to accommodate many people at any one time. Book trucks are virtually impossible in these aisles. Since the elevators were needed to move the manuscript boxes and media to upper floors, volunteers formed human chains, passing the books from one to another down the aisles and up to the second floor reading area using three staircases. There was neither time nor space to move all the collections out of the basement. The Associate Director for Collections and Scholarly Communication, the Head of Preservation, and one of the Access Services Supervisors formed a team to decide what would go and what would stay. Irreplaceable items were moved first, including the older University of Iowa thesis and dissertations, for which the University Libraries were the sole repository. Humanities books were also a priority. Back files of science journals and similar materials that were available online were left behind. There was little time to make these decisions and such "triage" was difficult, stressful, and tiring. It was also challenging to find space for all the books and special collections. Although the Main Library has five floors, the top two were already jam packed with books stacks that were overly full. In fact, the only viable space was a large reading room on the second floor since the films were taking over what little space was available on the first floor. The Manuscript boxes had already filled one reading room and were getting stacked down a large aisle on the third floor. Floor loading capacity was a key consideration in a building that was already too full of heavy book stacks. Finding space off campus was not feasible given the timeline and because those few available storage areas were being used by other campus or community needs resulting from flooding earlier that week. In the future, we plan to have a contract in place with a library book moving company so collections can be moved and stored in company trucks.

Just as the work in the basement was getting into full swing that morning, the University Librarian was notified that the Main Library staff members, over one hundred individuals, would also need to be evacuated by the end of that day. Earlier that morning, no one thought this would be necessary. So Main Library staff had to be pulled from the volunteer book chains to pack up what they needed to move their workspace. Fortunately, library administrators had already identified every study room, vacant office, computer lab or other space in the remaining libraries that could be used as temporary work space in anticipation that evacuation might be necessary. We were able to assign the space fairly quickly to departments and individuals. Those who could work from home were permitted to do so until the building could be reoccupied. Access services staff moved to a classroom in the Engineering Library; the Technical Services operation, to a computer lab in the Health Sciences library; Library Administration, to student group study rooms in the Business library, and so on. Many of these classrooms and labs already had computers, making it unnecessary to move many individual staff workstations. Libraries' IT staff moved in with campus IT operations and the library servers were moved into the Engineering Building. It was difficult to know how much work to take with us since no one really knew how long the staff would be displaced. In the absence of anything definitive, we were told to assume at least a couple of weeks.

Some of our systems operations, like our OPAC, run on campus Information Technology-managed servers that were not directly threatened, so these would continue to be fully operational. We reduced our library-managed servers from twelve to two. The library Web page, the staff intranet, and a few other operations were available in snapshot form in order to provide access, even if not in real time. These could be and were updated during subsequent weeks but only by our webmaster. Staff also had the ability to access and store shared files on one server. We had the campus Information Technology Services Telecommunication & Networking Department reroute the IPs so all vendors IP-based authentication could be preserved and users could get to the subscription databases. *Illiad* software (interlibrary loan), our scholarly digital repository collections, and our newly minted next generation catalog (*Primo*) were not initially available due to the amount of storage or hardware needed to make them operational.

By 9 p.m. that Friday, all Main Library staff members had been evacuated including the five staff from the Art and Music Libraries who had not yet even settled into their newly assigned space in Main. All of the media, ten percent of the 500,000 book collection, and enough manuscript boxes to clear the floor by five feet, had been moved from the basement to the upper floors of the Main Library. Library-managed servers had also been relocated along with assorted other critical equipment.

That weekend, three inches of ground water filled the Main Library basement. Fortunately, none of the remaining collections were water damaged. In fact, the only University Libraries collections that were destroyed during this flood were over one hundred books checked out to a graduate student whose basement apartment was totally destroyed. Luckily, the river crested the next Friday, earlier and at a lower level than expected, or there would likely have been considerably more damage to the Libraries, campus, and community.

After the Flood

Although the Main Library basement had only taken in about three inches of water, it still had to be drained, bio-cleaned, and inspected before the building could be reoccupied and open to the public. The University had a contract with two disaster recovery companies so both were already on-site to begin clean up. To bio-clean the basement, the recovery

company had to remove all of the bottom shelves to clean under the shelving. Initially, everyone thought we could reoccupy the building within a couple weeks. Commercial dehumidifiers were installed in the Art, Music, and Main Libraries to keep library collections and facilities dry as soon as it was possible to enter those buildings. Fortunately, the weather was unusually mild and dry for the rest of the summer, or the delay in getting dehumidifying equipment might have resulted in mold outbreaks. Library preservation staff monitored the dehumidifying equipment regularly, since keeping a relatively constant temperature in all three libraries proved nearly impossible. The campus power plant had been badly damaged, so air control in all the campus buildings was severely challenged for months. What little air conditioning was available, had to be initially directed to the university hospital. The university had closed for a week following the flood to all but essential staff to permit some preliminary clean up and provide time to reschedule summer session classes that had been held in flood damaged buildings. Once the campus reopened, the University Librarian had secured permission to let several carefully monitored volunteer staff members into the Main Library for less than one hour each day with flashlights, since there was no power, to retrieve books and films needed by students and faculty for summer session classes until the building could be reopened.

The Main Library staff was able to return and the building reopened to the public about a month after the flood. The staff moved in a couple of days earlier. This building had been a high priority for the University because of summer session classes and because it was the least damaged of those buildings that had taken in water. Library servers were moved back into the building several weeks ahead of the staff in order to get all our systems restored as quickly as possible. *Illiad* was critical so we could resume interlibrary loan. Library staff moved all those collections back to the basement within about a month or so after the Main Library reopened. Shortly after reopening, we discovered that the public computers in the second floor computer lab would not operate even though other public and staff computers in the Main Library were fine. Further investigation indicated that the water in the machine room had destroyed the transformer that powered that lab. Fortunately, there were enough computers in other areas of the Main Library to support the limited number of summer session enrollees and other users until that transformer could be replaced and working for fall semester.

The Art and Music collections were completely unavailable to the public throughout the summer. In fact, access to the Fine Arts campus was curtailed for some time. There were few, if any, summer session courses in these disciplines and with the Fine Arts teaching facilities completely out of commission, lack of summer access to these collections was not a big problem. As of fall semester, library staff began to retrieve materials for users on weekdays from these two libraries, once and often twice a day since the Fine Arts buildings could not be opened to the public. These two libraries, especially our Music Library, had been among our busiest branch libraries. There was really no workable space to accommodate them elsewhere on or near campus. Initially it was uncertain how long these buildings would be out of commission. Retrieving books every day was especially challenging because there had been no power, lights, water, or elevators functioning in those two buildings much of the fall semester. There were days when staff members retrieved over one hundred volumes daily from the Music Library, using head lighting similar to that used by miners. The only heating/cooling came from the dehumidifying units and, as noted earlier, it had been very difficult to keep the temperatures stable. At the end of the fall semester, the Music Library moved into the Main Library since it had become doubtful that the Music building would ever be reoccupied. The Music Department faced the likelihood of not offering

a critical course requiring extensive library usage if the library collection remained in the damaged building. Since the building that housed the Art Library was initially expected to be operational by January, 2010, it seemed feasible to all, including the Art Department, to leave the collection in the building and continue retrieving books for users until then. When that deadline began to seriously slip and after a faulty sprinkler head accidentally poured water on sections of the art collection, the decision was made to also move the Art Library into the Main Library the following summer, one year after the flood. In order to accommodate both the Music and Art Libraries in the Main Library, an additional five hundred seats had to be removed from an already overcrowded, heavily used building. Shortly thereafter, the University did lease collection storage space off campus, making it possible to move some other lesser used collections from the Main Library stacks and freeing up space for some of the lost seating. We expect the Art Library to be in the Main Library for about two years; the Music Library, about four or five years.

Role of Disaster Plan

The Libraries had an up-to-date collections disaster plan in place at the time of the flood. More importantly, we had the luxury of employing a number of professionals who had considerable experience dealing with a wide range of disasters included fire, water, and mold in our libraries, elsewhere on campus, regionally and nationally. Our Head of Preservation and our Conservator had also taught workshops around the state in disaster recovery. While we had an updated plan, I do not think that anyone had to consult it following the flood simply because the key information was so well known to them. However, the process of having created our plan some years earlier and keeping it updated was the reason the key contacts and procedures were so familiar. But no matter how thorough and up-to-date the plan, it can never cover every situation nor factor in every variable of a specific disaster. The most critical factors in a plan are knowing the contact names and numbers, knowing where to secure access to freezers and recovery companies, and knowing what to do or not do with various types of damaged materials.

Our Library Information Technology department had drafted an even more recent disaster plan and it was helpful since we had little previous experience dealing with this aspect of disasters. We did not have to move many of the staff workstations because we relocated so many staff into library computer labs and automated classrooms. In addition, we had just received a shipment of one-hundred fifty new staff computers that had not yet been installed. We moved this shipment out of the Main Library for protection so we knew that we could use them, if needed, instead of moving existing ones. We did miss an opportunity to simplify some of work involved in getting our staff back into operation since it did not occur to any of us until later that we had a couple of carts of laptop computers that we could have distributed to selected staff during the evacuation.

Because our flood was a campus and community wide disaster, we had the luxury of two experienced recovery companies at our immediate disposal and key staff all over campus who were solely directed to flood recovery during that summer. Much of the burden for various library arrangements became part of a larger campus recovery effort. For example, when it was time to evacuate the staff and relocate their work areas, others on campus made arrangements for a professional moving company to have a truck at the Main Library late afternoon to move everything needed to relocate staff workspaces temporarily. That made it possible for the library administrators to concentrate on where to relocate our staff, what needed to move, and the basement collections. When dealing with disasters solely within the library, some of these larger, external arrangements might need to be made more directly by library staff.

A Few Additional Lessons Learned

Unlike flash flooding and most other natural disasters, this kind of progressive flooding is a disaster in slow motion. With most disasters, there is barely time to get everyone to safety before the disaster hits. Then all you can do is deal with the damage left behind. With seasonal floods, there is some time for planning, albeit not a lot. Authorities are monitoring conditions regularly, progress up river is apparent, and forecasts are available. As a result we were able to move some materials from the basement and relocate staff in some semblance of order before the flood. However, authorities often do not agree and conditions change regularly. We ran the risk of needlessly exerting a lot of effort, and possibly looking a bit foolish by moving collections that, in the end, never needed to be moved. Until the river peaked and we knew that the worst was behind us, we had a persistent nagging concern that perhaps we should have moved even more from the basement. There was disagreement among knowledgeable individuals about whether it was wise to plug the floor drains in the basement in preparation. As it turns out, that would have been wise since the Library took in ground water through these drains. We had been advised not to plug the drains in case we were flooded with river water and that water had nowhere to drain. Had this been a tornado, we would have had little time to second guess decisions since we would have been able to do little more than get everyone to safety. In the end, we were very lucky. The following are a few additional lessons learned from the Flood of 2008:

- *Anticipate the unexpected and expect that to change regularly.* Flood preparation and recovery are the ultimate tests of flexibility. You need to be able to adjust quickly to a very unsettling environment and to help others do the same. Knowledgeable people disagree about what to do and when to do it. Information changes all the time and decisions are often awaiting specific outcomes that do not occur as planned. Even when you have a certain plan of action in place, unforeseen developments occur. Staff with technical responsibilities, not easily assigned to others, may have to leave during the day because their homes may be flooding or newly washed out roads and bridges would prevent them getting home later that day. The need to reassign tasks requiring specific expertise at the last minute can be especially challenging when the disaster is occurring throughout the region. Having a back-up with appropriate expertise, while difficult, is often necessary.

- *Relocation is disruptive even to those who normally managed change effectively.* Disaster recovery will take a toll on everyone no matter what their coping skills. This can be especially difficult as life begins to get back to normal for some but not for others. Both the University and the state of Iowa offered services to assist those dealing with the stress of the disaster. A number of University employees lost both their home and workplace. It is critical to watch for signs in co-workers, volunteers, and yourself that help might be needed. The impact often hits individuals much later than the initial disaster, even after their lives seem to be back to normal. It can seem impossible to take time out to de-stress, but it is essential.

- *Seeing is believing.* Although campus officials had assured us that the Art and Music collections were fine, it was important for the staff from those two libraries to confirm this for themselves. I arranged with campus officials a quick visit so these staff could evaluate their libraries. Because of the need for immediate asbestos abatement in the Music Building, it was not until June 24, over two weeks after staff had been evacuated from the Music Library, that they could get into that building. Nonetheless, this greatly eased everyone's peace of mind. The Main Library Facilities

Coordinator and I had the opportunity to enter the Main Library within a day or two of the flooding and I knew what a difference that had made for us.

- *Recognize that recovery from a disaster of this magnitude will take years and that there will be less tolerance for uncertainty and inconvenience as time goes on.* Initially, no one expects everything to work as it did before the disaster. Eventually, everyone wonders why it takes so long for decisions to be made, restoration to occur, and services to be back to normal. It is critical to manage expectations of progress and to recognize that there are a lot of players, including FEMA and insurance companies, if the institution has insurance. Many different parties need to be satisfied before restoration can occur. This is all you and others may be doing for a long time. Even small accommodations can take longer than expected to get back to normal. It took us weeks after we had reoccupied the Main Library to get all the packages that had been stockpiling in the Libraries temporary mail room established in the health sciences library during the month of evacuation.

- *Preparing for a pending disaster and the subsequent recovery efforts requires very careful planning and coordination.* It is critical to know who is in charge of what and to share information even if that information changes regularly. Both preparation before the disaster and its subsequent recovery efforts are much too large for any one person, so specific tasks need to be identified and assigned. But efforts need to be carefully coordinated. On June 13th, the Libraries administrators and I met together several times throughout the day to share progress and information on the work assigned to each and then adjust plans as necessary. On campus, a sizeable group of individuals initially met several times a day and then daily for months to update the others on progress and set-backs in their area of responsibility. These meetings eventually were decreased in frequency but occurred for over a year.

- *Staff and public communication is time-consuming but essential especially when information is changing daily.* Rumors thrive in the absence of authoritative information. During the week the University was closed, I sent library staff a daily update via e-mail on what was happening as of that day, warning in each message that this information could change, and often did, by the next morning. These continued for weeks after we were back on campus. The Libraries Public Relations Coordinator did an excellent job of keeping library information updated on Web sites and in campus news sources. She also worked with the campus public relations department on library news for the public media. There may be a lot of requests for interviews from the press during this time, and it is critical having someone managing these and screening for whom can best handle each request. Also, you need a consistent message and this is the easiest way to assure consistency. Old fashioned departmental phone trees work well to keep staff informed when the university is closed and e-mail may not available. One way or another, alternate provisions need to be in place if normal means of group communication are not operational.

- *Tasks that are normally simple can become a challenge.* We initially had some difficulty getting food and water to the volunteers in the Main Library who were moving books, some for eight hours or more. The Libraries charge card system cannot be used for food and a number of us used our personal funds (later reimbursed) to buy some refreshments until arrangements could be made with the appropriate person on campus to get some of the donated sandwiches and drinks that were already being delivered regularly to the campus sandbagging sites. This

became another task assignment for one of the staff to track down. When there are lots of similar volunteer efforts going on in many places around the town and campus, something that would normally be relatively easy to arrange, can prove challenging.

- *Celebrate even small successes.* We held a number of celebrations at various stages of progress on the flood recovery. It helps everyone mark progress, celebrate what has been accomplished to date, and be thanked for their efforts.

- *Share your expertise. University libraries often employ specialists not available at smaller institutions.* Since our own collections had so little damage, our preservation staff was able to provide leadership in the recovery efforts of two small museum/libraries in Cedar Rapids with badly damaged collections. Our preservation staff also posted information on our Libraries Web site for the public on what to do with their personal memorabilia that had been water damaged but might be salvageable. They also consulted with a number of public librarians and individuals throughout the state offering advice on damaged collections. The University and Libraries received very good press coverage for these efforts, fostering good will in the community and reenforcing our role as a state-wide resource.

- *Assess* what did and did not work when things settle down, but not too long after the disaster, lest memories fade in the meantime. Each disaster is its own learning experience.

- *Archive the event.* As soon as we were settled, we contacted appropriate individuals on campus to begin gathering photographs and other resources to establish the Flood of 2009 digital archive. Clearly this would be a major event in the history of our University and state and we had a responsibility to document it. We later invited Story Corps to come and conduct oral interviews. In addition to their interviews, they trained students in an anthropology class to conduct additional interviews for our archive.

Remember—*it could have been much worse*, and while no two disasters are identical, there are colleagues around the country who have been through similar experiences who may be your most useful resource.

THE ZIMMERMAN LIBRARY 2006 FIRE THAT LED TO THE 2007 LIBRARY FLOOD: AN OVERVIEW

Edward Castillo-Padilla, Nancy K. Dennis, Linda K. Lewis, and Frances C. Wilkinson

The University of New Mexico, founded in 1889, is the largest research university in New Mexico, and currently enrolls approximately 25,000 students at the main campus in Albuquerque, New Mexico, with an additional 7,000 students located at branch campuses throughout the state. Zimmerman Library, the Social Sciences, Education and Humanities library, is the largest branch of the University Libraries and is located on the main campus. The University Libraries is a member of the Association of Research Libraries with areas of strength in Latin American and Southwestern studies.

Zimmerman Library has 287,000 square feet of space which includes nine tower levels, four main floors, and two basement sub-levels. There are over one million volumes in the Zimmerman collections, and holdings include special collections, rare books, manuscripts, photos, microforms, posters, paintings, and artifacts. Approximately 100 full time employees work in Zimmerman Library. The library, designed by architect John Gaw Meem, is arguably one of the most distinguished and beautiful structures in the state of New Mexico and is considered the finest example of Spanish Pueblo Revival architecture.

The Fire

Just before 11 p.m. on Sunday, April 30, 2006 a fire started in the east section of the basement level in Zimmerman Library completely disrupting and shutting down all library operations. The cause of this fire has never officially been announced by the New Mexico State Fire Marshal's office (SFMO), but is still under investigation as arson.

The library staff on duty at the time of the fire immediately and efficiently evacuated the building within six minutes. Many students preparing for final examinations, just two weeks away, were in the library at the time of the fire. After ensuring that all patrons and library personnel had been safely evacuated, the responsibility for the building was relinquished to campus police and SFMO. The SFMO immediately announced that the library was a crime scene, and no one but firefighters, police and investigators from the SFMO office were permitted inside.

The city fire department, which has a substation, located only a few blocks from the library, dispatched fire fighters from three area stations. (See Figure 1.)

Fortunately, the blaze was confined to the basement periodicals shelving and microform locations, but the intense heat caused damage to sections of the first floor directly above the fire site. Unfortunately, the basement location of the fire, comprising approximately 44,000 square feet, presented the fire fighters with a challenge to contain. No electrical power or lights were available and intense smoke and soot quickly filled the basement, severely limiting visibility. At the time of the fire, Zimmerman Library lacked automatic control dampers to prevent smoke and soot from being distributed throughout the building or to exhaust the smoke from the building. Firefighters broke open two skylights located in the north and south sides of the basement to release the growing pressure of the hot smoke and soot. Smoke billowed up through the skylights, but even with that venting, smoke, some ash and soot were distributed throughout the entire building. The lingering

Figure 1: Firefighters Responding to Zimmerman Fire. Photo Courtesy of Edward Padilla.

smoke and fire odor was evident in every space in the library and could not be completely eradicated until a thorough cleaning was completed.

Emergency Response

The Deputy Dean, Fran Wilkinson, and Facilities Manager for the University Libraries, Ed Padilla, were on the scene within one hour of receiving the initial call. They met with SFMO and UNM Physical Plant personnel upon arrival to determine the extent of the fire. The Deputy Dean immediately started communicating with the University Libraries' administrators and the Disaster Recovery and Assistance Team (DRAT) members to inform and update them on the fire. DRAT members immediately activated the protocols indicated in the library's *Emergency Preparedness and Recovery Plan*. The library Facilities Manager assisted the Deputy Dean and first responders as the site was secured and the fire was contained. A temporary command center was established in the Social Sciences building located directly north of Zimmerman Library. This building lobby provided shelter from the smoke and a central point of contact,

but it had no phones available, so cell phones were instrumental in the extensive communications.

The fire generated much interest from local and regional media. Reporters arrived quickly and gathered in an area a safe distance from the library. The University's public relations personnel were onsite the night of the fire and in close contact with library administration throughout the response and recovery period. These personnel updated the media which began reporting on the fire in their early morning news broadcasts. Some library staff first learned about the fire from these early morning media broadcasts just as the DRAT members and supervisors were contacting their staff.

The University Libraries' *Emergency Preparedness and Recovery Plan* was instrumental in guiding the library emergency responses. The plan had recently been revised with updated contact numbers by the library administration so the information included in the document was current, a very important factor in communication. Although the document was posted on the library intranet, DRAT members were instructed to keep print copies of the disaster plan at home and in their vehicles. Having copies in multiple locations is vital since retrieving copies from a disaster scene may be impossible. The plan included the important and easily identifiable emergency information not only for DRAT members, but for all library personnel. Detailed evacuation procedures, campus and local emergency phone numbers, salvage priorities and specific information on responding to a variety of emergencies are included in the plan. Managers used the phone tree outlined in the plan to inform Zimmerman employees and non-library building tenants on the status of the fire, tell them whether they should report for work or to stay at home, and for those people coming to work inform them as to which building they should report. The plan also included contacts for immediate and long term emergency response and recovery actions related to the disaster and for local and global experts in disaster restoration. Other key contacts for DRAT were the University risk management department and local insurance claims representatives. In-

surer participation is vital for both the response and recovery process.

Very early on May 1st, the morning after the fire was contained, the SFMO permitted a select group from the library and the UNM administration comprising the Library's Deputy Dean, the Library's Facilities Manager, and the Director of University Communications and Marketing a short time to walk through and examine the fire damaged area. At that point, the group saw that a significant portion of the bound periodicals collection was a total loss and damage to the basement area was extensive due to fire and water. (Figure 2)

Because finals week was approaching, the library had to begin planning immediately to meet the needs of the students as well as planning the timely response and recovery to the disaster.

With the knowledge that the library had sustained significant damage, the library administration then assembled DRAT members at 8:00 a.m. that Monday morning in the Centennial Science and Engineering

Figure 2: Damaged Books from Fire. Photo Courtesy of Edward Padilla.

Library, one of the branch libraries of the University Libraries. The Deputy Dean provided a status report on the fire along with information that had been shared at the campus's emergency response group meeting at 7:00 a.m. that morning. Work began immediately to plan recovery activities as well as organize necessary actions to continue library services for the UNM students, faculty and staff. Careful and systematic plans were initiated for moving critical operations such as Interlibrary Loan, Circulation, Reserves, and Reference, as well as finding alternative work locations for over 100 displaced library employees. From that moment on and continuing for several days, a series of messages went to library employees who were staffing public desks and phones, providing them with the latest information on where services were located and how displaced library employees could be contacted. Maintaining open and frequent communication was imperative for library employees as well as the campus community.

On May 4th, the Library Dean called the first of many library-wide meetings at the UNM Student Union Building for a briefing on the fire and a status report on response and recovery efforts. Conveying to library staff that the situation was under control, and that all the necessary steps for organizing the recovery effort were in place so that the library could resume operations as soon as possible was extremely important. Library administrators set the tone for the response and recovery by acknowledging emotions, providing needed support and resources, while encouraging leadership to emerge at all levels throughout the library. These meetings during the recovery phase were important to demonstrate to the library staff and the broader community that the University and library administration were fully capable and skilled in reacting to the many challenges resulting from the fire.

Assessing the Damage

The primary concern during any emergency is for the safety of library users and staff. Fortunately there was no loss of life or injury to anyone associated with the fire. The second concern is for the extent of damage

Fig. 3: Destroyed Shelving and Books. Photo Courtesy of Edward Padilla.

to the collections. Once library staff were allowed access to the burned areas to do an initial visual review, they learned that a large portion of the History, Latin American studies, Native American studies, Hispanic studies, and African American studies subject areas were a total loss. Some areas adjacent to the heart of the fire, including geography, anthropology, archaeology, religion, philosophy, cultural studies, political science, sports and recreation, and education subject areas were also damaged. (Figure 3)

A detailed inventory later revealed that approximately 30,000 volumes were lost or severely damaged with an estimated value of $4.5 million. The Government Information reference collections situated adjacent to the fire required careful examination for potential damage. All microforms and cabinets in the fire area had to be cleaned and the microfilm boxes needed to be replaced. In order to make a reasonable assessment of the damage and/or loss to the collection, a detailed inventory had to be developed by library staff.

All furnishings and equipment either damaged beyond repair or in need of cleaning also had to be carefully inventoried for insurance purposes. Collections in the basement that were in areas not directly affected by fire or water still incurred heavy damage due to smoke and soot. Collections and artworks on all other floors in the library had surface smoke damage. All surfaces inside the library and all heating, ventilation and air conditioning components throughout the building were affected by smoke and soot.

Any disaster causes increased emotions, and that certainly happened as a result of this fire. The entire university community, from the President to the physical plant employees who worked daily in the library, were first shocked and then rallied to the support of the library. The intense emotional impact on library personnel was a cause for concern, and library administrators did everything possible to provide support services to those staff needing assistance. The counselors advised us that individuals recover at their own pace and in different ways. Heightened emotions

sometimes resurfaced long after the fire, and all managers dealt with such situations thoughtfully.

Recovery

Within just a few hours of containing the fire, an on-call local cleaning and disaster recovery company was immediately called to begin the initial cleanup work, which included providing air-scrubbers in the basement and first floor. Security services were scheduled for 24/7 coverage in the library, and a security fence was installed around the east side of the building.

Despite running air-scrubbers around the clock and removing burned materials, the strong odor of smoke and soot remained throughout the library as well as outside the perimeter of the building for several weeks. Throughout the entire response and recovery periods air quality testing was provided by the industrial hygienist working for the University Safety and Risk Services Department.

After the initial walk-through by University and library administrators, they concluded that an experienced disaster recovery company with the capacity and resources to manage and implement a large-scale materials pack-out and cleanup of a large public building was necessary. An RFP for these services was written within hours. This RFP required that the companies have the knowledge, resources and experience to remove, freeze-dry, deodorize, clean, and potentially store the collections in an offsite location; facilitate the cleaning of equipment and furniture and the de-humidification of the library space; and clean the complete HVAC system including filters and diffusers. All these required activities were to be accomplished efficiently and at an accelerated pace. On May 3rd, BMS CAT, a worldwide disaster restoration company, was selected. A local on-call contractor for UNM was hired for demolition of the burned basement area and first floor areas above the fire. The Library and University Physical Plant Department personnel met with BMS CAT and a local contractor to negotiate the scope of the work which included the initial clean-up, demolition, and removal of all of the remaining periodical volumes, microforms and cabinets, furnishings, and equipment. The basement pack-out work necessitated moving all the periodical volumes and microform collections and cabinets to the main BMS CAT headquarters in Fort Worth, Texas for cleaning and deodorizing. Over 200,000 volumes, in 17,632 boxes, and 147 pallets of boxed microforms were packed out in nineteen 53-foot tractor trailers in 17 days. Two large warehouses were leased near campus to store all surviving basement furnishings, equipment, and shelving. Throughout the whole recovery period, the Library Facilities staff made several trips each day to and from the storage facilities in order to retrieve items necessary for library staff to continue their duties and responsibilities on campus.

On May 1st, the library's first priority was to organize and plan to re-establish services for UNM students. The library developed a Web page that included information about the fire, response and recovery information, and a FAQ section. A reference and information service was established in the Student Union Building (SUB), where extended hours were negotiated for students to study in preparation for finals. Also negotiated were extended hours for the coffee shop in the SUB since the library's popular coffee shop was unavailable. Hours at two other branch library locations were extended and the interlibrary loan and reserve services were relocated. Information tables near both entrances into Zimmerman Library were set up and staffed. Many employees who had worked in the basement were relocated to work locations at the branch libraries, and some staff worked from home. After a week, a limited number of library personnel were permitted access. The Budget and Cost Management staff required access to their work areas on the second floor as soon as possible to retrieve budget and payroll records so that employees continued to receive paychecks. Facility services staff were allowed brief forays into the library to obtain important documents necessary for key staff to complete their work. They also retrieved critical

library materials left behind when the building was evacuated, as well as materials for faculty and graduate students from their assigned study carrels in the library. UNM's Safety and Risk Services managers were instrumental in helping staff obtain permission from the SFMO for entry into the library.

As a result of the fire, the fire detection and alarm system was destroyed throughout the whole building. Therefore, before the library could be granted occupancy from the SFMO, DRAT had to organize a manual fire watch for all spaces inside the building. Without this fire watch neither library staff nor customers would have been allowed in the building. Library personnel were called upon to provide the fire watch duties from the middle of May until the start of the fall semester in August. Eventually, funding from the insurance company was negotiated to hire a private security company to provide this critical service. Fire watch included staff or security personnel walking continuously throughout all building spaces, with a fog horn in hand, for the purpose of notifying building occupants in the event of an emergency. Three short blasts, delivered at intervals from the fog horn, was the alarm signal for an emergency. Fire watch required training from the SFMO and the UNM fire marshal, and an exhaustive scheduling routine that required rigid oversight. Fire watch had to be maintained until a new fire alarm system was installed, tested and approved by the SFMO; it lasted from May, 2006 through December, 2007.

Until the University and the library regained possession of Zimmerman Library on May 10, 2006 the SFMO only allowed limited numbers of library staff back into the library. Recovery teams from the library began to evaluate the Government Information Reference, microforms and periodical collections. The SFMO initially required all staff working in the building to wear hard hats and N-95 respirators, and use portable lights to access areas where only limited lighting was available. Special respirator training was provided by the campus Safety and Risk Services (SRS) department. SRS

Fig. 4: Pack-out under emergency lighting. Photo Courtesy of Nancy Dennis.

also provided fire extinguisher training. The library purchased extra hard hats, respirators, portable lights, rubber boots, eye protectors, batteries, gloves, and thermo-hygrometers for monitoring temperatures and relative humidity levels.

Before recovery work could begin, emergency lights had to be installed in the basement level and throughout the entire east side of the library, including three upper levels where reference and the general collections are located. (Figure 4)

All power to the upper levels of the building was affected because the main circuit panel electrical closet, located directly above the burned area, was completely destroyed by heat from the fire. The damage to the wiring continued up to the second and third floors. The fire-rated door of this electrical closet, although charred and damaged, fortunately prevented the fire from spreading to other areas on the first floor. Construction crews coordinated with UNM physical plant electricians to install the temporary lighting and emergency exit signs. While demolition and pack-out activities were in progress, many of the routine job duties by various depart-

ments were resumed as quickly as possible. Shipping and Receiving/Mail Room activities were relocated to other branch libraries, bindery shipments were delivered to branch libraries, cataloging work continued at the branches or from homes of staff members, and circulation and reference responsibilities were coordinated with branch libraries. Within three days, the Interlibrary Loan department moved into a small office in a branch library. Vendors were requested to hold invoices and shipments of materials until staff were settled in their temporary work locations.

Fortunately the library's data servers had been relocated to the main campus Information Technology building just weeks prior to the fire so access to the OPAC and electronic resources were not adversely affected. Desktop computers, printers, scanners and most peripheral devices located within the basement and first floor reference areas were declared a total loss from, heat, water, or smoke damage.

Within just a few days, the library developed an automated materials paging system for books still located in Zimmerman Library for students and faculty on campus. This service required staff to wear hard hats and respirators and use flashlights to retrieve materials. This service was very much appreciated by the campus community. Cell phones and laptops borrowed from other campus departments and area companies and libraries were provided to staff who had no access to a telephone or office space. Through careful planning, organization, hard work, and the dedication of the library employees, the library was able to provide most necessary services to the students so they could complete their assignments and final examinations.

When it became evident that the damage to the basement was extensive, the library began planning the complete renovation of the area. Employees whose offices and work areas had been adjacent to the fire were given 15 minutes to remove their personal possessions which would not be cleaned by the companies employed to clean the library materials. Employees were asked to identify the work-related materials that were priorities; those would be cleaned first. As it turned out, many work materials would not be returned to employees for months. Since these 15 minute visits were the first time most of the employees had been in the building since the fire, and since everyone knew that their areas would be totally rebuilt, intense emotions abounded.

As soon as the areas of Zimmerman Library that were not directly affected by the fire were cleaned and determined safe by the SFMO, portions of the building were re-opened to the public. On June 26, 2006, the first day of the summer session, the west end of the first floor of Zimmerman was opened. On July 17th the second and third floors containing the majority of the monograph collection were opened for public use.

Throughout the summer of 2006, the library, BMS CAT, the Office of Capital Project, and UNM Physical Plant personnel held meetings to coordinate a schedule for the demolition, pack-out of materials, and planning for the renovation of the damaged space. (See end of this chapter for a detailed time line of events.) Once library staff were permitted access to the damaged areas, work began to identify library materials that were damaged beyond repair and those materials that could be salvaged for future use. Library staff worked closely with BMS CAT personnel and construction crews because demolition was in progress at the same time, and fire-damaged and collapsed shelving ranges had to be carefully monitored and braced before staff could access them. The staff working on this part of the recovery had to endure formidable working conditions that included soot, dust and debris from fire and demolition, severely damaged shelving ranges, poor lighting, and very strong smoke odors.

Moving materials and debris out of the basement became problematic because the library service elevator was damaged by water during the fire. Construction crews quickly determined that a crane-operated lift could be used to remove demolished and burned materials through a large skylight that was opened by firefighters to release smoke during the initial fire response efforts. Once demolition was completed the surface cleaning project started. Not only were all inside library surfaces and HVAC units cleaned, the library also hired a professional conservator to clean all the murals and oil paintings that had been exposed to smoke. (Figure 5)

All furnishings and equipment not damaged were removed, cleaned, and stored at remote storage facilities. All computers were collected, inventoried, and examined by experts recommended by the insurer, and a determination was made on exactly how many computers would be discarded.

Parallel to the evaluation and restoration of the building, the evaluation and restoration of the collections were underway. The University needed the original cost of the lost materials in order to remove that amount from its total asset valuation. The insurance companies required more precise costs for replacing lost materials. The campus community wanted to know which titles had been lost. And everyone wanted the information immediately. The Collection Development Director worked with the online shelf list to identify the titles, with the check-in records to identify the holdings, and with the information compiled by the staff doing the triage on damaged collections in order to provide the information being demanded. The library IT department created a relational database that consolidated all information about the lost titles—the bibliographic information, the holdings lost, the alternate locations, the alternate formats, potential sources of replacements, estimated costs, and recommendations for replacements. Subject specialists worked with campus departments to identify which titles were priorities to replace. A summary list of the titles that were lost was created and posted on the library Web site for the campus and public to review. Offers of donations from across the country were reviewed. While the library was able to accept some donations immediately, storage capacity was limited; therefore, some donors were asked to keep their materials until the library was able to resume accepting large donations. Donations that were complete collections and could be bound were sent

to the commercial binder who agreed to store materials for the library for over a year. Collection development staff began working with vendors to obtain new digital resources that could replace materials in the areas that were most heavily damaged. Absolute Backorder Service, Inc. was selected to provide shelf-ready print replacements of some titles. They processed and stored the materials until the library facility was restored and able to accept delivery.

Because there was extensive damage to the first floor as well as the basement level, the library administration decided this would be an opportune time to redesign both floors. Library personnel, in conjunction with architects and the Office of Capital Projects, designed spaces that addressed the need for additional open study spaces, group study rooms, a computer classroom, a meeting room, a digitization room, and up to 70 new additional computers and workstations. The first phase was to expand and remodel the first floor reference area as quickly as possible to reopen the area for students. Within seven months of the fire over 10,000 square feet of space

Figure 5: Art conservators cleaning Zimmerman murals. Photo courtesy of Edward Padilla.

was planned, remodeled and occupied. Former employee office spaces were converted to student group and individual study rooms, electrical and data wiring was replaced and expanded to accommodate 70 additional computers, new book shelving was installed, and finishes (carpet, tile, and paint) were completed. On January 16, 2007, the library reopened the first floor reference areas to the public.

Meanwhile, planning continued for the complete renovation of the basement area. During May and June 2006, the damage to the basement structure was assessed. Due to the extensive fire and smoke damage, all basement walls, floors, ceilings, wiring, and HVAC systems had to be removed. Structural engineers carefully inspected the floors and ceiling concrete and support structures for damage and determined the building was safe. The damage included spalling (flaking away of concrete) in the ceiling concrete slab due to the intense fire/water conditions. The east decking insulation and protective membrane (above east basement area) had melted due to the fire and heat. Several large cracks in the floor slab of the basement were discovered and repaired.

In July 2006, an overall budget was calculated based on the existing structures and finishes before the fire. The insurance company approved the budget for approximately $5 million for the replacement of the more than 44,000 square feet of public and office space. With funding in place, an accelerated planning process began. Library personnel began working with planners, architects and engineers to create and design a completely new Zimmerman basement area that expanded student study space, offered a 40-seat computer classroom, increased capacity for over 60,000 linear feet of compact shelving and provided new work spaces and offices for 50 library employees. Within one year of the fire, an RFP for the construction was issued. The contractor began construction of the new basement area in July of 2007.

As part of the total renovation, a new fire alarm and fire sprinkler system was mandated for the basement and first floor areas by the SFMO. The design

and installation of these two systems were critical components in the recovery process, and for obtaining complete access to the library. The majority of the work to install a replacement fire alarm system throughout the entire library was accomplished at night so disruptions to our staff and patrons could be minimized. A thorough testing of each system was reviewed and certified by the SFMO. The basement elevators were fitted with new smoke and fire curtains that automatically drop to shield the elevator when a fire alarm is activated.

Parallel to the planning and construction of the basement rebuild project was the installation of compact shelving in the burned areas as well as in the two additional basement levels. Previous to the fire, plans were already underway to expand shelving in the two sub-basements. By combining previously allocated funding for the new compact shelving with insurance recovery funds for fire-damaged shelving, the library was able to increase shelving capacity dramatically. Through an RFP process, the University issued a contract in May 2007 for the planning and installation of the compact shelving in four locations of Zimmerman Library. This project was complicated and difficult due to the location of the compact shelving installations (three basement levels), and the collections that needed to be moved from seven tower levels to the location of the new compact shelving. This move included manuscripts, special collections, drawings, monographs, newspapers, periodical volumes and government documents. It was extremely important for library personnel to communicate and coordinate effectively with all recovery and construction contractors on both the fire recovery project as well as the compact shelving installation. The complexity and scope of each of these projects required full-time oversight by library personnel. (Figure 6)

Once the compact shelving was installed in the lower levels, the moving of the collections from the tower levels began. One of the requirements of that move was that the materials had to be available for use at all times, and re-shelved in exact call

Figure 6: Compact shelving installation in restored area of Zimmerman basement. Photo Courtesy of Nancy Dennis.

number order. The library acquired the services of a professional library moving company with experience in large scale academic library moves to assist with the pack-in duties including the distribution and shelving of library materials. The library provided detailed inventory information for staff and work crews. Library staff updated these inventories continuously during the pack-in period. The need for meticulous oversight by library personnel during this phase of recovery cannot be overstated.

Flooding in Basement

Construction of the renovated basement space continued apace with an anticipated occupancy for early November 2007. The return of materials that had been removed from Zimmerman and stored in warehouses in Texas was being actively organized.

The day before the library was to obtain the certificate of occupancy for the newly remodeled basement, the new wet-pipe fire suppression system was being tested. A 10" water main line broke open in the new basement fire sprinkler riser room flooding the basement floor with 5-7 inches of water. The irony that the flood was caused by the installation of a fire suppression system that was installed in response to the fire did not escape notice by all involved in the recovery. This major flooding episode required another disaster response and recovery operation. This was an unsettling setback that library personnel and work crews had no time to dwell on; recovery actions similar to the responses to the fire event commenced immediately. (See Figure 7)

At the time of the flood in the basement all the materials at the BMS CAT headquarters in Fort Worth, Texas were en-route back to the library so additional warehouse space had to be arranged immediately in Albuquerque to store these materials. The collection pack-back plans needed to be immediately modified to account for yet another warehouse stop before the 17,632 boxes of materials could be returned to the fire and flood-repaired basement beginning in February 2008.

Figure 7: Flooding in Zimmerman basement during renovation. Photo Courtesy of Nancy Dennis.

After the clean-up by a local disaster recovery company and construction crews, a new rebuilding project was launched in the basement. All new carpet (over an acre) was removed, all sheetrock and insulation up to three feet above the floor level was replaced, all electrical and data wiring was replaced, all new staff modular units were cleaned, all surfaces were checked for rust damage, millwork on columns was replaced, and walls were repainted. (Figure 8)

The compact shelving project temporarily stopped while crews cleaned and removed any rust residue within the floor tracks and carriages.

All the risk factors associated with water damage had to be considered for both the health of individuals working in the flood area as well as library collections. The Safety and Risk Services industrial hygienist periodically tested for mold residue and air quality.

Thankfully, none of the periodical collections had been returned to the basement shelving areas at the time of the flood. The only materials in the basement were a few government documents that had been moved there temporarily as part of the on-going shifts related to the compact shelving installation. With further irony, the only items damaged were some documents related to flooding.

Fortunately the construction company was able to reconstruct the basement back to the pre-flood condition in less than three months time, and turned it over to UNM and the library by January, 2008. The compact shelving project was also successfully completed. An accelerated pack back of collections commenced from January through March 2008. See Part IV for an in-depth case study on the recovery and return of library collections after the UNM Zimmerman Library fire and flood.

The newly renovated basement was opened quietly to students March 24, 2008 with very little publicity or fanfare. An official opening celebration was held April 30, 2008 (on the 2-year anniversary of the fire) with all appropriate dignitaries in attendance. More than just a few tears were shed by library employees who had endured this incredible professional and personal experience in a short two

Figure 8: Cleaning up after the Zimmerman basement flood. Photo Courtesy of Nancy Dennis.

years. University Libraries history is often referred to as BTF (before the fire) and ATF (after the fire). (Figure 9)

Lessons Learned

Lessons learned that might help others if they face a similar disaster:

- Have an updated disaster preparedness plan. All managers must have copies at home, in personal vehicle, and at work. If you have an intranet, put a copy there.

- Know where water shut off valves are located or be sure the building has a post indicator valve (P.I.V.), which is a valve located above ground that controls the flow of water into a building and has an indicator showing the valve is either open or closed.

- Know the location of air handling units, and familiarize yourself with how they operate.

- Have current building plans in multiple locations because they may be needed by fire fighters and/or police.

- Periodically review your emergency evacuation procedures, and be sure all employees are familiar with these procedures and the emergency exits near their work areas. This information is particularly important for night and weekend personnel.

- Know who to call: parent organization's, administration, library staff, police and fire departments, physical plant maintenance people and insurance company representatives.

- Deploy only competent staff in the response and recovery stages. Individuals must maintain composure and common sense throughout intensified physical and emotional circumstances. Staff must be able to follow directions carefully and completely, and also be able to think and act constructively on their own without ego issues interfering.

- Establish and maintain good relationships with all other campus departments. Library staff never know when they may need assistance from others, and during emergencies it

Figure 9: New student space in Zimmerman's restored basement. Photo Courtesy of Nancy Dennis.

is very helpful to have positive relationships to call upon for assistance.

- Be sure all library emergency responders and facilities personnel have cell phones.
- Always protect art and artifacts as much as possible.
- Be sure that fire doors are rated and located properly at electrical closets and fire separation points in the building. Check with campus safety personnel for assistance.
- Have physical plant check to be sure all cracks or holes in the floor and ceiling slabs where fire, smoke and water could penetrate are properly filled to help prevent spread of fire. Also, check open spaces around conduits or pipes running through slabs.
- Confirm with library IT personnel that all server and desktop PC files are properly backed-up with copies stored offsite.
- Have someone available for interviews and to communicate with the media.
- Use technology to keep in touch: cell phones, e-

mail, instant messaging, Twitter, Facebook, etc.

- Have additional batteries and chargers available to recharge cell phones and laptop computers.
- Communicate continuously with employees. Have staff meetings in addition to web pages, e-mail, chat, blogs etc. Meetings are especially crucial when people are scattered and working in different locations.
- Know that some decisions will have to be made quickly and keep moving forward. Document and share those decisions with the recovery team.
- Patience is imperative. Know that some things will seem to take forever. While some things do take a long time, such as investigations of what caused the disaster, others just seem to take longer because it is a crisis situation.
- Accept the emotional aftershocks. Some people will go through many of the seven stages of grief (shock, denial, bargaining, guilt, anger, depression, and acceptance). Others may have some post-traumatic stress reactions. Respect that, and

do not dismiss it. Some people will be helped by informational meetings. Use pizza and ice cream parties as an opportunity for staff scattered in several buildings to come together. Depending upon the situation, counseling referral services may be helpful. A group of UNM library employ-

ees organized gatherings and compiled a Fire Book, creatively documenting the fire, the recovery and employee responses. Library employees also created a quilt, with each square made by a different person depicting their various memories and impressions of the experience.

Timeline—Key Dates

April 30, 2006—Fire event, just before 11:00 p.m.

May 1, 2006—Disaster Recovery Assistance Team meets for first time-8:00 a.m., and RFP for emergency recovery is issued.

May 2, 2006—Contractors visit and inspect RFP scope of work.

May 3, 2006—RFP awarded to BMS CAT.

May 5, 2006—Library regains partial possession of library, and on-call contractor begins demolition and removal of destroyed furnishings, equipment, etc.

May 10, 2006—Library regains temporary occupancy of building. Access limited to administrative staff and DRAT members. Library staff begins providing fire watch.

May 30, 2006—Smoke and soot damage so extensive in basement that the entire 44,000 square feet must be completely demolished and rebuilt.

June 26, 2006—Zimmerman lobby and West Wing reopened to the public. First floor and basement remain closed for construction.

Aug. 23, 2006—Santa Fe Protective Services, a private security company, takes over full fire watch responsibilities until new alarm system is installed and certified. Second and third floors reopened to the public.

December 2006—Fire alarm system installation completed and certified by SFMO.

January 2007—Zimmerman first floor reference area reopened to the public.

May, 2007—RFP awarded to general contractor for basement construction with estimated completion date of October 8, 2007.

May 2007—Contract for compact shelving project for basement levels one, two and three awarded to Improve Group/Spacesaver.

June 5, 2007—Construction began in basement.

October 31, 2007—Construction completed, new fire alarm and fire suppression system installed, awaiting certificate of occupancy expected in two days. A 10" main water riser pipe/flange disengages, flooding the newly rebuilt basement level, with water also entering sub levels two and three.

November 1, 2007—Pack back begins. Return of cleaned periodicals, microfilm/cabinets from BMS CAT headquarters in Fort Worth, Texas. Library on fast track to obtain storage warehouses to store materials unable to be returned to basement due to flood conditions. Pack back duration was from November, 2007 thru March, 2008.

November 2007 through February 2008—Basement re-build and compact shelving projects completed.

March 24, 2008—Basement reopens to the public.

April 30, 2008—Official opening celebration.

August 2009—Final recovery project punch list completed.

April 2010—Still awaiting final insurance settlement.

ZIMMERMAN LIBRARY FIRE: A CASE STUDY IN RECOVERY AND RETURN OF LIBRARY COLLECTIONS

Anne D. Schultz and Teresa Y. Neely

The basement of Zimmerman Library reopened to the public in March of 2008, nearly two years after the April 30, 2006 fire, and six months after the October 31, 2007 flood caused by a failure of equipment installed to bring the building up to code and protect the facility from future fires. To date, an official cause of the April 2006 fire has not yet been released by the New Mexico State Fire Marshal's office. See the UNM case study, "The Zimmerman Library 2006 Fire That Led to the 2007 Library Flood: An Overview," in this volume for a complete description of the events surrounding the disaster.

Planning for the pack back began shortly after the fire with the creation of the Pack Back Team. The team used the term "pack back" to describe the return of materials to the basement of Zimmerman Library after it had been renovated from fire damage, and eighteen months later, from water damage. Although challenging, the fire presented the opportunity to consolidate collections previously shelved on separate floors, and in some cases, in separate branch libraries. As a result, the material to be returned to the space was not limited to the collections housed there prior to the fire—print periodicals and newspapers, New Mexico and United States government documents print and audio-visual collections, and University Libraries (UL) microform collections. Not satisfied with the seemingly insurmountable task of determining the most efficient method for returning more than 13,000 boxes of journals; 200 microfilm cabinets, most still filled; and hundreds of boxes of microfilm, the pack back team decided to integrate other collections into the

pack back. These other materials included print abstracting and indexing bibliographic resources that probably should have been shelved along with the periodicals instead of in the reference collection one floor away from the journals they indexed. Other items to be moved to the basement during the pack back included:

- print and micro-format materials acquired to replace titles lost in the fire. These materials would be arriving in shipments at various times so shelving consideration for replacement volumes and growth would need to be taken into consideration in planning the pack back;
- gifts received for replacement titles; these were held by our library bindery contractor until basement renovations were completed. These materials would be arriving from the bindery along with our regular bindery shipments, also at various times;
- items received post-fire as a result of ongoing subscriptions, shelved elsewhere in Zimmerman Library during the renovation; and
- micro-format resources being transferred from the Fine Arts and Design branch library.

Seizing the opportunity to accomplish other collection management projects simultaneously with the pack back, a decision was also made on how best to treat print journal titles owned in other formats, particularly those titles represented in JSTOR, Project MUSE, and other full text databases with perpetual access. One wonders what we were thinking!

We would later find that we made many assumptions about the state of the pack out; however, upon cold sober reflection, we found we had more questions than answers about what to expect when it was time for collections to return. This chapter will share the efforts of UL staff and others to plan for the orderly and organized return and re-shelving of materials to the newly renovated basement of Zimmerman Library in record time.

The Environment
The UL had the misfortune to experience two significant disasters within an eighteen month period. During the winter holiday break in December 2004, a pipe broke in the Centennial Science and Engineering Library (CSEL), dumping 40,000 gallons of water into the lower level where books and maps were housed. While relatively few volumes and maps were lost, all collections on this level had to be removed for remediation of the facility. The UL did have a disaster plan, but several inadvertent mistakes were made by the salvage contractor's pack out of the collections, causing unforeseen complications for the return of the materials three months later. For example, boxes were labeled with incomplete call numbers causing confusion during the return of the material and repeated shifting as books were shelved.

Having barely recovered from the CSEL flood, the Zimmerman Library fire started in the basement, late on the evening of April 30, 2006—a Sunday near the end of the spring term. The library was evacuated quickly when the alarms sounded, and fire and rescue responded immediately to suppress the fire. Library administrators and the Facilities Services Manager were contacted and on the scene within an hour. The UL's disaster plan was immediately set into motion. Because the library was declared a crime scene, library staff, with few exceptions, had no access to any area of the building over the next ten days. Safety concerns and investigations into the cause of the fire by the State Fire Marshal's office delayed the initial steps for collection

analysis, salvage, and recovery efforts until May 10, 2006.

It is worth mentioning that life as we knew it in the UL continued despite the Zimmerman fire and subsequent flood. Among other things, faculty searches in progress for the new dean and the resident in Research and Instruction Services continued, as did planning for the installation of compact shelving in five separate spaces in Zimmerman Library—basement levels two and three for collections held by the Center for Southwest Research, Special Collections and Archives; basement west for circulating and non-circulating New Mexico State and Federal government documents collections; and basement east, the future home for social science, humanities, and education print periodicals, and collections in various micro-formats. Planning for the pack back was dependent upon completed basement renovations including the installation of this compact shelving. Additionally, Zimmerman Library basement planning efforts occurred simultaneously with plans to move the Fine Arts Library (FAL) to its new location in the George Pearl Hall, home to the School of Architecture and Planning and the Fine Arts and Design Library. Construction began in 2006 and the Fine Arts and Design Library (FADL) reopened in February of 2008 in its new home.

In order to plan for the return of materials to a facility post-disaster, it is critically important to have an understanding of the pre-disaster physical layout of your library building(s), particularly the collections. What exactly is shelved where? How tall are the shelves? How many ranges do you have in a particular area? How many shelves are on each range? Are all of those shelves completely filled? What is in those microfilm/fiche cabinets? How many pieces of fiche per inch do you have? How many reels of film? Unfortunately, this experience revealed how little we knew about the physical collection layout in the basement of Zimmerman Library, information critical to the determination of how many physical volumes we owned, how many we had lost, how many we were bringing back, and how best to proceed in the planning to bring them back to a differently organized space with the addition of compact shelving. And most importantly, how do we plan this mammoth effort with the knowledge that many volumes are gone, some never to be replaced, and the uncertainty of how much we would be able to replace in print (at the request of some faculty), or how much space to leave for growth of continuing print subscriptions?

Review of the Literature

The published library literature on disaster recovery does not include detailed evidence of a process for the organized and orderly return of non-damaged or salvaged materials post-disaster. Overwhelmingly, the literature tends to focus on news-like announcements of the disaster, the state of the organization affected, disaster planning, preservation, and salvaging damaged materials.[1] Unfortunately and sadly, published accounts of the devastation suffered by libraries in the December 2004 Indian Ocean tsunami,[2] and the destruction caused by Hurricane Katrina on August 29, 2005, and Hurricane Rita in September of that same year[3] do not include accounts of pack backs as library collections in these instances were either completely destroyed or as in the case of the tsunami in Sri Lanka, were "re-taken by the ocean in the wake of the tsunami,"[4] or in the aftermath of Katrina "simply washed away or left behind to become part of the piles just called 'debris'?"[5]

There is a body of literature addressing libraries recovering from fire,[6] and water,[7] however, there is scant evidence of the planning or process to return materials after a disaster, particularly of the magnitude of the Zimmerman Library basement pack back.

In 1978, the Stanford University Meyer Library's basement stacks were flooded due to a ruptured water main. Approximately 50,000 of the 400,000 books housed there were affected. Nine months after the flood "32,000 books had been returned to

the library. Approximately 1,500 were scheduled for rebinding, 1,000 were waiting for repair and 15,000 remained to be sorted."[8] Although this article does not discuss the pack back in great detail, it is useful because it describes the more complicated process of identifying and quarantining wet books; transporting them to freezers; transporting them from freezers to a vacuum chamber for drying; identifying and preparing a staging area for book repair and assessment post-drying; and finally, returning them back to the Meyer Library.

In August of 1978, excessive rains overwhelmed the roof of the College of Physicians of Philadelphia Library. Library staff and volunteers, under the watchful eye of William Spawn, a Philadelphia resident and an "expert in the restoration of water-damaged books," sorted, packed, and loaded 3,235 wet books in 379 borrowed milk crates into a refrigerated trailer. Also damaged were nineteen cases of pamphlets and 269 folios. The books were freeze-dried in small batches and then fumigated before being returned to the College. There is no other mention of pack out or pack back procedures.[9]

A 1985 fire and subsequent mishandling of books left 100,000 jumbled volumes at the Dalhousie University Law Library in Halifax, Nova Scotia. The article focuses specifically on automating the task of organizing the mixed up titles, but does not address the actual pack back of the titles.[10] The April 1986 fire in the Los Angeles Central Library destroyed 375,000 books, however, they were able to freeze 700,000 others. The article notes the packing of wet books into boxes, moving the boxes onto pallets, and using forklifts to move pallets to trucks for the trip to the freezer; however, there is no mention of a pack back. Unfortunately, the same library was the victim of arson again in September of that same year, destroying nearly 25,000 books.[11]

In 1988, multiple fires destroyed 400,000 volumes and 3.6 million volumes were damaged by water at the Library of the Academy of Sciences of the USSR (Union of Soviet Socialist Republics) in Leningrad. Conflicting reports at the time had the library director, V. A. Filov, "estimate(ing) the losses at three thousand rubles and said the library would reopen in a few days," and a different scene described by Likhachev, "a respected scholar of Russian culture,"—"a bulldozer moving huge piles of charred books and newspapers, volunteers who tried to help being locked out, and the staff forbidden from trying to save books from the heap in the courtyard."[12] Although the article includes a discussion of the disinfectant treatment of 8.1 million items for preservation purposes, applied without removing the books from the shelves, as well as drying methods, in packets of ten to fifteen books, for the volumes that had been frozen, there is no mention of a pack back.[13]

A June 1989 thunderstorm hit the University of Port Harcourt Library in Nigeria damaging 70,000 volumes of books and bound periodicals and 20,000 documents. Two hundred fifty volunteers formed a single line to move wet books from the damaged library wing to the newly designated temporary storage area after the roof was blown off the library. The move of materials was completed in three days. There is no other mention of a pack out or pack back.[14]

In 1990, two weeks after a two year refurbishment project, a fire in another part of the building left soot on everything in the Pilkington Technology Centre Library and Information Centre in the UK. The author writes about the unprofessionalism of 'Disasterco,' the name he gave to the salvage company hired to clean everything from collections to carpets to equipment. Upon delivery of 340 crates of cleaned books, the author and three other staff were forced to unpack and re-shelve 10,000 books in four and one half hours, while staff from 'Disasterco' waited for the crates to be emptied.[15]

A 1992 flood at the Oklahoma Department of Libraries resulted in the return of 1,622 boxes by the salvage company; however there is no mention of a pack back.[16] An arson fire occurred at Illinois

State University's Milner Library in 1992; however the scale of loss and damaged titles (1,638) was far below that suffered at Zimmerman Library. They lost 558 titles, they were able to save 135 by freezing, and 945 were air dried. No pack back was discussed.[17]

The July 1997 flash flood damaged half of the collections at Colorado State University's (CSU) Morgan Library. Approximately 462,500 volumes were damaged including monographs and bound periodicals. The pack out was completed in fourteen days, yielding more than 7,000 pallets of boxed materials destined for cold storage lockers.[18] Efforts to recover and restore this number of volumes were 'pioneering' as "no one had ever attempted to recover and restore close to 500,000 water-damaged volumes and return them to the collection."[19] Unique to the published disaster recovery literature is the aggressive and highly successful gift program employed by the CSU Morgan Library staff that resulted in nearly one million items, which along with the salvaged items would need to be processed and make up the eventual pack back of materials.[20] Unfortunately, the authors do not address the pack back of gifts or salvaged items.

In August 2002, approximately fifty libraries in the Czech Republic were flooded, resulting in the freezing of 150,000 volumes. The National Library of the Czech Republic assumed the leadership role of coordination and contacted companies ready to move the materials that were soaked and placing them, where possible and necessary, in cooling plants; however, there is no other specific mention of a pack out or a pack back.[21]

The October 30, 2004 flood by the University of Hawaii at Mānoa's Hamilton Library resulted in the loss or damage to "approximately 800,000 documents in paper, 1.6 million microforms, several thousand CD-ROMs and DVD products, 165,000 maps and 92,000 aerial photographs" from the Government Documents and Maps Department "which includes the regional federal documents depository, a large United Nations collection and the map collection." Library staff and volunteers numbering in the hundreds, including faculty and students "sloshed through the muck to retrieve as much as they could." They retrieved about 1/3 of the map collection and also aerial photographs, some of which were sent to the Libraries Preservation unit to be washed and dried. Some materials were frozen in refrigerated shipping containers and others were shipped to a restoration company in Texas.[22] There is no other mention of a pack out or pack back.

A January 2006 burst steam pipe caused sprinklers to activate at the Yale University Sterling Memorial Library. With a 98.97 percent recovery rate, only forty-six volumes salvaged either by air drying in house or vacuum freeze-dried needed to be replaced; there is no mention of a pack back.[23]

This review of descriptions of library disasters shows a profound lack of information about the return of salvaged materials to the respective libraries. Clearly some description of packback operations would have been useful to Zimmerman staff but finding none we realized we should take on the responsibility of describing a large-scale packback. This case is a description of our experience.

The Initial Collection Assessment Post-Disaster

By May 12, 2006, nearly two weeks after the fire, the UL had hired BMS CAT, a salvage company, different from the one used in the CSEL flood in 2004, to begin efforts to remediate the entire building and deal specifically with cleaning the basement collections. The salvage operation took thirteen days. After library staff were allowed access to the building, BMS CAT staff, along with selected UL employees, managed to pack over 13,000 boxes of print periodicals, hundreds of boxes of microfilm, and more than 200 microfilm and microfiche cabinets into multiple semi-tractor trailer trucks to be shipped to the BMS CAT warehouse in Fort Worth, Texas for cleaning and storage until Zimmerman was ready to receive

them back. Although the UL's federal depository collection was housed in the basement on the west side, at the time of the pack out, it was believed that these materials had been spared from fire and water damage, and thus, were not included in the pack out nor were they included in the materials shipped out to the storage facility in Texas.

No disaster plan can provide detailed steps for every potential crisis a library might face. A broad and flexible framework is critical.[24] Also important is a commitment to training for the appropriate staff who would be mobilized to respond, should a disaster occur.[25] The UNM UL found, as have many others, that when a catastrophe happens, the library's desired response may be affected by external conditions beyond its control. In this case it is critical that the staff deployed by the library to act during the response and recovery phases have both the ability to make decisions in a challenging and ambiguous environment, and the support of upper management to follow through with decisions made on the ground.[26]

Several members of the library's initial response team for Zimmerman collections recovery had worked on the efforts following the CSEL flood. In the case of the CSEL flood, these team members had either volunteered to assist in the recovery effort, had knowledge of the UL integrated library system (ILS) system to assist in the effort to automate the organization of materials prior to their return, or significant knowledge of CSEL collections. This type of knowledge also proved to be instrumental in the recovery of materials from the Fawcett Library at London's Guildhall University.[27] Skills gained and lessons learned in the CSEL flood recovery effort were critical to the management of the materials from the Zimmerman fire.

We learned from the CSEL experience that an organized plan for removing collections is critical, and that it is not safe to assume that a recovery contractor will remove library materials with care in regard to labeling and sorting boxes. The Zimmer-

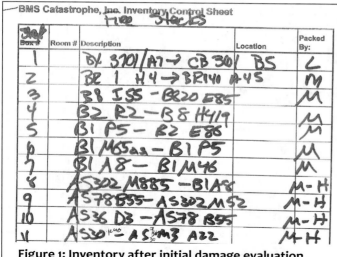

Figure 1: Inventory after initial damage evaluation. Courtesy Anne D. Schultz.

man basement fire had been contained in the north end of the basement in the periodical stacks, some of which had collapsed from the combined effects of the intense heat and the water used to put out the fire. All collections in the basement were at risk for smoke, thermal, and/or water damage. After seeing the area directly affected by the fire, the recovery team determined that it would be necessary to map out the condition of the collections to prioritize the salvage efforts. Since the most severe damage to collections had occurred in the periodical stacks, work began there. The fire and its aftermath had obliterated some of the signage in the stacks and many journals had obviously been destroyed. We determined that our first step should be numbering the ranges and making an effort to link call numbers to the new range numbers. We labeled the stacks in the burned and proximate area with numbers less than 100, and numbered the other stacks, in the south section of the periodicals wing, with numbers greater than 100. This tactic allowed us to distinguish between sections that were relatively unharmed by the fire and sections that had sustained terrible damage.

After numbering and labeling both sides of each range of stacks with a unique number, a list was created correlating call numbers to the stack labels. We also estimated, in the stacks close to the burned area, what level of damage volumes had sustained, recording this information along with the numbering system. A copy of an existing map of the stacks was edited to include the "new" range numbers. The area with stack labels in or near the burned area became known as the "fire stacks," and the periodicals at the south end of the building were called the "non-fire stacks." Figure 1 shows part of the inventory list that resulted from the initial evaluation of the periodicals.

The next step was to evaluate in more detail the condition of the volumes on the shelves in both the fire and non-fire periodical stacks. This process was quite challenging as all electrical power to the basement was out, and the demolition contractor, hired to begin work in the basement, had only been able to provide limited lighting. Our initial evaluation of the collections was done with battery operated lanterns and flashlights in dirty, hot conditions. (See Image 1.)

State and Federal government information reference collections and microfilm cabinets housed in the basement were mapped in a similar way. The government reference stacks were given stack labels, and fortunately, the microfilm cabinets had already been numbered sequentially due to a recent carpet installation project. In addition to the government documents reference collection, also housed in the basement were the circulating documents collections; however, that collection was shelved behind a fire door and thus unharmed. Parts of the documents reference collection were comprised of historical materials such as early *Census Reports*, early *Supreme Court Reports*, and the *United States Statutes at Large*. Based on a number of discussions taking place between library staff and BMS CAT contractors, the decision was made to not ship these materials to Fort Worth or to ozone them on site because it was believed at the time that the process would further deteriorate these fragile materials.

Image 1: Working conditions in Zimmerman basement after fire. Courtesy Nancy K. Dennis .

The collection was boxed and stored with the government document circulating collections behind the fire door. In hindsight, we should have obtained a second opinion from an outside preservation expert because there was disagreement between in-house preservation experts and the vendor, who had limited experience remediating fragile historical materials that had been affected by fire. When the materials were unboxed and re-shelved for public access, there was a very strong smoke odor that took months to dissipate naturally.

In the area proximate to the fire where shelving had not collapsed, we began to work our way through the ranges, removing volumes from the shelf to check for water and thermal damage. When we found material too damaged to save, we discarded the volumes and kept an inventory of what was lost when the items could be identified. In the area of the fire origin, twelve complete ranges had been damaged beyond recovery and the burned remnants were already being removed by the demolition contractor. In the remaining collapsed stacks on that side, salvage would have to be done shelf by shelf, as the condition of the volumes ranged from moderately damaged to unsalvageable.

We had to decide quickly what we might be able to save, and what was beyond hope. We decided to make every effort to try to save materials in certain areas of strength at the University—largely, materials relating to our Latin American studies program as well as periodicals dealing with southwestern United States and Native American issues. In general, we discarded volumes that had burned into the text block, items that had fallen onto the floor and become saturated with water during the fire suppression, and volumes that had been crushed by collapsed shelving. In many cases, thermal and fire damage was limited to the buckram casing of the bound volumes. We decided to keep those volumes with the intent to re-bind them after remediation work had been done.

Remediation Efforts and the Pack Out

Since collection cleaning would primarily be carried

out at the contractor's facilities out of state, it was necessary to rapidly begin to pack up and prepare the various collections in the basement for shipping to the BMS CAT facility in Fort Worth, Texas. We had learned after the CSEL flood to be sure that boxes were labeled consistently with all of the relevant information. After the CSEL flood we discovered that most boxes had been packed with only partial call numbers, making it impossible to reorder the boxes without opening them first to determine the contents, thereby complicating that pack back.

Six teams of BMS CAT staff were assigned to work on the packing and removal of collections from the Zimmerman basement. Although the library's response team was available to answer questions, we were focused on continuing our work evaluating materials in the fire area and could not directly supervise each packing team. In an attempt to ensure boxes were packed in order and labeled correctly, we developed a packing protocol. Each team was asked to be sure to follow the call number order, working from left to right on each shelf, and from the top to bottom of each section on a side of a shelving range. Boxes were to be labeled first with the stack number we had assigned: the section number (first section on the left side to be numbered one, etc.); the shelf number, with shelves numbered one to seven from top to bottom; and a box number. These procedures were time consuming, but we knew it was the only hope of having some type of order to the collections when they were returned to us. The pack out crews also kept detailed lists of the boxes associated with each stack number. The recovery team kept copies of these lists as well, which proved to be invaluable in staging materials for their eventual return to the library.

Nineteen semi-tractor trailer trucks were loaded with pallets of microform cabinets and boxed journals in under three weeks. It would be nearly two years before renovations to the basement were com-

Image 2: Packed semi-tractor trailer truck. Courtesy Nancy K. Dennis.

pleted and all materials returned to the library, but preparations for the pack back began as soon as the recovery phase was completed. (See Image 2.)

As the pack back team discussed strategies for the return of the collections, we relied heavily on several tools generated by the pack out process. Figure 2 shows the map of the periodical stacks that was annotated with the stack numbers assigned during the initial collection evaluation after the fire.

The map was correlated with a list of stack numbers and call number ranges that also contained descriptive information on the condition of the materials in that section. The in-

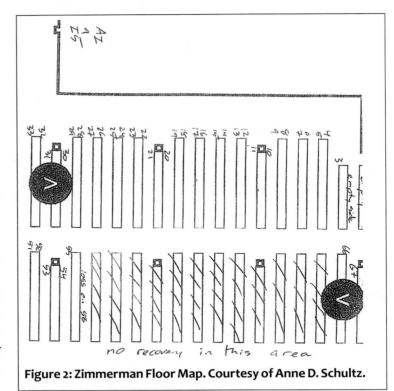

Figure 2: Zimmerman Floor Map. Courtesy of Anne D. Schultz.

Box #	Room #	Job # JH 3052 Description STACK # 22	Location	Packed By:
		Sec. SECTION : 1	Basement	N.T.
		Shelf : 1 EMPTY	Bsmt.	N.T.
1		Shelf : 2 → AP 20 B3 1893	Bsmt.	N.T.
2		Shelf : 2 cont → AP 20 R3 v.125	Bsmt.	N.T.
3		Shelf : 3 → AP 20 R3 V.132	Bsmt.	N.T.
4		Shelf : 4 → AP 20 R3 1897	Bsmt.	N.T.
5		Shelf : 5 → AP 20 R3 V.134	Bsmt.	N.T.
6		Shelf : 5 cont → AP 20 R3 v.162	Bsmt.	N.T.
7		Shelf : 6 → AP 20 R3 1902	Bsmt.	N.T.
8		Shelf : 6 cont → AP 20 R3 1904	Bsmt.	N.T.
9		Shelf : 7 → AP 20 R3 1905	Bsm.	N.T.

Figure 3: Box inventory sheet. Courtesy Anne D. Schultz .

ventory sheets (see Figure 3) created by the salvage contractor's crews provided detailed information on the number of boxes packed per stack as well as call numbers for the materials in each box.

One thing we failed to consider during the pack out process was how the boxes would be loaded into the trucks. When the contractors loaded pallets of journals, the boxes came from all six crews working in various sections of our stacks. We had not thought to cluster these boxes since at the time emphasis was placed on the rapid removal of materials. When materials were unboxed and cleaned at the contractor's facility, they were returned to the original (but cleaned) boxes and returned to the pallets on which they had arrived. Fortunately, the contractor had kept a list with information about the boxes on each pallet. While this list did not perfectly capture all the detail on the boxes, it would provide us with enough information to organize the return of the pallets.

Zimmerman Library Reference Collection—The Pack Out

Although the fire occurred in the northeast part of the basement, the first floor was also affected. At that time, the first floor area directly over the location of the fire was occupied by staff from technical services and the e-resources team. The fire provided an opportunity to evaluate the use of the entire first floor area. Materials such as print abstracting and indexing sources were identified to be transferred from the reference collection to compact shelving in the basement. The entire Zimmerman reference collection was packed into boxes and stored temporarily inside Zimmerman Library until the first floor reference area reopened to the public in spring 2007. To complicate matters, the collection was divided between those items to be returned to the collection, and DNR's (do not returns), items not intended to be returned to the reference collection such as the aforementioned print abstracts and indices. The last of the DNR's were not returned from storage to be shelved in their final locations until spring 2010.

The teams conducting the pack out of the basement were also responsible for the pack out of the first floor reference area, and were given the same protocol developed for the basement collections. The way the pack out protocol was or was not followed was not discovered until the DNR's had been moved off site and requests for materials to be paged were received. At that time, it was discovered that the contract employees packing out the print reference collection did not follow appropriate protocol. To put it simply, instead of marking the boxes with the call numbers represented in the boxes, multiple boxes were labeled with the same call number range which was later discovered to be the call numbers for the entire side of the shelving range. This discovery made it quite challenging to page materials from this collection. As a result, closer supervision and specific guidelines for packing of library materials and labeling of said boxes is strongly recommended, particularly if access to those packed materials is expected prior to re-shelving.

The Pack Back Team

The pack back team was first convened in spring 2007. The initial membership was made up of individuals from throughout the UL based on a number of factors. Naturally, the team included individuals who were experienced with disaster recovery from the CSEL flood, as well as staff from UL facilities services, reference, government documents, circulation, collection development, cataloging, and acquisitions services. Additionally, the newly hired resident was appointed to the team, and the associate dean for facilities and access services, also responsible for the Zimmerman building renovation efforts overall, was a team member as well. University Libraries employees from other departments and branches, including the Fine Arts Library, who needed staff for their upcoming move; e-resources; library and information technology; access services; selectors for the lost/damaged collections; and the UL ILS system administrator attended meetings as needed.

The team included members from across the UL, selected for their subject or functional expertise without regard for their rank or level within the organization. In disaster recovery situations, it is critically important to select team members who are the most knowledgeable about the project or have the particular expertise needed to move the project forward. Often, this will not be the director or manager. In these instances, the team needs to think in terms of one organization, rather than a library with multiple branches and/or departments. Disasters affect entire organizations, not just one department or branch, and a successful recovery is dependent upon everyone working together.

In order to facilitate communication among group members, a group electronic distribution list and a project wiki were created to post meeting notes, pictures and other supporting information. The group met regularly for nearly a year to plan the pack back. The team leader scheduled weekly meetings on team members' calendars through spring 2008. The importance of having meetings scheduled well in advance cannot be stressed enough. The core pack back team included nearly twenty members and trying to schedule a group of that size at the last minute would have been very difficult. Scheduling and holding regular meetings, taking and distributing/posting meeting notes, establishing a communication tool (electronic distribution list), and a place where all information about the project can be posted (wiki) and accessed ensured all team members had all the same information about the project. The wiki became an invaluable tool because it was a place where we could post pictures of progress, floor plans for the affected space, and meeting notes— not just for the team, but for UL staff not directly involved in the pack back effort so that everyone had access to the same information as the project progressed.[28]

At the first meeting, the group reviewed the timeline for the project, identified sub-projects and assigned responsibility, discussed plans and methods for inventorying materials involved in the pack back, and discussed a field trip to Fort Worth, Texas to tour the warehouse where salvaged materials had been taken for cleaning and storage post-fire. Prior to the field trip and in order to best prepare for the pack back, the group wanted to know:

- *Will we be receiving an electronic inventory of the bound volumes taken to Fort Worth?* At the time of the fire, UL practice was to check-in individual serial issues, send individual issues to the bindery as appropriate, then place volumes of issues on the shelf once returned from the bindery. Bound volumes were not checked in and rarely circulated. Subsequently, the UL was unable to generate an inventory of actual physical volumes owned prior to the fire from Millennium, the UL integrated library system (ILS). It was generally understood that a searchable database would be created by the salvage company during the cleaning and storage process.

- *Could we inspect the boxes that contained materials that bordered the fire damaged areas to determine the condition of those titles?* There was always concern about the condition of the materials shelved closest to the epicenter deemed 'keepable' by the team conducting the initial collection assessment.

- *Can we get a list of what is returning on each truck?* The team wanted to know if they could plan the pack back with the knowledge of which call numbers would be returning when.

- *What will be on the box labels? Same as what went out? The stack scheme designed during the pack out?* Two of the UL expert veterans of the CSEL flood developed a scheme for labeling boxes during the Zimmerman pack out based on their experience with the CSEL disaster. The pack back team's understanding was the materials packed in boxes and labeled on site would be transported to the Fort Worth facility, cleaned, then re-packed and returned in boxes according to the same scheme. The pack back team wanted confirmation that the same design would be followed so they could best plan for the pack back.

Finally and most practically,

- *What microfilm titles are in the orange cabinets?* The UL, like many libraries, had microfilm holdings in a variety of types and styles of cabinets, and at the UL different types and styles of cabinets most likely held different categories of collections—e.g., journals vs. newspapers. The orange cabinets were deemed not returnable by the pack back team for a variety of reasons including the damage that they had sustained over the years and during the pack out, so it was imperative to determine what used to live in those cabinets and what we

needed to do to return those materials to the UL sans cabinets. (See Image 3.)

At the next few meetings, the team discussed the logistics of returning thousands of boxes to Albuquerque. Would BMS CAT return them directly to Zimmerman Library or would there be an opportunity to return them to an interim space in order to better organize, prepare and control the pack back? There seemed to be more unknowns than knowns at that point. Also adding to stress levels was a UL-wide decision that print titles that were held in perpetual access databases such as JSTOR and Project MUSE would not be returned to the basement. Teaching and research faculty expecting all "their" lost print titles to be replaced with print were temporarily sidetracked by this decision. Some faculty confused the discussions of which destroyed titles would be replaced in print with the discussions of

Image 3: Orange cabinets. Courtesy Teresa Y. Neely.

which titles would be shelved in the periodicals area. There is much that can be said about tactful and strategic relationship-building between librarians and faculty, particularly during the disaster recovery process and in dealing with "their print journals." Unfortunately, we learned much by trial and error. In any case, be sure to keep the faculty informed and never underestimate the power of a face to face meeting with an academic department where there is concern, to answer questions and allay fears. It will certainly make your work-life go a little smoother!

The Fort Worth Field Trip

In late July 2007, some members of the pack back team visited the contractor's facility in Texas to determine whether it would be feasible to reorder the

boxes on the pallets before they were delivered. The team returned from Fort Worth armed with pictures of our boxed, shrink wrapped collections, lots of great information, and a 'to do' list for the pack back team.

The team discovered that the collections stored in Texas included 413 pallets of periodicals, thirty-two boxes per pallet, approximately 13,216 boxes; and 147 pallets of microfilm and microfiche, and 213 microfilm and microfiche cabinets. Our collections (on pallets) covered 8,816 square feet in the Fort Worth facility, most were stored on vertical shelving up to four levels high. (See Image 4.)

The team estimated that we would need between 15,000 and 20,000 square feet of horizontal space if all shipments were returned to an interim space at one time, prior to moving them to Zimmerman.

Image 4: Fort Worth warehouse storage. Courtesy Nancy K. Dennis.

The 25,000 square foot warehouse in Fort Worth was not climate controlled and the processing plant was not air conditioned. It was ninety degrees and ninety percent humidity when the team members visited. They found boxes were labeled the same way they were during the pack out, box number, stack number, call number, etc. At least ninety percent of the boxes were labeled and approximately ninety-nine percent of the pallets contained mixed call numbers. The pallets were also labeled with job number, pallet number, and were labeled, "UNM Zimmerman Library Cleaned and Ozone Completed." The team also returned with a 400 page hand written inventory of the boxes on each pallet. The inventory was not available electronically, but at least we now knew we could control the order in which pallets were returned—very good news to us. They reported that some items had a smoke odor and there were some cabinets that had been locked and/or damaged so they had not been cleaned nor inventoried.

The "to do" list included possibly converting the inventory to an electronically accessible format, such as Access or Excel, finding someone who was savvy in Access or Excel, creating a list of JSTOR/Project MUSE titles to remove prior to the pack back, acquiring warehouse space with appropriate amenities, and creating an inventory of microfilm titles not returning to Zimmerman such as newspaper titles now available digitally.

Meanwhile, discussions began to see if there was an affordable space to return the pallets in order to allow organizing prior to the return to Zimmerman. After seeing 413 pallets of boxed journals plus all of the microfilm cabinets, we revised our plan to offload and organize boxes in the library's parking lot. Basic amenities such as a loading dock, heat and air conditioning, lights, functioning bathrooms and the possibility of long term storage on the UNM campus for other collections would be ideal. In addition to the interim storage space, other items adding to the cost of the pack back included the availability of a Bobcat and forklifts and someone to drive them, a moving company, and UNM licensed drivers. The pack back team also continued to discuss a plan that involved using smaller trucks to return materials from Fort Worth, that could back up to the Zimmerman Library loading dock, bypassing the need for an interim storage space. As the pack back process evolved, costs were estimated, explained and communicated to the campus risk management department and the insurance adjustors assigned to this claim. Frequent and clear communication is strongly encouraged to reduce any funding surprises along the way.

By early August 2007, the pack back team was working under the assumption that there would be an interim storage space in Albuquerque, to be secured by September 1, and that the manpower for getting the boxes from the trucks to the warehouse would be contracted out. Once the boxes arrived at the Zimmerman Library loading dock and made their way down to the basement, UL staff would take over with unpacking the boxes and re-shelving materials based on the original pack out scheme enhanced with information about what was being replaced, retained and/or continued in print. In our naiveté, we simplified the steps in the process of the pack back as we thought it would be at that time:

- unload pallets from the truck using a forklift or pallet jack
- break down pallets and sort boxes by stacks using hand trucks
- sort boxes into call number order within the stacks at the warehouse
- identify and remove JSTOR/Project MUSE titles
- identify and remove any damaged boxes for processing
- transport boxes to Zimmerman Library
- offload into basement
- stage boxes at the end of stacks/compact shelving bays
- unpack boxes and place volumes on shelves

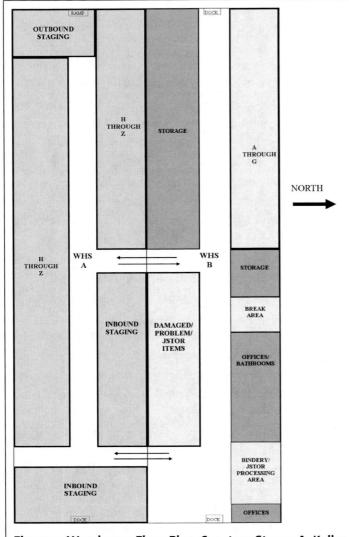

Figure 4: Warehouse Floor Plan. Courtesy Steven A. Keller.

- Warehouse Maintenance (e.g., recycling and trash bins)

At that meeting we learned that the expenditure for leasing the warehouse had indeed been approved and hoped to be able to occupy it by September 1, 2007. We also discussed dismantling shelving in Zimmerman Library and installing it in the warehouse. At that time, the team was still operating under the assumption that we would use UL staff for the pack back. The logistics group determined we would operate on an 8 am to 5 pm schedule with our expert warehouse mover (an access services staff member) as supervisor, and that we would receive two to three semi-trucks of pallets per week. At our next meeting on August 31, 2007 we discussed a floor plan, designed by the warehouse mover, showing how things could be potentially laid out in the warehouse and also discussed the re-shelving tool, described later in this case study. At that time it was reported we were about five weeks away from having the basement renovations completed. Compact shelving installation was scheduled to begin in early September 2007. (See Figure 4.)

Fortunately, we were able to rent warehouse space near the University for staging materials as they were returned from Texas. Our contractor loaded pallets in the order we specified and arranged for deliveries to be made on our schedule. We decided to receive the material that had been furthest away from the fire first, thinking it would be faster to re-shelve those volumes first as the condition of volumes in the fire area was uncertain.

Fortunately, our in house expert warehouse mover also had a talent for organizing pallets of materials. We were also able to hire additional labor from a

At the August 21, 2007 meeting, sub-groups were identified to develop procedures and processes as a part of the pack back.

- Bindery group—for damaged materials triage
- Logistics group—staffing including contracted movers and UL staff
- Inventory group—not activated immediately
- JSTOR/Project Muse Group
- Microfilm—not activated immediately
- Mapping the collections
- Supply Team/Equipment

local company, NRG, who also arranged for forklift rental and a forklift operator. We received one truckload of pallets from the Fort Worth warehouse delivered to the local warehouse, approximately twenty-four pallets per shipment, twice weekly beginning the week of September 14, 2007 and ending on October 31 2007, a total of sixteen deliveries. When each truck arrived, pallets were quickly offloaded and broken down, and then boxes were re-sorted by the stack number from our original labeling system. Initially. We did not attempt to order the boxes within each stack number, thinking this step would occur as the boxes returned to Zimmerman.

At the October 19, 2007 meeting, it was reported that we had received fifty pallets, representing 28 stacks, and we were ahead of where we thought we would be in sorting boxes and "re-palletizing" (a UL created phrase) them at the warehouse. Compact shelving installation was on schedule for Zimmerman basement, and a review of two pallets of materials shelved closest to the fire was promising, indicating little heat, water or damage from crushing.

At the October 26, 2007 meeting, procedures for training UL staff for the pack back were discussed and scheduling dates were set: Monday, October 29, Tuesday, October 30, and Wednesday, October 31. We reviewed the supplies we would need for the pack back and finalized how many people we would need from NRG to deliver the re-palletized materials from the local warehouse. Since the basement was not yet open to the public, procedures to ensure security and safety were developed and put into place.

Mapping the Collection

Prior to returning materials to the basement, the collection needed to be remapped to the new configuration with compact shelving. Before compact shelving was installed in the basement of Zimmerman Library, the periodicals were shelved in approximately 24,876 linear feet of cantilever shelving. After compact shelving was installed, the available space increased to 36,071 linear feet.

Additionally, mapping had to be completed without final knowledge of which titles could or would be replaced in print, if at all; and also, room needed to be left for growth of continuing print subscriptions and all of the materials being transferred to the basement from other parts of the UL. In order to address this, the "pack back tool" was born—a 253 page 11" x 17" inch, mammoth, color coded document based on title disposition. The team leader had a vision of what the pack back tool could be, however, the UL resident, was expected to translate the vision into a physical object that could be easily used and interpreted by shelvers, and she delivered with honors! The overarching goal of the pack back was to get all of the BMS CAT boxes of materials back on the shelf and then integrate other collections such as purchased and donated replacements, continuing subscriptions, abstracts and indexes, etc; however, the tool needed to account for these anomalies so that the pack back team would know where to leave space for growth, etc. The color coded legend for the pack back tool, representing the color highlighting the titles, was as follows:

- Active title (leave growth space)
- Not in a BMS box (leave space for materials coming from other locations)
- Oversized material (do not leave space, will be shelved elsewhere in the basement)
- Do Not Replace (titles lost in fire not being replaced in print)
- Should be in CSEL Library (do not leave space, materials already moved to another physical location but still remained in LIBROS [our ILS] with Zimmerman Periodical location)
- Will be moving to FADL Library (do not leave space, materials will be moving to another physical location but still remained in LIBROS with Zimmerman Periodical location)
- DILARES titles (titles lost in fire, it was unclear if they would be available to be replaced, leave space) [29]

The tool also included notes and codes for whether a title was active, or currently in reference or in some other space to assist pack back team members. Additionally, the tool included stack numbers as represented on the boxes during the pack out; the number of volumes we should find in the boxes; the number of volumes lost, if known; and any additional notes that may have been necessary for a particular title. Although not perfect, it would have been difficult to tackle the pack back without this tool. (See Image 5.)

However, the best laid plans sometimes go awry. On October 31, 2007, less than a week away from the start of returning materials to the basement, an equipment failure caused a ten inch water main to empty itself into the newly carpeted, painted, and renovated basement of Zimmerman Library. An enormous amount of water covered the basement floor from the east end where rails for compact shelving had been installed, to the main stairwell and elevator shaft on the west side of the basement. Ironically, pack back team members were in the basement training UL staff for the pack back which was scheduled to commence the following week. This obviously delayed our plans somewhat. (See Image 6.)

After the water pipe failure in the riser room, we decided to take advantage of the delay to complete a special project and to re-palletize the boxes in the warehouse, which would speed up the process as boxes eventually returned to Zimmerman. We had identified titles in both Project MUSE and JSTOR, and armed with this list of titles and call numbers, the warehouse team went through each set of pallets for stack numbers containing these titles. We opened boxes to double-check and separated those boxes from the rest of the material to be returned to

Image 5: Pack Back Tool. Courtesy Teresa Y. Neely.

Image 6: Flooded Zimmerman basement. Courtesy Nancy K. Dennis.

Zimmerman. Boxes were then re-palletized in box number order and pallets were shrink-wrapped and staged. Because we knew from the pack out inventory how many boxes had been packed per stack, we were also able to confirm that we had received all boxes for each section. After sorting through all stacks with JSTOR and Project MUSE titles, we went through the same reorganization process with boxes in the other stacks. At this point, we now knew we would return boxes in call number order, from A to Z, since all compact shelving had been installed in the basement and there was no need to work with the "easier" non-fire stack titles first.

The team also moved the materials that had been removed from reference (DNR's) from a separate site to the warehouse and integrated them into the pallets. Other tasks completed included pulling the

JSTOR and Project MUSE microfilm, emptying the orange microfilm cabinets that were not returning to Zimmerman Library, and boxing up the microfilm that would be returning.

After the delay caused by the flooding on October 31, the pack back team began to discuss new strategies for the most efficient and rapid return of materials once the basement was ready—for the second time. Improve Group, the company hired to install compact shelving, had hired a team of library movers, American Library Consultants (ALC), to handle moving collections as compact shelving was installed in various areas of Zimmerman Library. Since ALC was finishing up with moving collections for Improve Group, and was familiar with our collections anyway, we asked them to give us a bid on participating in the pack back. We gave

ALC owners a tour of the warehouse where materials were staged in pallets ready to be transported to Zimmerman, explained the circumstances surrounding the pack out, and our expectations and concerns of the possible condition of materials closest to the fire epicenter. We hoped, as professional library collection movers, they could complete the job in a shorter timeframe than we could using library staff volunteers. They assured us they could and that they were up to the task. Upon submitting a bid, the insurance company agreed to pay the cost of hiring ALC as contractors for the pack back. With that decision, the pack back team proceeded to refine a procedure for getting materials from the warehouse back into the Zimmerman basement.

We had two teams of outside labor—contractors from NRG, a local moving company, to work at the warehouse and also to load and offload pallets from the warehouse to the Zimmerman loading dock, and down the conveyor belt into the basement; and ALC, for the actual opening of boxes and re-shelving of material. The workflow was arranged as follows:

- NRG staff, with a representative from the pack back team, will load pallets at the warehouse and drive the delivery truck to campus.
- When the truck arrives at Zimmerman, NRG staff will help us to offload and break down pallets at the loading dock. A conveyor belt will be used to safely transport the boxes from the loading dock into the basement.
- In the basement, ALC employees and NRG staff will load boxes onto hand trucks and move them into the compact shelving area.
- An ALC crew member will organize and stage boxes strategically on ALC carts to expedite the unpacking of the journals.
- ALC crews will follow our map for the collections and use the pack back tool to unpack and re-shelve journals.

Although this procedure seemed quite straightforward there were, of course, some complications in the implementation. As ALC began to open and unpack boxes beginning with the A call numbers, it soon became clear that library staff with knowledge of the collection and the ability to solve problems and make decisions on the spot were critically needed. The work ALC did with moving collections for the compact shelving installation was fairly straightforward in that they emptied shelves temporarily, then later re-shelved collections without having to reorder the volumes. The pack back was not quite the same animal. As in any large periodical collection, there were runs of complete bound volumes and other titles composed of single issues, or "lots of pieces of paper," as was noted during the pack back. Additionally, the volumes were not coming out of the boxes in strict volume order as they probably weren't packed in volume order. Additionally, if volumes were mis-shelved or just sitting on the shelf, they were packed into boxes as well, as if they were in the correct shelf order. Pack back team members anticipated these inconsistencies; however, they still slowed ALC's work., In the end, members of the pack back team along with UL staff volunteers tackled the most difficult areas which included those closest to the fire; while ALC re-shelved non fire stacks. Work on the difficult stacks continued long after ALC had departed on Wednesday, February 27, 2008.

Integrating Journal Replacements, Gifts, and Continuously Received Subscriptions

The first three shipments from Absolute Backorder Service, Inc., the vendor selected to supply us with replacement volumes for lost titles, arrived on March 19, 2008, and we received our tenth and final shipment in late April 2009. All total, we received 9,525 (mostly bound) volumes to be integrated into the pack back, along with continuing print subscriptions received post-fire, and regular shipments from the bindery that also contained approximately 7,000 volumes of gift replacements.

Returning the Microform Collections

In many ways, the most challenging aspect of the pack back was the return of the microfilm and microfiche cabinets and their contents. Most cabinets of fiche and film were removed from the building and shipped to Texas with their contents in the drawers. Although this was the recommended mode of removal by BMS CAT, and it did speed up the pack out process considerably, there were challenges for the return.

Like many libraries, Zimmerman had an eclectic collection of fiche and film cabinets acquired over many years. We had a set of large, orange cabinets with two part sets—one set of drawers opened vertically and was stacked on top of another cabinet, with drawers that opened horizontally. These cabinets were finicky, sometimes didn't open at all, and sometimes, well, you know... The top cabinets had had their contents emptied and boxed at the time of the pack out as it would have been both difficult and dangerous to move them loaded. The pack back committee debated whether or not to return these cabinets to our remodeled facility. After several discussions, we agreed not to return these cabinets to the building but to use them in our temporary remote storage to house runs of film for long term storage. Because we had rented warehouse space to receive and stage our journals, we were also able to have the orange cabinets shipped directly there.

The remaining cabinets were to be returned directly to Zimmerman after the boxed journals had been shelved. It would take three semi-tractor trailers to return them, so we planned three separate delivery days. The deliveries would have to be scheduled after midnight, so the Zimmerman loading dock could be used without causing traffic problems. We did know, because of the pack out inventory, how many cabinets to expect for each smaller collection (government documents, New Mexico newspapers, periodical microfilm, etc), but we did not know the size of each individual cabinet. Mapping the new locations of each collection was

done based on the likely dimension of the cabinets in their new configurations, including a substantial margin for error. The cabinets for each type of material were numbered, and the inventory pack out sheets did tell us how many cabinets belonged in each subgroup. We made our best efforts to map out three sections for microform cabinets, and waited to test our plan with the first delivery.

The first truckload of microfilm cabinets was difficult to deal with. Three members of the pack back team agreed to be at Zimmerman at one a.m. to manage the return of the cabinets. NRG, our local labor company, usually very reliable, was expected to send four people to offload the truck and move the cabinets from the loading dock to the basement. We had mapped out our sections, stopped for donuts and coffee, and were ready to go at the loading dock in the middle of the night.

The first thing to go wrong was the semi-truck that was nearly two hours late. Our second problem was our NRG crew—we had two experienced, hard-working guys and two who were not as motivated. Our third problem was a load of boxes of microfilm shipped outside of cabinets—we had forgotten that some film boxes had been packed separately, and these were included in pallets on the first truck. One member of the pack back team concentrated on hauling loads of boxes to the basement using the staff freight elevator while the others helped offload cabinets. Our two reliable workers moved most of the film cabinets on furniture dollies from the loading dock through the public areas of Zimmerman using the only elevator large enough to hold film cabinets. This worked fairly well, although it was exhausting labor. We had to reposition a few cabinets on the dollies as they exited the elevator. Pushing them out of the elevator was more difficult than loading them onto the elevator. We had some near misses, but never dropped a cabinet in the basement. However, the most dramatic moment of the night involved a fiche cabinet that fell from the furniture dolly as it was being wheeled across the

Zimmerman lobby. Fortunately, the drawers that opened were empty, and the cabinet itself missed the glass doors of the library's Starbucks café by a good six inches.

We were fairly successful at following our plan for arranging the cabinets in the basement. As expected, we did need to make some modifications as we hadn't known the exact dimensions of each cabinet before it arrived back in Albuquerque. Of course, they did not return in order, either, so we guessed at the amount of space to leave between cabinets and hoped for the best. One unanticipated problem was moving the loaded cabinets on carpet after removing them from the furniture dollies. The carpet laid in the basement was actually composed of square carpet tiles rather than long rolls of carpeting. This was a practical decision in terms of replacement, but we found that the adhesive backing in some cases was inadequate, and as we pushed the heavy cabinets, the carpet tile moved. We solved this problem by using flattened cardboard boxes as furniture glides. The cardboard produced less friction sliding across the carpet, and as the cabinet was correctly placed we could tip it up and pull out the cardboard.

Because of the unintended time delay, we were still moving cabinets and boxes as the library opened the following morning. Fortunately, the basement was still closed to the public and we were able to recruit library helpers (who had slept through the night) to assist us in finishing up the cabinet replacement before noon. Our next two deliveries were far less eventful, and we were able to complete the work more quickly and get some sleep!

Final Thoughts

For us the success of the pack out, pack back, and additional side projects can be attributed to four principles: organization, flexibility, trust, and collaboration. At every step, from salvage to re-shelving of materials, we were able to maintain some level of organization, even when it wasn't perfect. Each ef-fort to track and categorize materials and processes paid off. We were able, in the end, to do several key things efficiently. Materials were removed rapidly from the challenging conditions post-fire; we were able to receive and sort materials at the warehouse prior to the pack back and despite the large volume of materials being returned and the limited space for temporary storage; and we were able to return the majority of the collections to the basement in under a month, despite complications.

All team members were able to adapt to constantly changing conditions outside of the team's control. The ability to plan and work in an ambiguous environment was critical. During the pack out and the planning phase of the pack back, we made constant rapid adjustments to plans and procedures as circumstances required. Several different contractors and subcontractors were involved in both processes, and changes and delays in the work flow of others often affected our goals and timelines.

Trust, at all levels, was also a key to our success. Because many members of the team did not hold a high rank in the organization, we had to have the trust of the administrative level to work effectively. It would have been impossible to clear every small decision with higher ranking employees. The members of the team trusted each others' judgment, skills, and work ethic, regardless of the position each person held during their "normal" job duties. We were able to work effectively with each other and to see and respect the special skills that each member brought to the overall process.

For us, this project was, in many ways the most satisfying work we have ever done in our library careers. We had clearly identifiable goals and challenging work environments. All members of the team had an opportunity to lead when appropriate, to share ideas, and contribute time and effort. The members of the team developed strong relationships with each other, and got to know people with whom they would not ordinarily have a chance to work. We were able to collaborate successfully with university employees outside the library, various contractors, safety personnel, and others to meet our goals and restore Zimmerman to a fully functioning library serving the entire UNM community.

This project was certainly the most complex that we have ever worked on. The key elements were planning and people. It just would not have come together if those elements had not been in place. Planning was essential from the day after the fire until the day the basement reopened to the public and continues today with the last shipment of Absolute materials making its way to the shelves within the last few months. Working with people from throughout the UL and outside the UL and the university was a true and satisfying learning experience—one that we sometimes remember with fondness, and sometimes from a distance as if we did not—could not possibly have—experienced that and made it to the other side. Recovering from a disaster in the workplace is not easy and not something we would wish on anyone, but the experience, insight, collegial relationships and friendships developed and maintained are immensely rewarding side effects.

Notes

1. See Lydia Preiss, "Learning from disasters: A decade of experience at the National Library of Australia," *International Preservation News* 20 (1999): 19-26; Carolyn Hoover Sung, Valerii Pavlovich Lenov, and Peter Waters, "Fire recovery at the Library of the Academy of Sciences of the USSR," *American Archivist* 53 (1990): 298-312.

2. Upali Amarasiri, "Rising from the wreckage: Development of tsunami-affected libraries in Sri Lanka," *IFLA Journal* 31 (2005): 307-314.

3. Jamie Ellis, "Lessons learned: The recovery of a research collection after Hurricane Katrina," *Collection Building* 26, no. 4 (2007): 108-111; Tom Clareson and Jane S. Long, "Libraries in the eye of the storm: Lessons learned from hurricane Katrina," *American Libraries* 37, no. 7 (2006): 38-41; Alma Dawson and Kathleen de la Peña McCook, "Rebuilding community in Louisiana after the hurricanes of 2005," *Reference & User Services Quarterly* 45 (2006): 292-296; Kathy L. Bailey, "When books were debris," *Reading Today* 27, no. 1 (2009): 21.

4. Amarasire, "Rising from the wreckage," 309.

5. Bailey, "When books were debris," 21.

6. John Morris, "Los Angeles Library fire—Learning the hard way," *Canadian Library Journal* 44 (1987): 217-22; Sung, Lenov, and Waters, "Fire recovery at the Library of the Academy of Sciences of the USSR," 298-312; Kevin Green, "The case of the Pilkington Technology Center fire," *ASLIB Information* 21, no. 2 (1993): 72-75; Mike Holderness, "Back from the brink of disaster," *Library Manager* 3 (1995): 16-17; Hillary Hammond, "Norfolk and Norwich Central Library: The emerging phoenix," *New Library World* 97, no.6 (no.1130), (1996): 24-31; Peter Cullhead, "The Linkoping Library fire," *International Preservation News* 31 (2003) : 4-8; Richard Battersby, "Recovering from disaster: The loss of Edinburg's AI Library," *Library + Information Update* 4 (2005): 36-38; James G. Milles, "Managing after a disaster: Or there and back again," *Legal Reference Services Quarterly* 25, no.1 (2006): 59-75.

7. M. G. Carbery, "The libraries of Florence-after," *The Catholic Library World* 41, no. 2 (1969): 94-101; Philip D. Leighton, "The Stanford flood," *College and Research Libraries* 40 (1979): 450-459; Sally Buchanan, "The Stanford Library flood restoration project," *College and Research Libraries* 40 (1979): 539-548; Eileen Brady and John F. Guido, "When is a disaster not a disaster?" *Library & Archival Security* 8, no. 3/4 (1988): 11-23; Gary Harrington, "Flood recovery in Oklahoma City," *Conservation Administration News* 54 (1993): 10-11; Camila A. Alire, ed., *Library disaster planning and recovery handbook* (Chicago: University of Chicago Press, 2000); Vojtech Balík and Jirí Polišenski, "The National Library of the Czech Republic and the floods of 2002," *Alexandria* 16, no. 1 (2004): 17-24; Dawson

and McCook, "Rebuilding community in Louisiana after the hurricanes of 2005," 292-296; Mabel Suzuki and Ross Togashi, "Halloween flood at University of Hawaii Library," *Western Association of Map Libraries Information Bulletin* 36, no. 2 (2005): 101-110; G. M. E., "Northeastern flooding takes toll on archives, libraries," *American Libraries* 37, no. 7 (2006): 16-17.

8. Buchanan, "The Stanford Library flood restoration project," 539-548.

9. Christine Rugger, and Elliott Morse, "The recovery of water-damaged books at the College of Physicians of Philadelphia, *Library & Archival Security* 3, no. 3/4 (1980): 23-28.

10. Fred W. Matthews, "Sorting a mountain of books," *Library Resources and Technical Services* 31, no. 1 (1987): 88-94.

11. Morris, "Los Angeles library fire—learning the hard way," 217-221.

12. Sung, Leonov, and Waters, "Fire recovery at the Library of the Academy of Sciences of the USSR," 299-300.

13. Ibid., 308-310.

14. N. P. Obokoh, "Coping with flood disaster; The experience of a university library," *Library Review* 4, no. 6 (1991): 22-29.

15. Green, "The case of the Pilkington Technology Centre fire," 72-75.

16. Harrington, "Flood recovery in Oklahoma City," 10-11.

17. Elizabeth Schobernd, "Lessons from a library fire," *College and Undergraduate Libraries* 5, no. 2 (1998): 43-51.

18. Carmel Bush and Diane Lunde, "The disaster-recovery process for collections," in *Library Disaster Planning and Recovery Handbook,* ed. Camila Alire (New York: Neal-Schuman Publishers, Inc., 2000), 57-90.

19. Camila A. Alire, "The silver lining: Recovering from the shambles of a disaster," *Journal of Library Administration* 38, no. 1/2 (2003): 101-107.

20. Patricia Smith, "Upstairs/downstairs: Implementing a processing center for restoring the collection," in *Library Disaster Planning and Recovery Handbook,* ed. Camila Alire (New York: Neal-Schuman Publishers, Inc., 2000), 361.

21. Balík and Polišensky, "The National Library of the Czech Republik and the floods of 2002," 17-24.

22. Suzuki and Togashi, "Halloween flood at University of Hawaii Library," 101-110. See also Andrew Albanese, "Floods cripple University of Hawaii Library," *Library Journal* 129, no. 20 (2004): 19; A.S., "Flash floods drench University of Hawaii Library," *American Libraries* 35, no. 11 (2004): 16.

23. Tara D. Kennedy, "Steamy situation: Water emergency in Sterling Memorial Library," *Public Library Quarterly* 25, no. 3/4 (2006): 89-97.

24. Adrienne Muir and Sarah Shenton, "If the worst happens; the use and effectiveness of disaster plans in libraries and archives," *Library Management* 23, no. 3 (2002): 115-123; Holderness, "Back from the brink of disaster," 17.

25. Paul Eden and Graham Matthews, "Disaster management in libraries," *Facilities* 15, no. ½ (1997): 42-49.

26. Constance L. Foster, "Damaged periodicals: A wet trial yields dry results," *Serials Review* 22, no. 1 (1996) : 33-39.

27. Holderness, "Back from the brink of disaster," 17.

28. University of New Mexico, University Libraries, "Zimmerman Library Basement Pack Back," https://libwiki.unm.edu//zimpackback/doku.php.

29. The Division of Latin American Resources and Services, a multi-departmental unit within the UNM University Libraries.

BIBLIOGRAPHY

SELECTED BIBLIOGRAPHY AND SUGGESTED READINGS

"The ABCs of Business Continuity and Disaster Recovery Planning." CSO: the Resource for Security Executives, 2008. http://www.csoonline.com/article/204450/Business_Continuity_and_Disaster_Recovery_Planning_The_Basics (December 14, 2009).

"ABTAPL Conference on Conservation and Disaster Planning, 31 March-2nd April 1989." *Bulletin of the Association of British Theological and Philosophical Libraries* 2, no. 6 (1989): 4–33.

"Acts of God (and Others)." CIO, 2008. http://www.cio.com/specialreports/infotechhorror/god.html ((December 14, 2009).

Adinku, Sarah. "Towards Disaster Preparedness and Recovery Planning Procedures for Libraries: A Survey of Staff and Users of the Balme Library, University of Ghana." *African Journal of Library, Archives and Information Science* 15, no. 1 (2005): 75–79.

Akussah, Harry. "The Preservation of Traditional Library and Archival Materials in the 'Harsh' Ghanaian Environment." *African Journal of Library, Archives and Information Science* 1, no. 1 (1991): 19–28.

Alder, G. Stoney. "Managing Environmental Uncertainty with Legitimate Authority: A Comparative Analysis of the Mann Gulch and Storm King Mountain Fires." *Journal of Applied Communication Research* 25, no. 2 (1997): 98–114.

Alegbeleye, Bunmi. "Disaster Control Planning in Nigeria." *Journal of Librarianship* 22, no. 2 (1990): 91–106.

Alexander, David. "Regional Disaster Preparedness and Recovery: A Project Proposal." *Colorado Libraries* 7, no. 3 (1981): 33–38.

Alire, Camila A. "And on the Eighth Day... Managing During the First Week of Library Disaster Recovery." *Colorado Libraries* 24, no. 3 (1998): 10–12.

————. *Library Disaster Planning and Recovery Handbook*. New York: Neal-Schuman, 2000.

————. "The Silver Lining: Recovering from the Shambles of a Disaster." *Journal of Library Administration* 38, no. 1/2 (2003): 101–107.

Amarasiri, Upali. "From Golden Water to Salvation: Tsunami-Affected Libraries in Sri Lanka." *Alexandria* 18, no. 3 (2006): 119–133.

————. "Rising from the Wreckage: Development of Tsunami-Affected Libraries in Sri Lanka." *IFLA Journal* 31, no. 4 (2005): 307–314.

American Association of Museums. "American Association of Museums." http://www.aam-us.org (December 14, 2009).

American Hospital Association. *American Hospital Association Resource Center Disaster Plan*. Chicago: American Hospital Association, 1993.

American Institute for Conservation of Historic & Artictic Works. http://www.conservation-us.org (December 14, 2009).

American Red Cross. "Picking up the Pieces after a Disaster." http://www.redcross.org/services/disaster/0,1082.0_23_,00.html (December 14, 2009).

Arnesen, S. J., V. H. Cid, J. C. Scott, R. Perez, and D. Zervaas. "The Central American Network for Disaster and Health Information." *Journal of the Medical Library Association* 95, no. 3 (2007): 316–322.

Arnoult, Jean-Marie. "Les Bibliotheques Irakiennes En 2003: Un Nouveau Chapitre De L'histoire Interminable Des Desastres. Libraries in Iraq in 2003: A New Chapter in the Never-Ending Story of Disasters." *International Preservation News* 30 (2003): 20–29.

Ashbaugh, E. "The Effects of Disasters Upon the Rural Library." *Rural Libraries* 23, no. 1 (2003): 7–20.

Ashley-Smith, Jonathan. *Risk Assessment for Object Conservation.* Oxford: Butterworth Heinemann, 1999.

Ashman, John. "Conservation Piece—Disaster Planning." *Scottish Libraries* 28, no. 91 (1991): 7.

Association of Moving Image Archivists. "AMIA." http://www.amianet.org (December 14, 2009).

Association of Research Libraries. Systems and Procedures Exchange Center. *Preparing for Emergencies and Disasters.* Washington, D.C.: Systems and Procedures Exchange Center, Association of Research Libraries Office of Management Studies, SPEC Kit 69, 1980.

Badu, Edwin Ellis. "The Preservation of Library Materials: A Case Study of University of Science and Technology Library in Ghana." *Aslib Proceedings* 42, no. 4 (1990): 119–125.

Baker, Richard C. "Ark Building Workshop for Worcester Librarians." *Conservation Administration News* 21, no. 85 (1985): 1–2.

Balas, Janet L. "No Rest for the Weary, or, a Systems Administrator's Work Is Never Done." *Computers in Libraries* 26, no. 1 (2006): 17–19.

Balík, Vojtech and Jirí Polišenski. "The National Library of the Czech Republic and the floods of 2002." *Alexandria* 16, no. 1 (2004): 17–24.

Ballofett, Melly, and Jenny Hille. *Preservation and Conservation for Libraries and Archives.* Chicago: American Library Association, 2004.

Barkley, Dan. "Emergency Preparedness During a Renovation." *dttp: Documents to the People* 35, no. 3 (2007): 25–26.

———. "The University of New Mexico, Zimmerman Library Fire." *dttp: Documents to the People* 35, no. 3 (2007): 28–30.

Barlak, K. "Emotional Coping Mechanisms in Times of Disasters." *New Jersey Libraries* 28, no. 3 (1995): 15.

Barr, Jean. "A Disaster Plan in Action: How a Law Firm in the World Trade Center Survived 9/11 with Vital Records and Employees Intact." *Information Management Journal* 37, no. 3 (2003): 28–29.

Batchelor, Keith. *Records Management: A Guide to Disaster Prevention and Recovery.* London: British Standards Institution, 1999.

Bazerman, Max H., and Michael D. Watkins. *Predictable Surprises: The Disasters You Should Have Seen Coming, and How to Prevent Them.* Boston MA: Harvard Business School Press, 2004.

Behrendt, Elizabeth C. " 'Drying-out' the U.S.G.S. Collection." *Colorado Libraries* 7, no. 3 (1981): 30–32.

Beinhoff, Lisa A. "Library Earthquake Preparedness Planning: How to Make Sure That Your Library Is Ready for the Big One." *Journal of Library Administration* 31, no. 1 (2000): 67–83.

Bell, Nancy. "Guidelines for Disaster Planning in the Oxford Colleges Conservation Consortium: 1—Disaster Prevention." *Bulletin of the Association of British Theological and Philosophical Libraries* 2, no. 6 (1989): 77–80.

Bender, Nathan E. "Recovering from Disasters: Restoration of Libraries." *Idaho Librarian* 58, no. 1/2 (2008).

Benefiel, C. R., and P. A. Mosley. "Coping with the Unexpected: A Rapid Response Group in an Academic Library." *Technical Services Quarterly* 17, no. 2 (1999): 25–36.

Bertot, John Carlo, Paul T. Jaeger, Lesley A. Langa, and Charles R. McClure. "Public Access Computing and Internet Access in Public Libraries: The Role of Public Libraries in E-Government and Emergency Situations." *First Monday* 11, no. 9 (2006): np. http://firstmonday.org/htbin/cgiwrap/bin/ojs/index.php/fm/article/view/1392/1310 (December 14, 2009).

Birkland, Thomas A. *Lessons of Disaster: Policy Change after Catastrophic Events*. Washington, D. C.: Georgetown University Press, 2006.

Blackwell, P. R. "A First Hand Account of the Columbia Space Shuttle Response and Recovery." *Western Association of Map Libraries Information Bulletin* 34, no. 2 (2003): 66–69.

Bohem, Hilda, and University of California (System). Task Group on the Preservation of Library Materials. *Disaster Prevention and Disaster Preparedness*. Berkeley: Office of the Assistant Vice President—Library Plans and Policies, Systemwide Administration, 1978.

Bolger, Laurie. "Scared or Prepared? Disaster Planning Makes the Difference." *Information Outlook* 7, no. 7 (2003): 26–30.

Boorstein, Michell. "Fire Claims Library, and Pieces of the Past." *Washington Post* May 1, 2007 (2007): 1.

Boutros, David, Michael Patrick Gillespie, and Sharron Uhler. *A Disaster Preparedness Manual for Eastern Kansas and Western Missouri: A Bibliography and Checklist for Archives, Libraries, Manuscript Collections, and Museums*. Kansas City, Mo.: Kansas City Area Archivists Publications Committee, General Services Administration, Federal Archives and Records Center (OIRM), 1983.

Boyd, J. "Disaster Recovery Plans: The Nottinghamshire Experience." *Managing Information* 1, no. 7/8 (1994): 33–35.

Brady, Eileen E. and John F. Guido. "When Is a Disaster Not a Disaster?" *Library and Archival Security* 8, no. ¾ (1988(: 11–23.

Brady, Mary Louise, Ilene F. Rockman, and David B. Walch. "Software for Patron Use in Libraries: Physical Access." *Library Trends* 40, no. 1 (1991): 63–84.

Breeding, Marshall. "Defending Your Library Network." *Information Today* 18, no. 8 (2001): 46–47.

Breighner, Mary, William Payton, and Jeanne M. Drewes. *Risk and Insurance Management Manual for Libraries*. Chicago: American Library Association: Library Administration & Management Association, 2005.

"British Library Announces Endangered Archives Program." *Advanced Technology Libraries* 33, no. 5 (2004): 7.

Britt, Phillip. "Taking Steps for Disaster Recovery." *Information Today* 22, no. 9 (2005): 1–21.

Brodart. http://www.brodart.com (December 14, 2009).

Brokerhof, Veerle Meul, Stefan Michalski, and Pedersolik Jose Luiz Jr. "Advancing Research in Risk Management Applications to Cultural Property." *ICCROM Newsletter*, no. 33, June 2008 (2007): 10–11.

Brooks, Constance, Pamela W. Darling, and Association of Research Libraries. *Disaster Preparedness*, Preservation Planning Program. Washington, DC: Association of Research Libraries, 1993.

Broughton, Susan. "Crisis Aftermath: A Role for the Public Library?" *Public Library Journal* 4, no. 4 (1989): 85–89.

Buchanan, Sally. "The Stanford Library Flood Restoration Project." *College and Research Libraries* 40, no. 6 (1979(: 539–548.

Buchanan, Sally A., and Toby Murray. "Disaster Planning, Preparedness and Recovery for Libraries and Archives: A RAMP Study with Guidelines." Paris, UNESCO, General Information Programme and UNISIST, 1988.

Burgess, Dean. "The Library Has Blown Up!" *Library Journal* 114, no. 16 (1989): 59–61.

Burst, Deb. "The New Ice Age." *Fine Books & Collections*, Sept/Oct (2007): 59–61.

Butler, Randall. "The Inland Empire Libraries Disaster Response Network." *Conservation Administration News* 34, no. 88 (1988): 8–9.

Butler, Randall, and Sheryl Davis. "IELDRN Stages Disaster Recovery Workshop." *Conservation Administration News* 40, no. 90 (1990): 1–3

Cady, Susan A. "Insuring the Academic Library Collection." *Journal of Academic Librarianship* 25, no. 3 (1999): 211–215.

Canadian Conservation Institute. "Canadian Conservation Institute." http://www.cci-icc.gc.ca (December 14, 2009).

Canos, J. H., G. Alonso, and J. Jaen. "A Multimedia Approach to the Efficient Implementation and Use of Emergency Plans." *IEEE Multimedia* 11, no. 3 (2004): 106–110.

Carpenter, Kathryn H. "Dealing with Disaster: An Interview with Camila Alire." *Library Administration & Management* 14, Fall (2000): 188–190.

Casey, Mary Lu. "Report on a Flood and Recovery Operations at Western Wyoming College." *Colorado Libraries* 7, no. 3 (1981): 18–23.

Cassell, Gracelyn. "Library Experiences with Natural Disasters: Hurricanes and Volcanoes (Monserrat)." *International Preservation News* 34 (2004): 4–11.

Cervone, H. Frank. "Disaster Recovery and Continuity Planning for Digital Library Systems." *OCLC Systems & Services* 22, no. 3 (2006): 173–178.

Chadwell, Faye A. "Planning for the Worst: When Disaster Strikes." *OLA Quarterly* 6, no. 3 (2007): 16–17.

Chartrand, R. L. "Emergency Preparedness and Response Challenges for Special Libraries." In *Proceedings of the 1995 Clinic on Library Applications of Data Processing, Graduate School of Library and Information Science, Illinois University at Urbana-Champaign, 10–12 Apr 1995.* Edited by Linda C. Smith and Myke Gluck, 173–9. Graduate School of Library and Information Science, Illinois University at Urbana-Champaign, 1995.

Cheng, Kirby. "Surviving Hacker Attacks Proves That Every Cloud Has a Silver Lining." *Computers in Libraries* 25, no. 3 (2005): 6–8.

Chiesa, Adele M. "Identifying the Emergency Management Profession." *Special Libraries* 78, no. 2 (1987): 88–92.

Childress, S. "Planning for the Worst: Disaster Planning in the Library." *Southeastern Librarian* 44, no. 2 (1994): 51–55.

Chua, Alton Y. K. "A Tale of Two Hurricanes: Comparing Katrina and Rita through a Knowledge Management Perspective." *Journal of the American Society for Information Science and Technology*, 58, no. 10 (2007): 1518–1528.

Clareson, Tom, and Jane S. Long. "Libraries in the Eye of the Storm: Lessons Learned from Hurricane Katrina." *American Libraries* 37, no. 7 (2006): 38–41.

Clifton, Gerard. "Risk and Preservation Management of Digital Collections." *International Preservation News* 36, Sept (2005): 21–23.

Cloonan, Michele V. "The Moral Imperative to Preserve." *Library Trends* 55, no. 3 (2007): 746–755.

Coates, P. R. "Planning for Disaster Control." In *Books in Peril: Proceedings of the Symposium on the Preservation of Library and Archival Materials in Southern Africa Held at the South African Library, Cape Town,*

51–61. Cape Town: The Library, 1987.

"Collection Protection." *Library of Congress Information Bulletin* 67, no. 1/2 (2008): 16.

Collins, Janet. "One Approach to Earthquake Preparedness." *Information Bulletin (Western Association of Map Librarians)* 27, July (1996): 128–129.

Colorado Library Association. *Disaster Planning.* Ft. Collins, Colo.: Colorado Library Association, 1981.

Computer Information Security and Protection. 1975-March, 1982 (Citations from the International Information Service for the Physics and Engineering Communities Data Base). Springfield, VA., National Technical Information Service, (1982).

Condic, Kristine S. "Using Second Life as a Training Tool in an Academic Library," *The Reference Librarian,* 50, no.4 (2009): 333–345.

Conservation Center for Art and Historic Artifacts "CCAHA." http://www.ccaha.org (December 14, 2009).

Conservation OnLine. "Conservation Online (Cool)." http://www.conservation-us.org (December 14, 2009).

Corrigan, Andy. "Disaster: Response and Recovery at a Major Research Library in New Orleans." *Library Management* 29, no. 4/5 (2008): 293–306.

———. "With a Bucket of Extremes: Saving an ARL-Size Library Collection in New Orleans." In *Sailing into the Future: Charting Our Destiny. Proceedings of the 13th National Conference of the Association of College & Research Libraries,* edited by Hugh A. Thompson, 83–91. Chicago: ALA, 2007.

Cotera, Maria. "Around the World in 20 Years: International Co-Operation Projects." *Library + Information Update* 6, no. 9 (2007): 38–41.

Coult, G. "Disaster Recovery." *Managing Information* 8, no. 8 (2001): 36–39.

Courtois, Martin P., and Claire B. Rubm. "Crisis, Disaster and Emergency Management." *College & Research Libraries News* 63, no. 10 (2002): 723–726.

Cravey, Pamela. *Protecting Library Staff, Users, Collections and Facilities: A How-to-Do-It Manual.* NY: Neal-Schuman Publishers Inc, 2001.

Cullhead, Peter. "The Linkoping Library Fire." *International Preservation News* 31 (2003): 4–8.

Cunha, George. "Disaster Planning and a Guide to Recovery Resources." *Library Technology Reports* 28, no. 5 (1992): 533–624.

Curley, M., and S. Hartman. "Disaster Response in a Small Institution: Labor Week Flood." *Colorado Libraries* 24, no. 3 (1998): 9.

Curzon, Susan Carol. "Coming Back from Major Disaster: Month One." *Public Library Quarterly* 25, no. 3/4 (2006): 17–29.

Cuthbert, S., and J. Doig. "Disaster Plans: Who Needs Them?" *Australian Academic and Research Libraries* 25, no. 1 (1994): 13–18.

Davis, Lynn Ann. "Riding the Surf: Dealing with Library Disasters in Island Communities." *Public Library Quarterly* 25, no. 3–4 (2006): 99–112.

Davis, Mary B., Susan Fraser, and Judith Reed. "Preparing for Library Emergencies: A Cooperative Approach." *Wilson Library Bulletin* 66, no. 3 (1991): 42–44.

Davis, Mary, and Ellen Kyger. "Flood Destroys North Dakota State University's Main Library." *College & Research Libraries News* 61, no. 8 (2000): 661.

Dawson, Alma, and Kathleen de la Pena McCook. "Rebuilding Community in Louisiana after the Hurricanes of 2005." *Reference & User Services Quarterly* 45, no. 4 (2006): 292–296.

Dearstyne, Bruce W. "Taking Charge: Disaster Fallout Reinforces RIM's Importance." *Information Management Journal* 40, no. 4 (2006): 37–42.

DeCandido, Robert, Cheryl Shackelton, New York Metropolitan Reference and Research Library Agency., and New York Metropolitan Reference and Research Library Agency, Conservation/Preservation Advisory Council. *Who Ya Gonna Call? A Preservation Services Sourcebook for Libraries and Archives*, Metro Miscellaneous Publication, New York: METRO, 1992.

Delaney, Tom. "Necessity Is the Mother of Virtuality." *Colorado Libraries* 24, no. 3 (1998): 13–15.

———. "The Day It Rained in Fort Collins, Colorado: Flood Damage and ILL at Colorado State University." *Journal of Interlibrary Loan, Document Delivery and Information Supply* 8, no. 4 (1998): 59–70.

DeLong, Linwood R. "Collecting Material on Natural Disasters: A Case Study in Co-Operative Collections Development." *Collection Management* 24, no. 1/2 (2000): 175–183.

DeLong, Linwood R. "Collections Development and the Red River Flood of 1997: A Case Study in Collecting Information on a Natural Disaster." *Feliciter* 43, no. 10 (1997): 18–21.

DePew, John N. "A Statewide Disaster Preparedness and Recovery Program for Florida Libraries." *Conservation Administration News* (1988) 33, no. 88.

———. "The Statewide Disaster Preparedness and Recovery Program for Florida Libraries: An Update." *Conservation Administration News* 37, no. 89 (1989): 6–7.

Diamond, Tom. "The Impact of Hurricanes Katrina and Rita on 3 Louisiana Academic Libraries." *Library Administration and Management* 20, no. 4 (2006): 192–200.

Dimattia, Susan Smith. "A Gem of a Plan." *Information Outlook* 11, no. 6 (2007): 26–32.

DiMattia, Susan Smith. "Planning for Continuity: Disaster Plans." *Library Journal* 126, no. 19 (2001): 32–34.

"Disaster Preparedness. (special issue)" *Southeastern Librarian* 44, no. 2 (1994): 47–74.

"Disaster Puts Focus on It, Electronic Information Systems." *Information Management Journal* 40, no. 4 (2006): 42–43.

Disaster Recovery Directory. Ashton MD: Edwards Information, 2008.

"Disaster Recovery Resource List." *Colorado Libraries* 24, no. 3 (1998): 31–36.

"Disaster Resource Guide." http://www.disaster-resource.com (December 14, 2009).

Doig, Judith. "Evacuation Procedures for Libraries." *Australasian College Libraries* 7, no. 1 (1989): 13–16.

Donnelly, H., and M. Heaney. "Disaster Planning—a Wider Approach." *Aslib Information* 21, no. 2 (1993): 69–71.

Dorge, Walerie, and Sharon L. Jones. *Building an Emergency Plan; a Guide for Museums and Other Cultural Institutions*. Los Angeles: Getty Conservation Institute, 1999.

Drabek, T. E. "Disaster Warning and Evacuation Responses by Private Business Employees." *Disasters* 25, no. 1 (2001): 76–94.

Dropkin, Murray. "Continuing Series on Disaster Planning: Fundraising in the Aftermath." *Nonprofit Report* 11, no. 8 (2002): 1–3.

———. "Crisis Intervention for Nonprofits: Responding to the Events of September 11, 2001 and Updating Your Organization's Disaster Plan." *Nonprofit Report* 11, no. 5 (2001): 1–4.

Dryden, D. "Disaster Plan for a Hospital Library." *Bibliotheca Medica Canadiana* 14, no. 3 (1993): 139–145.

Dubicki, Eleonora. "Surviving the Loss of Access to Print Periodicals." *Technical Services Quarterly* 23, no. 2 (2005): 1–17.

Eden, Paul, and Graham Matthews. "Disaster Management in Libraries." *Library Management* 17, no. 3

(1996): 5–12.

Ellis, Jamie. "Lessons Learned: The Recovery of a Research Collection After Hurricane Katrina." *Collection Building* 26 (2007): 108–111.

Eng, S. "How Technology and Planning Saved My Library at Ground Zero." *Computers in Libraries* 22, no. 4 (2002): 28–32.

England, Claire, and Karen Evans. *Disaster Management for Libraries: Planning and Process*. Ottawa: Canadian Library Association, 1988.

Enssle, H. "Security Following a Disaster: The Experience at Colorado State University Libraries." *Colorado Libraries* 24, no. 3 (1998): 16–18.

Ezennia, S. E. "Flood, Earthquake, Libraries and Library Materials." *Library and Archival Security* 13, no. 1 (1995): 21–27.

Faber, Michael J. "The Evolving Commercial Records Center Industry." *Information Management Journal* 35, no. 3 (2001): 4–9.

Fackerell, Reita. "So You Think You Are Ready for a Disaster? Don't Be So Sure…" *OLA Quarterly* 14, no. 4 (2008): 15–16.

Featherstone, Robin M., Becky J. Lyon, and Angela R. Ruffin. "Library Roles in Disaster Response: An Oral History Project by the National Library of Medicine." *Journal of the Medical Library Association* 96, no. 4 (2008): 343–350.

Ferguson, M. P. "Now What Do We Do? Training People to Manage Disasters." *Colorado Libraries* 24, no. 3 (1998): 27–30.

Fernandez de Zamora, Rosa Maria, and R. M. Fernandez de Zamora. "Libraries in the Mexico City Earthquake." *Information Development* 6, no. 3 (1990): 140–143.

"Few Organizations Have Effective Community Plans." *Information Management Journal* 37, no. 3 (2003): 7.

Fichter, Darlene. "Planning for the Unexpected." *Online* 29, no. 2 (2005): 51–53.

Fisher, S. "The Library Arsonist." *Colorado Libraries* 24, no. 3 (1998): 7–8.

Fisher, S. P., and T. K. Fry. "Security and Emergency Preparedness in a University Library: Planning Works." *Colorado Libraries* 23, no. 1 (1997): 9–11.

Fithian, Gail. "The Aftermath of the Flood at the Boston Public Library: Lessons Learned." *Proceedings of the 8th Annual Federal Depository Library Conference, April 12–15, 1999* (1999). http://www.access.gpo.gov/su_docs/fdlp/pubs/proceedings/99pro30.html (December 14, 2009).

Fleischer, S. Victor, and Mark J Heppner. "Disaster Planning for Libraries and Archives: What You Need to Know and How to Do It." *Library & Archival Security* 22, no. 2 (2009): 125–140.

Foot, Mirjam M. "Report of the Preservation Management Summer School Held at the Public Record Office and the British Library, 19th–23rd July 1999." *Liber Quarterly : the Journal of European Research Libraries* 9, no. 4 (1999): 511–515.

Forbes, Heather. "Preparation, Prevention and Practice: Attempting to Avoid Disasters at Canterbury Cathedral Archives." *Journal of the Society of Archivists* 24, no. 2 (2003): 189–197.

Fortson, Judith. *Disaster Planning and Recovery: A How-to-Do-It Manual for Librarians and Archivists*. NY: Neal-Schuman Publishers Inc, 1992.

Foster, Constance L. "Damaged periodicals: A wet trial yields dry results." *Serials Review* 22, no 1 (1996): 33–39.

Fritz, Mark. "Online Content: Mitigates Disasters." *EContent* 29, no. 1 (2006): 12–13.

Frost, Gary, and Randy Silverman. "Disaster Recovery in the Artifact Fields—Mississippi after Hurricane Katrina." *International Preservation News*, no. 37 (2005): 35–47.

Fu, Paul S. "Handling Water Damage in a Law Library." *Law Library Journal* 79, no. 4 (1987): 667–687.

Gallagher, Amanda Hall. "Communicating During Times of Crises: An Analysis of News Releases from the Federal Government before, During and after Hurricanes Katrina and Rita." *Public Relations Review* 33, no. 2 (2007): 217–219.

Gandy, Shawna. "Don't Go It Alone—Building Networks for Collaborative Emergency Preparedness." *OLA Quarterly* 14, no. 4 (2008): 2–4.

Ganong, Ray. "The Emergency of E-Vaulting." *Information Management Journal* 37, no. 1 (2001): 21–30.

Gee, Pat. "Kahuku Library Patrons Fuming at Vandals." *Star Bulletin* (September 8,2006) 11, no. 251. http://archives.starbulletin.com/2006/09/08/news/story11.html (December 16, 2009).

Genovese, Robert, Trish Taylor, and Edward White. *Disaster Preparedness Manual*. 2006 Revision. Buffalo NY: W. S. Hein, 2006.

George, S. C. "Library Disasters: Are You Prepared?" *College and Research Libraries News* 56, no. 2 (1995): 82–84.

George, Susan C. *Emergency Planning and Management in College Libraries*, Clip Note 7. Chicago: Association of College and Research Libraries, 1994.

George, Susan C., and Cheryl T. Naslund. "Library Disasters: A Learning Experience." *College and Research Libraries News* 47, no. 4 (1986): 251–257.

Georges, Jo-Ann. "Skills Development and Management for Disaster Mitigation Planning: The Specific Case of Electronic Equipment and Digital Data." *International Preservation News*, no. 34 (2004): 12–14.

Getty Conservation Institute. "The Conservation Institute." http://www.getty.edu/conservation (December 14, 2009).

Gibson, Ruth. "Disaster Planning: An Annotated Bibliography." *Bulletin of the Association of British Theological and Philosophical Libraries* 2, no. 6 (1989): 70–77.

Gillespie, Karen. "Elements in Developing a Library Emergency Plan." *Kentucky Libraries* 58, Summer (1994): 10–11.

Gorman, G. E., and Sydney J Shep, eds. *Preservation Management for Libraries, Archives and Museum*. London: Facet Pub, 2006.

Grabel, Joyce Ann. *Employer's Guide to Disaster Readiness and Recovery*. NY: Aspen Publishers, 2007.

Green, D. "After the Flood—Disaster Response and Recovery Planning." *Bulletin of the Medical Library Association* 78, no. 3 (1990): 303–305.

Greene, H. "Build It and They Will Come: Libraries and Disaster Preparedness." *North Carolina Libraries* 52, no. 1 (1994): 6–7.

Gregory, Peter. *IT Disaster Recovery for Dummies*. Chichester: John Wiley, 2007.

Griffen, Agnes M. "Potential Roles of the Public Library in the Local Emergency Management Program: A Simulation." *Special Libraries* 78, no. 2 (1987): 122–130.

Guerin, Lyn. "Canadian Emergency Preparedness Initiatives." *Library & Archival Security* 18, no. 2 (2003): 3–5.

Gugliotta, Terry. "Fire at University of New Mexico Library." *Public Library Quarterly* 25, no. 3/4 (2006): 61–69.

Gulik, S. H. "Your Disaster Plan: Does It Cover Everything?" *New Jersey Libraries* 28, no. 3 (1995): 6–7.

Haddow, George D., *Disaster Communications in a changing Media World*. Burlington, VT.: Elsevier Butterworth-Hein, 2009.

Haddow, George D., Jane A Bullock, and Damon P. Coppola. *Introduction to Emergency Management*. 3rd ed. Amsterdam: Elsevier/Butterworth-Heinemann, 2008.

Hadgraft, Nicholas. "Disaster Planning in Small Libraries." *Bulletin of the Association of British Theological and Philosophical Libraries* 2, no. 6 (1989): 21–33.

Haines, M. "Physical Hazards and Post-Trauma Problems." *New Jersey Libraries* 28, no. 3 (1995): 11–12.

Halsted, Deborah D., Richard P. Jasper, and Felicia M. Little. *Disaster Planning: A How-to-Do-It Manual for Librarians*. NY: Neal-Schuman Publishers Inc, 2005.

Hammond, Hillary. "Norfolk and Norwich Central Library: The Emerging Phoenix." *New Library World*. 97, no 6 (1996): 24–31.

Harrison, Alice W. "Conservation of Library Materials [Clip No. 10]." *APLA Bulletin* 43, no. 1 (1979).

Harvey, Ross. "Lessons from 'Lessons from Leningrad'." *Australian Academic and Research Libraries* 20, no. 3 (1989): 149–153.

Hendrix, Lolita. "Will You Be Ready When Disaster Strikes?" *Nonprofit World* 18, no. 3 (2000): 32–37.

Henson, Stephen. "Writing the Disaster Response Plan: Going Beyond Shouting "Help! Help!." *Proceedings of the 9th Annual Federal Depository Library Conference, October 22–25* (2000). http://www.access.gpo.gov/su_docs/fdlp/pubs/proceedings/00pro28.html

Heritage Preservation. *A Public Trust at Risk: The Heritage Health Index Report on the State of America's Collections*: Heritage Preservation, 2005.

———. "Emergency Response and Salvage Wheel." 2005.

———. *Field Guide to Emergency Response*. Heritage Preservation, 2006.

———. "Heritage Preservation." http://www.heritagepreservation.org (December 14, 2009).

Hewison, Hazel. "Disaster Planning and Recovery—the Caribbean Experience." *Legal Information Management* 5, no. 3 (2005): 185–188.

Higginbotham, Barbra B. "Before Disaster Strikes; Be Prepared." *Technicalities* 15, July (1995): 4–5.

———. "It Ain't over 'Til It's Over: The Process of Disaster Recovery." *Technicalities* 16, no. 5 (1996): 12–13.

———. "Practical Preservation Practice—Managing Emergencies; Small Construction Projects." *Technicalities* 16, no. 9 (1996): 12–14.

Holden, Paul. " 'Heaven Helps Those Who Help Themselves': The Realities of Disaster Planning." *Journal of the Society of Archivists* 25, no. 1 (2004): 27–32.

Houk, Judy. "Cardboard Was the Culprit." *Colorado Libraries* 7, no. 3 (1981): 28.

Howes, Robert. "After the Disaster: Drawing up the Insurance Claim." *Aslib Proceedings* 55, no. 3 (2003): 181–187.

Image Permanence Institute. "Image Permanence Institute." http://www.imagepermanenceinstitute.org (December 14, 2009).

"International Committee of the Blue Shield: What's New?" *International Preservation News* (2000): 25.

International Preservation News #34 Dec 2004. (Special Issue on disasters).

"Iowa Libraries Bear Brunt of Midwest Floods." *American Libraries* 39, no. 7 (August) (2008): 22–23.

Jaeger, Don, Kristen Kern, and Susan E. Parker. "What to Do When Disaster Strikes: The California State University, Northridge, Experience." *Serials Librarian* 44, no. 3/4 (2003): 237–242.

Janis, Irving L. *Crucial Decisions: Leadership in Policymaking and Crisis Management*. NY: Free Press, 1989.

Jokilehto, Jukka. "Training as an Essential Part of Risk Preparedness." ICOMOS International Council on Monuments and Sites, http://www.international.icomos.org/risk/2001/training2001.htm (December 14, 2009).

Jones, K. "Disaster! Experience, Recovery, Mitigation." *Colorado Libraries* 24, no. 3 (1998): 3–36.

Jones, Virginia A. "How to Develop an Emergency Management Plan." *Information Management Journal* 42, no. 2 (2008): 52–56.

Jones, Virginia A., and Kris E. Keyes. *Emergency Management for Records and Information Programs.* Prairie Village, KS: ARMA International, 2001.

Jones, Willie M. "Trial by Tornado." *InfoPro,* March 2000 (2000): 37–39.

Kahn, M. "Fires, Earthquakes and Floods: How to Prepare Your Library and Staff." *Online* 18, no. 3 (1994): 19–24.

Kahn, Miriam B. *Disaster Response and Planning for Libraries.* 2 ed. Chicago: ALA, 2003.

———. *Protecting Your Library's Digital Sources: The Essential Guide to Planning and Preservation.* Chicago: American Library Association, 2004.

———. *The Library Security and Safety Guide to Prevention, Planning, and Response.* Chicago: American Library Association, 2008.

Kahn, Miriam B., and Barbra B. Higginbotham. "Disasters for Directors: The Role of the Library or Archive Director in Disaster Preparedness and Recovery." *Advances in Preservation and Access* 2 (1995): 400–412.

Kallenberg, Greg. "Using the Web to Respond to 9/11." *Information and Referral* 24, no. 28 (2002): 27–34.

Kane, Kim. "You Too Can Do a Disaster Plan." *Library Mosaics* 12, no. 2 (2001): 12–13.

Kautzman, Amy. "LOMS Risk Management & Insurance Committee." *Library Administration & Management* 22, no. 1 (2008): 56.

Kelly, Michael. "Library Disaster Planning in Colorado." *Colorado Libraries* 7, no. 2 (1981): 18–25.

Kennedy, Tara D. "Steamy Situation: Water Emergency in Sterling Memorial Library." *Public Library Quarterly* 25, no. 3/4 (2006): 89–97.

Kern, Kristen. "Along the Oregon Trail: Disaster Preparedness in Oregon Libraries and Archives." *OLA Bulletin* 14, no. 4 (2008): 17–19.

———. "It's an Emergency: The Portland State University Library Flood." *OLA Quarterly* 14, no. 4 (2008): 11–14.

Kidd, T. "United Kingdom Serials Group: Nineteenth Annual Conference and Exhibition." *Library Acquisitions: Practice and Theory* 20, no. 4 (1996): 475–482.

King, Ian P. G. "Disaster Librarianship: The Bradford City Fire Disaster Information Service." *Health Libraries Review* 3, no. 3 (1986): 160–163.

Klasson, Maj. "Psychological Effects of the Linkoping Fire (and Some Strategies for Overcoming the Problems in the First Few Months)." In *Disaster and After: the Practicalities of Information Service in Times of War and Other Catastrophes,* edited by Paul Sturges and Diana Rosenberg, 51–70. London: Taylor Graham, 1999.

———. "Rhetoric and Realism: Young User Reactions on the Linkoping Fire and Its Consequences for Education and Democracy." *Library Review* 51, no. 3/4 (2002): 171–180.

Klieman, Aaron S. "Crisis Leadership and Non-Communication: Marcos of the Philippines." *Political Communication & Persuasion* 1, no. 1 (1980): 43–78.

Knisely, Susan, and Shannon Behrhorst. "Disaster Planning for Your Library." *Nebraska Library Association Quarterly* 37, no. 1 (2006): 8–14.

Knoche, Michael. "The Herzogin Anna Amalia Library after the Fire." *IFLA Journal* 31, no. 1 (2005): 90–92.

Koivunen, Hannele. "Tsunami, Ethics and Information: The Right to Information as an Ethical Civil Right." *Scandinavian Public Library Quarterly* 1 (2005): 4–7.

Kulczak, Deborah E. "A Decade of Disaster: A Selected Bibliography of Disaster Literature 1985–1991." *Library & Archival Security* 15, no. 1 (1999): 7–66.

Kuzyk, Raya. "Serving through Disaster." *Library Journal* 132, no. 5 (2007): 26–29.

LEED Management Services. *How-To Guide to LEED® Certification for New Mexico Buildings.* Lafayette, CO: LEED Management Services, 2007.

Lashley, Beverley. "Cooperative Disaster Planning for Libraries: A Model." *International Preservation News* 31 (2003): 26–33.

Law, D. "Disaster and After: An Introduction." In *Disaster and after: the practicalities of information service in times of war and other catastrophes. Proceedings of an international conference sponsored by IGLA (The International Group of the Library Association), 4–6 September 1998, University of Bristol,* edited by Paul Sturges and Diana Rosenberg, 3–7. London : Taylor Graham, (1998).

Lazarev, V. S. "Chernobyl-Related Databases in the Republic of Belarus: Their International Potential." *Health Libraries Review* 15, no. 1 (1998): 41–44.

Lederer, N., and D. J. Ernest. "Managing the Media During a Library Crisis." *American Libraries* 33, no. 11 (2002): 32–33.

Lee-Hsia Hsu Ting. "Library Services in the People's Republic of China: A Historical Overview." *Library Quarterly* 53, no. 2 (1983): 134–160.

Leighton, Philip D. "The Stanford Flood." *College and Research Libraries* 40, no 5 (1979): 450–459.

Leighton, Philip D., and David C. Weber. *Planning Academic and Research Library Buildings.* Chicago: American Library Association, 1999.

Lewis, A. "The Newcastle Earthquake Library and Database: An Initiative of the Newcastle Region Public Library." *Australasian Public Libraries and Information Services* 6, no. 3 (1993): 101–106.

Liebsch, Bill, and Janet Liebsch. *It's a Disaster—and What Are You Gonna Do About It: A Disaster Preparedness, Prevention & Basic First Aid Manual.* 4 ed. Tucson AZ: Fedhealth, 2005.

Line, M. B. "Management Musings 9: Extracting Pearls from Rotten Oysters." *Library Management* 23, no. 8/9 (2002): 435–436.

Littlefield, Robert S., and Andrea M. Quenette. "Crisis Leadership and Hurricane Katrina: The Portrayal of Authority by the Media in Natural Disasters." *Journal of Applied Communication Research* 35, no. 1 (2007): 26–47.

Loewenstein, P. "Montserrat Book-Aid Project: The Final Lap." *Assistant Librarian* 86, no. 4 (1993): 52–53.

Loftus, Joan. "Disasters: Plans, Clean-up and Recovery at Stanford University Libraries." *Proceedings of the 8th Annual Federal Depository Library Conference, April 12–15, 1999,* (1999). http://www.access.gpo.gov/su_docs/fdlp/pubs/proceedings/99pro32.html (December 16, 2009).

Lunde, Diane B. "Aftermath of a Disaster: Establishing a Rebinding Program." *New Library Scene* 17, June (1998): 10–13.

———. "The Disaster at Colorado State University Libraries: Recovery and Restoration of the Collection." *Colorado Libraries* 24, no. 3 (1998): 22–26.

————. "Preservation: Staff Training for Disaster Response." *Colorado Libraries* 34, no. 4 (2008): 29–30.

————. "What Do You Do With 426, 500 Wet Books: Or, Options for Restoring a Water-Damaged Collection." *Library Journal* 129, Dec. Supplement (1999): 6–7.

————. "When Disaster Strikes: A Case Study: Colorado State University Libraries, July 28, 1997." *Serials Librarian* 26, (1999): 363–382.

Lunde, Diana B, and Patricia A Smith. "Disaster and Security: Colorado State Style." *Library & Archival Security* 22, no. 2 (2009): 99–114.

MacKenzie, G. P. "Working for the Protection of the World's Cultural Heritage: The International Committee of the Blue Shield." *Journal of the Society of Archivists* 21, no. 1 (2000): 5–10.

McCarthy, Richard C., *Managing Your Library Construction Project: A Step-by-Step Guide.* Chicago: American Library Association, 2007.

Manley, Will. "Facing the Public." *Wilson Library Bulletin* 55, no. 9 (1981): 686–687.

Martin, Susan K. *Insuring and Valuing Research Library Collections.* Washington, D.C.: Systems and Procedures Exchange Center, Association of Research Libraries Office of Management Studies, ARL SPEC Kit 272 (2002).

Maslen, Colin. "Testing the Plan Is More Important Than the Plan Itself." *Information Management and Computer Security* 4, no. 3 (1996): 26–29.

Massey, Mary E. (Tinker). "Something to Think About—a Moment's Destruction." *Against the Grain* 19, no. 1 (2007): 55.

Matthews, Fred W. "Sorting a mountain of books." *Library Resources and Technical Services* 31, no 1 (1987): 88–94.

Matthews, Graham. "Disaster Management: Sharing Experience, Working Together across the Sector." *Journal of Librarianship and Information Science* 37, no. 2 (2005): 63–74.

Matthews, Graham. "Disasters in Libraries: Guidelines from Loughborough." *Serials* 9, no. 3 (1996): 245–250.

Matthews, Graham, and John Feathers, eds. *Disaster Management for Libraries and Archives.* Aldershot, Hampshire, UK: Ashgate, 2003.

Matthews, Graham, Yvonne Smith, and Gemma Knowles. "Disaster Management in Archives, Libraries and Museums: An International Overview." *Alexandria* 19, no. 1 (2007): 1–22.

————. *Disaster Management in Archives, Libraries, and Museums.* Aldershot, Hants, England; Burlington, VT : Ashgate, 2009.

————. "The Disaster Control Plan: Where Is It At?" *Library & Archival Security* 19, no. 2 (2004): 3–23.

McClung, Scott. "OCC Annual Meeting." *Conservation Administration News* 45, no. 91 (1991): 14–15.

McColgin, Michael, Bonnie E. Farnon, Sid Freyer, Jim Nocera, Linda Slusar, Pam Klein, College of DuPage., College of DuPage. Satellite Network., and American Library Association. *Disaster Planning.* Chicago: American Library Association, 2000.

McCracken, Peter H. "The Critical Inadequacy: Disaster Planning in Libraries and Museums." University of North Carolina, 1995. MA thesis.

McEntire, David A. *Disaster Response and Recovery: Strategies and Tactics for Resilience.* Hoboken, NJ: Wiley, 2007.

McGinty, John. "Insuring Libraries against Risk." *Library & Archival Security* 21, no. 2 (2008): 177–186.

McGlown, K. Joanne. *Terrorism and Disaster Management: Preparing Healthcare Leaders for the Reality.* Chicago: Health Administration Press, 2004.

McIlwaine, John. *IFLA Disaster Preparedness and Planning: A Brief Manual*, International Preservation Issues. Paris: International Federation of Library Associations, 2006.

McIntyre, John E. "A Dual Approach to Risk Management." *Liber Quarterly : the Journal of European Research Libraries* 8, no. 4 (1998): 448–457.

———. "Disaster Control Planning." *Serials* 1, no. 2 (1988): 42–46.

———. "Disaster Control Planning: A National Concern?" *Alexandria* 2, no. 2 (1990): 51–60.

McKnight, Michelynn. "Health Sciences Librarians' Reference Services During a Disaster: More Than Collection Protection." *Medical Reference Services Quarterly* 25, no. 3 (2006): 1–12.

McNutt, John G. "Electronic Government, the Internet, and Disasters." *dttp: Documents to the People* 34, no. 1 (2006): 17–21.

Merrill, Andrea T. *The Strategic Stewardship of Cultural Resources: To Preserve and Protect*. NY: Haworth Information Press, 2003.

Meyer, Lars. *Safeguarding Collections at the Dawn of the 21st Century: Describing Roles and Measuring Contemporary Preservation Activities in ARL Libraries*. Washington DC: Association of Research Libraries, 2009.

Miller, R. Bruce. "Libraries and Computer: Disaster Prevention and Recovery." *Information Technology and Libraries* 7, no. 4 (1988): 349–358.

Miller, William. "Natural Disasters in the Academic Library." *Library Issues* 28, no. 3 (2008): 1–2.

Miller, William, and Rita M. Pellen. *Dealing with Natural Disasters in Libraries*. Binghamton, NY: Haworth Information Press, 2006.

Milles, James G. "Managing After a Disaster: Or There And Back Again." *Legal Reference Services Quarterly* 25, no 1 (2006): 59–75.

Moon, Myra Jo. "A Report on the Colorado Disaster Prevention and Preparedness Workship." *Colorado Libraries* 7, no. 3 (1981): 39–44.

Moothart, Tom. "Muddy Waters Bring the Library Blues and Enhanced Electronic Access to Journals." *Serials Review* 23, Winter (1997): 79–82.

Morgan, G., and J. G. Smith. "Disaster Management in Libraries: The Role of a Disaster Plan." *South African Journal of Library and Information Science* 65, no. 1 (1997): 62–71.

Morris, John. *The Library Disaster Preparedness Handbook*. Chicago: American Library Association, 1986.

Morton, D. "Natural Hazards Research and Applications Information Center." *Colorado Libraries* 19, no. 4 (1993): 25.

Muir, Adrienne, and Sarah Shenton. "If the Worst Happens: The Use and Effectiveness of Disaster Plans in Libraries and Archives." *Library Management* 23, no. 3 (2002): 115–123.

Mullin, Christopher G., C. Peake, Anne Van Sickle, Karen Labuik, and Bruce Evans. "[Special Issue on Planning for Disaster.]." *PNLA Quarterly* 60, no. 3 (1996): 11–15.

Murray, Toby, and Oklahoma Conservation Congress. *Basic Guidelines for Disaster Planning in Oklahoma*. [Oklahoma: Oklahoma Conservation Congress?], 1991.

Murray-Rust, Catherine. "President's Column." *Library Administration and Management* 20, no. 1 (2006): 2.

Musser, L. "Internet Information on Hazards and Disasters: Resources for Researchers." *Science and Technology Libraries* 16, no. 1 (1996): 11–18.

Musser, L., and L. Recupero. "Internet Resources on Disasters." *College and Research Libraries News* 58, no.

6 (1997): 403–407.

Myers, James N., and Denise D. Bedford. *Disasters: Prevention and Coping. Proceedings of the Conference, 21–22 May, 1980.* Stanford, CA.: Stanford University Libraries (1981).

Myers, Kenneth N. *Business Continuity Strategies: Protecting against Unplanned Disasters.* 3 ed. Hoboken, NJ: Wiley, 2006.

Myree, Simone. "Fire Suppression and Water Mist Systems." *Library & Archival Security* 21, no. 2 (2008): 169–174.

Nannestad, E. "Emergency Planning: Report of a Workshop." *Local Studies Librarian* 21, no. 1 (2002): 7–9.

National Preservation Institute. "National Preservation Institute." http://www.npi.org . (December 14, 2009).

National Trust for Historic Preservation. "National Trust for Historic Preservation." http://www.preservationnation.org (December 14, 2009).

Nelson, J. "Safety in the Public Library." *Show Me Libraries* 44, no. 2 and 3 (1993): 36–38.

Nevins, Kate, and Sandra Nyberg. "Solinet's Gulf Coast Libraries Recovery Projects for Public and Academic Libraries." *Public Library Quarterly* 25, no. 3–4 (2006): 215–223.

Ngulube, Patrick, and Lindiwe Magazi. "A Stitch in Time Saves Nine: Emergency Preparedness in Public Libraries of Kwazulu-Natal, South Africa." *Innovation*, no. 32 (2006): 110–124.

———. "Protecting Documents against Disasters and Theft: The Challenge before the Public Libraries in Kwazulu-Natal, South Africa." *South African Journal of Libraries and Information Science* 72, no. 3 (2006): 185–197.

Norris, Debbie Hess. *Disaster Recovery. Salvaging Photograph Collections.* Philadelphia: Conservation Center for Art and Historic Artifacts, 1998.

Northeast Document Conservation Center. "Northeast Document Conservation Center." http://www.nedcc.org/home.php (December 14, 2009).

Norton, Judith. "Disaster Planning Resources." *OLA Quarterly* 14, no. 4 (2008): 23–26.

———. "Nuts and Bolts of Writing a Disaster Plan." *OLA Quarterly* 14, no. 4 (2008): 6–10.

Nowakowski, A. "The Polish Floods of 1997: The Poznan Perspective." *Disaster and after: the practicalities of information service in times of war and other catastrophes. Proceedings of an international conference sponsored by IGLA. (The International Group of the Library Association), 4–6 September 1998, University of Bristol,* edited by Paul Sturges and Diana Rosenberg, 81–89. London: Taylor Graham, (1998).

O'Connell, Mildred. "Disaster Planning: Writing and Implementing Plans for Collections-Holding Institutions." *Technology & Conservation* 8, Summer (1983): 18–24.

O'Neill, R. K. "Management of Library and Archival Security: From the Outside Looking In." *Journal of Library Administration* 25, no. 1 (1998): 1–112.

Obokoh, N. P. "Coping with flood disaster; The experience of a university library." *Library Review* 40, no. 6 (1991): 22–29.

Obokoh, N. P. "Disaster Control Planning in Nigerian Libraries and Archives." *African Journal of Academic Librarianship* 7, no. 1 and 2 (1989): 41–48.

Oehlerts, Beth. "Inventory: Risk Identification and More." *Library & Archival Security* 22, no. 2 (2009): 73–83.

Ogawa, Chiyoko. "Disaster Planning and Assistance Activities in the Field of Archives and Records Management." *Journal of Information Processing and Management* 48, no. 1 (2005): 390–395.

Ogden, Sherelyn. "Security from Loss: Water and Fire Damage, Biological Agents, Thefts, and Vandalism." *Rare Books & Manuscript Librarianship* 11, no. 1 (1996): 43–47.

Ogden, Sherelyn, and Northeast Document Conservation Center. *Preservation of Library & Archival Materials: A Manual*. 3rd ed. Andover, Mass.: Northeast Document Conservation Center, 1999.

Oliber, Marshall. "A Librarian Copes with Disaster in New Orleans." *Library Media Connection* 24, no. 7 (2006): 18–21.

Olle-LaJoie, Maureen. "Hurricane Katrina." *dttp: Documents to the People* 35, no. 3 (2007): 35–37.

Owens, Brian M., and Christopher Brown-Syed. "Not in Our Stars: The University of Windsor Archives and Library Disaster Plan." *Library & Archival Security* 14, no. 1 (1998): 61–66.

Page, Julie A. "Exercising Your Disaster Plans: A Tabletop Drill." *Conservation Administration News* 54, no. 93 (1993): 8–9.

Page, Julie A. "In an Emergency: Salvaging Library Collections." *Serials Librarian* 40, no. 1/2 (2001): 19–30.

Page, Julie A. "Ten Things You Need to Know before Disaster Strikes." http://www.infopeople.org/training/webcasts/webcast_data/196/index.html (December 14, 2009).

———. "When Disaster Strikes: First Steps in Disaster Preparedness." *Serials Librarian* 36, no. 3/4 (1999): 347–361.

Pagel, S. B., and J. L. Hoover. "Collection Management in the Automated Law Library." In *Law librarianship. A handbook for the electronic age*. Edited by Patrick E. Kehoe, Lovisa Lyman and Gary Lee McCann, 445–477. Littleton, CO: Fred B. Rothman and Co. for the American Association of Law Libraries, 1995.

Palmer, Gayle. "Digitization, Can It Play a Role in Disaster Preparedness? Notes from the Field." *OLA Quarterly* 14, no. 4 (2008): 20–22.

Palmer, Michael. "North Wales Coast Flood Disaster. Crisis Information Provision." *Public Library Journal* 6, no. 2 (1991): 33–39.

Pampel, Fred C. *Disaster Response*. NY: Facts on File, 2008.

Partridge, S., and K. Jones. "Disaster Resources in Colorado Courtesy of the Colorado Preservation Alliance." *Colorado Libraries* 24, no. 3 (1998): 42.

Paton, Douglas, and Rhona Flin. "Disaster Stress: An Emergency Management Perspective." *Disaster Prevention and Management* 8, no. 4 (1999): 261–267.

Patterson, Robert H. "Disaster Planning in Wyoming: Preface." *Colorado Libraries* 7, no. 2 (1981): 26–28.

Patton, Susannah. "Disaster Recovery: Captain Contingency." *CIO*, March 1, (2006). http://www.cio.com/article/17927/Logistics_Expert_Yossi_Sheffi_Talks_Disaster_Recovery (December 14, 2009).

Payton, Annie Malessia, and Theodosia T. Shields. "Insurance and Library Facilities." *Library & Archival Security* 21, no. 2 (2008): 187–193.

Perry, Ryan. "The Great University of Georgia Libraries Fire of '03: Lessons Learned and Questions Raised." *Public Library Quarterly* 25, no. 3–4 (2006): 71–88.

Emergencies." *Agricultural Libraries Information Notes* 4, no. 12 (1978): 1–3.

Plassard, Marie-France, and Marie-Therese Varlamoff. "Survey on Disaster Planning in National Libraries." *International Preservation News* 34 (2004): 23–28.

Plotnik, Art, and Susan Brandehoff. "Major Database Disasters; Could They Happen Here?" *American Libraries* 14, no. 10 (1983): 645–647.

Pollonais, Steve. "Risks Associated with Hurricanes in the Caribbean." *International Preservation News*, no. 34 (2004): 15–18.

Preiss, Lydia. "Learning from Disasters: A Decade of Experience at the National Library of Australia." *International Preservation News* 20 (1999): 19–26.

Press, Nancy Ottman. *Expect the Worst : Disaster Planning for the Small Library*. Seattle, Wash.: National Network of Libraries, Pacific Northwest Region, 1992.

Protext. http://www.protext.net (December 14, 2009).

Ragsdale, K. W., and J. Simpson. "Being on the Safe Side." *College and Research Libraries News* 57, no. 6 (1996): 351–354.

Ratcliffe, Fred W. "Conservation, Preservation, Disasters and Disaster Planning." *Bulletin of the Association of British Theological and Philosophical Libraries* 2, no. 6 (1989): 4–12.

Rayward, W. Boyd, and Christine Jenkins. "Libraries in Times of War, Revolution, and Social Change (a Special Issue)." *Library Trends* 55, no. 3 (2007).

Rea, Gavin. "Open 24 Hours at the University of Bath Library and Learning Centre." *Assignation* 20, no. 4 (2003): 47–49.

Regional Alliance for Preservation. "Regional Alliance for Preservation." http://www.rap-arcc.org (December 14, 2009).

Reinsch, M. "Library Disasters and Effective Staff Management." *Conservation Administration News* 55, no. 93 (1993): 4–5.

Rhodes, Barbara J. "Preservation at the AMNH Library." *Conservation Administration News* 44, no. 91 (1991): 27–29.

Rice, Diane B. "First Response to Disasters for Small Museums and Libraries." *PNLA Quarterly* 70, no. 3 (2006): 4.

Rightmeyer, S. P. "Disaster Planning, or, the 'What Next' Attitude." *New Jersey Libraries* 28, no. 3 (1995): 3.

Rike, Barb. "Prepared or Not: That Is the Vital Question." *Information Management Journal* 37, no. 3 (2003): 25–33.

Riley, Julie, and A. J. Meadows. "The Role of Information in Disaster Planning: A Case Study Approach." *Library Management* 16, no. 4 (1995): 18–24.

Ritzenthaler, Mary Lynn, and Diane Vogt-O'Connor. *Photographs: Archival Care and Management*. Chicago: Society of American Archivists, 2006.

Roberts, Barbara O. "Speaking Out: Establishing a Disaster Prevention/Response Plan: An International Perspective and Assessment." *Technology & Conservation*, Winter (1992/3): 15–7, 35–36.

Robertson, Davenport. "SLA's Response to Natural Disasters." *Information Outlook* 9, no. 10 (2005): 22–26.

Robertson, Guy. "A Van and a Plan: How Consortium Offices Can Contribute to Disaster Recovery." *Feliciter* 49, no. 6 (2003): 302–304.

———. "Beyond Band-Aid Solutions: Dealing with Medical Emergencies in Your Library." *Feliciter* 53, no. 1 (2007): 34–36.

———. "Disaster? No Plan? What a Library Director Should Do." *Feliciter* 54, no. 4 (2008): 175–177.

———. "Hoping for the Best, Preparing for the Worst: A Disaster Planner's Experience." *Feliciter* 41 (1995): 20–25.

———. "Investigating Risk: Assessing and Analyzing Trouble before It Strikes." *Feliciter* 48, no. 1 (2002): 30–32.

———. "Lights Out! Dealing with Power Outages in Your Library." *Feliciter* 50, no. 4 (2004): 156–158.

———. "People, Paper, Data: Disaster Planning for Libraries." *Disaster Recovery Journal* 10, no. 1 (1997):

38–43.

———. "Postponing Alexandria: Dealing with Catastrophes and Disasters in Your Library." *Feliciter* 51, no. 6 (2005): 277–279.

———. "Water Finds a Way: Dealing with Leaks and Floods in Your Library." *Feliciter* 51, no. 2 (2005): 83–85.

Robison, B., and G. E. Marlatt. "Libraries in the War on Terrorism." *Online* 30, no. 5 (2006): 39–42.

Rosenberg, D. "Disaster and After: IGLA's 1998 Residential Conference." *Focus on International and Comparative Librarianship* 29, no. 3 (1998): 195–197.

Rosenwinkel, Heather G., and Oregon Health Sciences University. Library. *Oregon Health Sciences University Library Disaster Preparedness and Recovery Plan.* Portland, OR.: Oregon Health Sciences University Library, 1991.

Rugger, Christine, and Elliott Morse. "The recovery of water-damaged books at the College of Physicians of Philadelphia." *Library and Archival Security* 3, no. 3/4 (1980): 23–28.

Ruyle, Carol J., and Elizabeth M. Schobernd. "Disaster Recovery without the Disaster." *Technical Services Quarterly* 14, no. 4 (1997): 13–26.

Ruzicka, Glen. *Disaster Recovery: Salvaging Books.* Philadelphia: Conservation Center for Art and Historic Artifacts, 2002.

Safran, Franciska, and Barbara Vaughan. "The Charting of the Western New York Disaster Preparedness Network." *Conservation Administration News* 61, April (1995): 10–13.

Samek, Toni, Keith McPherson, Jeanne Buckley, Phil Gold, and Elaine Harger. "[Destruction of United Talmud Torah Grade School Library]." *School Libraries in Canada* (special issue) 23, no. 4 (2004).

Sannwald, William W. *Checklist of Library Building Design Considerations.* Chicago: American Library Association, 2009.

Savage, Noelle. "Facing up to Library Security." *Wilson Library Bulletin* 58, no. 8 (1984): 562–564.

Schink, Michael Lee. "Selecting Disaster Recovery Software." *Colorado Libraries* 25, no. 1 (1999): 38–39.

Schlotzhauer, Nonny. "Disaster Relief: Starting Points for Learning." *College & Research Libraries News* 67, no. 2 (2006): 91–96.

Schmidt, Fred C. "Disasters: Plans, Clean-up, and Recovery—the Colorado State Experience." *Proceedings of the 8th Annual Federal Depository Library Conference, April 12–15, 1999* (1999).

Schobernd, Elizabeth. "Lessons from a library fire." *College and Undergraduate Libraries* 5, no 2 (1998): 43–51.

Schoenberg, Allan. "Do Crisis Plans Matter? A New Perspective on Leading During a Crisis." *Public Relations Quarterly* 50, no. 1 (2005): 2–6.

Schultz, Anne. "The University of New Mexico, Centennial Science and Engineering Library." *dttp: Documents to the People* 35, no. 3 (2007): 26–28.

Scott, R. "FEMA and NHC Web Sites." *North Carolina Libraries* 57, no. 3 (1999): 121.

Shankar, Kalpana. "Wind, Water and Wi-Fi: New Trends in Community Informatics and Disaster Management." *Information Society* 22, no. 2 (2008): 116–120.

Shaw, Graham. "Assessment of Damage to Libraries and Archives in Iraq." *Library Times International* 19, no. 4 (2003): 11.

Sheldon, Ted P., and Gordon O. Hendrickson. "Emergency Management and Academic Library Resources." *Special Libraries* 78, no. 2 (1987): 93–99.

Shimmon, Ross. "The International Committee of the Blue Shield 1998–2004: An Overview." *Alexandria* 16, no. 3 (2004): 133–141.

Shorley, D. "Disaster Planning: 'in the End You Just Cope'." *Library + Information Update* 2, no. 3 (March) (2003): 46–47.

Short-Traxler, Kristie. "Developing an Emergency Control Plan for Oxford University Libraries." *Sconul Focus* 35 (2005).

Shultz, Suzanne M. "Hospital Library Reference: Searching under Time Constraint." *Medical Reference Services Quarterly* 1, no. 3 (1982): 53–60.

Shuman, Bruce A. *Library Security and Safety Handbook: Prevention, Policies, and Procedures.* Chicago: ALA, 1999.

Siess, J. "It's Not the Fire, It's the Smoke." *One Person Library* 18, no. 1 (2001): 5–6.

Silverman, Randy. "A Litany of 'Terrible, No Good, Very Bad' Things That Can Happen after the Disaster." *International Preservation News* 33 (2004): 8–15.

———. "Comparing Mass Drying and Sterilization Protocols for Water-Damaged Books." *International Preservation News*, no. 42 (2007): 22–29.

———. "Fire and Ice: A Soot Removal Technique Using Dry Ice Blasting." *International Preservation News*, no. 39 (2006): 20–24.

———. "Report: Tsunami and Archives: The Unexpected Possibilities: Jakarta, Indonesia—17–18 July 2006." *International Preservation News*, no. 39 (2006): 30–33.

———. "The Day the University Changed." *Idaho Librarian* 55, no. 3 (2004).

———. "The Seven Deadly Sins of Disaster Recovery." *Public Library Quarterly* 25, no. 3/4 (2006): 31–46.

———. "Toward a National Disaster Response Protocol." *Libraries & The Cultural Record* 41, no. 4 (2006): 497–511.

Simmons, Laurie. "Water Damage and Restoration of the Jewish Consumptives' Relief Society Archives." *Colorado Libraries* 7, no. 3 (1981): 24–27.

Simmons, Sylvia, ed. *Civil Disasters: The Role of Public Libraries Following a Crisis in the Community.* London: Library Association Publications, 1993.

Sinclair, Gwen. "Regional Disaster: The Flood at the University of Hawaii at Mānoa Library." *dttp: Documents to the People* 35, no. 3 (2007): 31–35.

Skepastianu, M. "Library Disaster Planning: Prevention, Preparedness, Response, Recovery." *International Preservation News* 13, no. 96 (1996): 14–16.

Smith, Elizabeth H. "Mold Abatement in a Remote Storage Facility." *Library & Archival Security* 15, no. 1 (1999): 75–82.

Smith, Richard D. "Disaster Recovery: Problems and Procedures." *IFLA Journal* 17, (1991): 13–24.

Smith, Sharman Bridges. "Observations of Ground Zero: From the Outside." *Public Library Quarterly* 25, no. 3/4 (2006): 151–157.

Smith, Patricia, Beth Oehlerts, Glenn Jaeger, and Sandy Belskis. "Repurchasing Journals Lost in a Major Disaster: Library and Vendor Perspectives." *Serials Review* 32, no. 1 (2006): 26–34.

Smithsonian Institution. "Smithsonian Institution." http://www.si.edu (December 14, 2009).

Snedaker, Susan. *Business Continuity and Disaster Recovery Planning for It Professionals.* Burlington, MA: Syngress, 2007.

Society of American Archivists. "Society of American Archivists." http://www.archivists.org (December

14, 2009).

Soled, E. H., E. A. Vererka, J. Krieg, and J. Barrett. "Information Technology Utilization in Emergency Management at Exxon Research and Engineering Company." *Special Libraries* 78, no. 9 (1987): 116–121.

St Lifer, E. "Andrew's Aftermath: Hurricane `Saves' Public Library." *Library Journal* 119, no. 10 (1994): 48–50.

"State of Wyoming Disaster Recovery Plan." *Colorado Libraries* 7, no. 2 (1981): 29–36.

Stephens, David O. "Protecting Records in the Face of Chaos, Calamity, and Cataclysm." *Information Management Journal* 37, no. 1 (2003): 33–40.

Stevens, P. "Planning for Disasters in Archives, Libraries and Museums." *Local Studies Librarian* 14, no. 1 (1995): 14–16.

Stielow, F. J. "Disaster Preparedness and Response Manual: A Common Sense Guide to Risk Management." *LLA Bulletin* 56, no. 1 (1993): 29–34.

Stoker, D. "Planning Disasters for the Twenty-First Century." *Journal of Librarianship and Information Science* 28, no. 3 (1996): 129–131.

Stoker, David. "The Case of the Disappearing Books." *Journal of Librarianship and Information Science* 23, no. 3 (1991): 121–124.

Stovel, Herb. *Risk Preparedness: A Management Manual for World Cultural Heritage.* Rome: ICCROM, 1998.

Stremple, Rosalie, and Michael F Martone. "Disasters Come in All Sizes." *InfoPro*, March (2000): 29–35.

Strudwick, Jane. "A Selected Bibliography of Library Disaster Stories: Before, During, and After." *Public Library Quarterly* 25, no. 3–4 (2006): 7–16.

Sturges, Paul, and Diana Rosenberg. *Disaster and After: The Practicalities of Information Service in Times of War and Other Catastrophes: Proceedings of an International Conference.* London: Taylor Graham, 1999.

Sung, Carolyn Hoover, Valerii Pavlovich Lenov, and Peter Waters, "Fire Recovery at the Library of the Academy of Sciences of the USSR." *American Archivist* 53 (1990): 298–312.

Suzuki, Mabel and Ross Togashi. "Halloween flood at University of Hawaii Library." *Western Association of Map Libraries Information Bulletin* 36, no. 2 (2005): 101–110

Swartz, Nikki. "Dealing with Disaster." *Information Management Journal* 40, no. 4 (2004): 28–34.

———. "Six Months That Changed the Face of Information Management." *Information Management Journal* 36, no. 4 (2002): 18–25.

Switzer, Teri R. "The Crisis Was Bad, but the Stress Is Killing Me!" *Colorado Libraries* 24, Fall (1998): 19–21.

Tennant, Roy. "Coping with Disasters." *Library Journal* 126, no. 19 (2001): 28.

Thenell, Jan. *The Library's Crisis Communications Planner : A PR Guide for Handling Every Emergency.* Chicago: American Library Association, 2004.

Thomas, Marcia, and Anke Voss. *Emergency Response Planning in College Libraries,* CLIP Note no. 40. Chicago: American Library Association: Association of College and Research Libraries, 2009.

Thorburn, G. "Burning Books: The Work of DOCUMENT SOS." *Library Management* 15, no. 6 (1994): 23–25.

Threats to Your Collection: Preparing for Emergencies in Oklahoma. Oklahoma City: Oklahoma Department of Libraries, 2005.

Todaro, Julie. *Emergency Preparedness for Libraries.* Lanham, Maryland: Scarecrow Press; Government Institutes, 2009.

———. "Managing through Tragedy." *Library Administration and Management* 16, no. 1 (2002): 40–43.

Trinkaus-Randall, Gregor. "New Frontiers in Emergency Preparedness." *ALCTS Newsletter* 16, no. 1 (2005): 1.

"Two Years and Counting: New Orleans Libraries after Katrina." *American Libraries* 38, no. 8 (2007): 30–31.

UNESCO Cluster Office for the Caribbean. "Mitigating Disasters." http://webworld.unesco.org/mitigating_disaster/english/indexe.html (December 16, 2009).

Ungarelli, Donald L. "Are Our Libraries Safe from Losses?" *Library and Archival Security* 9, no. 1 (1989): 45–48.

Upton, M. S., and C. Pearson. *Disaster Planning and Emergency Treatments in Museums, Art Galleries, Libraries, Archives and Allied Institutions.* Canberra, Institute for the Conservation of Cultural Material Incorporated (1978).

U. S. Library of Congress. "U. S. Library of Congress Preservation." http://www.loc.gov/preserv (December 14, 2009).

U. S. National Archives and Records Administration. "ABCs of Modern Fire Suppression in Cultural Institutions." National Archives and Records Administration, http://www.archives.gov/preservation/conferences/2008/presentations.

———. "National Archives and Records Administration." http://www.archives.gov/ (December 14, 2009).

U. S. National Park Service. http://www.nps.gov/history/preservation.htm (December 14, 2009).

van der Hoeven, Hans, and Joan van Albada. *Lost Memory—Libraries and Archives Destroyed in the Twentieth Century.* UNESCO, 1996. http://unesdoc.unesco.org/images/0010/001055/105557e.pdf (December 16, 2009).

Varlamoff, M. T. "Coping with Disasters: IFLA's Role in the ICBS (International Committee of the Blue Shield) and in Co-Operative Initiatives to Preserve the Memory of the World." *Disaster and after: the practicalities of information service in times of war and other catastrophes. Proceedings of an international conference sponsored by IGLA* (1998): *(The International Group of the Library Association), 4–6 September 1998, University of Bristol*, edited by Paul Sturges and Diana Rosenberg, 161–165. London: Taylor Graham, (1998).

———. "The Blue Shield Initiative. Joining Efforts to Preserve Our Cultural Heritage in Danger." *Liber Quarterly : the Journal of European Research Libraries* 12, no. 2/3 (2002): 275–282.

Villadsen, Alice W., and Gerardo E. De los Santos. *Hoping for the Best While Preparing for the Worst: Disasters, Emergencies and the Community College.* Phoenix AZ: League for Innovation in the Community College, 2007.

Volesko, Michele Mary. "It Wasn't Raining When Noah Build the Arc: Disaster Preparedness for Hospitals and Medical Librarians Post September 11." *Internet Reference Services Quarterly* 6, no. 3/4 (2002): 99–131.

Voss, Brian D. "What Would Ozymandias Think About Disaster Planning?" *EDUCAUSE Review* 41, no. 2 (2006): 76–77.

Wall, Kay L. "Lessons Learned from Katrina: What Really Matters in a Disaster." *Public Library Quarterly* 25, no. 3–4 (2006): 189–198.

Wallace, Michael, and Lawrence Webber. *The Disaster Recovery Handbook: A Step-by-Step Plan to Ensure Business Continuity and Protect Vital Operations, Facilities and Assets.* NY: AMACOM Books, 2004.

Weiser, Philip J. "Communicating During Emergencies: Toward Interoperability and Effective Information Management." *Federal Communications Law Journal* 59, no. 3 (2007): 547–573.

Wellheiser, Joanna G., and Nancy E Gwinn, eds. *Preparing for the Worst, Planning for the Best: Protecting Our Cultural Heritage from Disaster*, IFLA Publications. Munich: K. G. Saur, 2005.

Wellheiser, Johanna G., and Scott Jude. *An Ounce of Prevention: Integrated Disaster Planning for Archives, Libraries, and Record Centers.* 2nd ed. Lanham MD: Scarecrow Press, 2002.

Wesley, Cecile. "Library and Information Services in the Sudan." In *Information and libraries in the Arab World*, edited by Michael Wise and Anthony Olden, 181–89. London: Library Association Publishing, 1994.

Wessling, Julie, and Thomas Delaney. "After the Flood, Colorado State Reaps a Harvest of Invention." *American Libraries* 31, Nov (2000): 36–37.

Wettlaufer, B. "Preparing a Library Disaster Plan." *Library Mosaics* 6, no. 6 (1995): 8–10.

Whaley, Monte. "Flood Had Benefits for CSU Libraries." *Denver Post*, July 30, 2007. http://www.denverpost.com/news/ci_6495586 (December 15, 2009).

Wilkinson, Frances C. and Linda K. Lewis, "Developing a Safety Training Program," *Library & Archival Security* 21, no. 2 (2008), 77–85.

Wilkinson, Frances C. and Linda K. Lewis, *Writing RFPs for Acquisitions: A Guide to the Request for Proposal.* Chicago: American Library Association, 2008.

Will, B. H. "The Public Library as Community Crisis Center." *Library Journal* 126, no. 20 (2001): 75–77.

Winston, Mark D., and Susan Quinn. "Library Leadership in Times of Crisis and Change." *New Library World* 106, no. 9 (2005): 395–415.

Witten, I. H., M. Loots, M. F. Trujillo, and D. Bainbridge. "The Promise of Digital Libraries in Developing Countries." *Electronic Library* 20, no. 1 (2002): 7–13.

Wong, Yi Ling and Ravonne Green. "Disaster Planning in Libraries." *Journal of Access Services* 4, no. 3 (2008): 71–82.

Wood, L. "What Lessons Have We Not Yet Learned About Disasters?" *Colorado Libraries* 24, no. 3 (1998): 4–6.

Wood, Larry. "1000 Easy Steps toward Developing a Disaster Recovery Plan; or, the Boss Must Like Me Because He Gave Me the Job of Writing the Disaster Plan." *Conservation Administration News* 58–59, July/Oct (1994): 16–20.

Wrobel, Leo A. *Disaster Recovery Planning for Communications and Critical Infrastructure.* Boston: Artech House, 2009.

Xing, Wei, Marios D. Dikaiakos, Hua Yang, Angelos Sphyris, and George Eftichidis. "Building a Distributed Digital Library for Natural Disasters Metadata with Grid Services and RDF." *Library Management* 26, no. 4 (2005): 230–245.

Young, Richard F., and Bibliotech (Oakton Va.). *Library and Archival Disaster Preparedness and Recovery.* Oakton, Va.: Bibliotech,, 1986.

Young, Terrence E. "If I Only Knew Then." *Library Media Connection* 24, no. 7 (2006): 22–23.

GLOSSARY

This glossary is a selective list of major terms used in disaster preparedness, emergency response, and disaster recovery literature. For more extensive information, please consult the following resources.

California Preservation Program: http://calpreservation.org. Glossary: calpreservation.org/disasters/generic/salvage_glossary.rtf.

Disaster Recovery Journal and the DRI Institute for Continuity Management. Glossary: http://www.drj.com/index.php?option=com_glossary

National Library of Australia: Library Preservation. Glossary: http://www.nla.gov.ay/chg/gloss.html.

ICS: Incident Command System. Glossary: http://training.fema.gov/EMIWeb/IS/ICSResource/ICS-ResCntr_Glossary.htm.

The terms provided below are not meant to serve as all-inclusive definitions, but rather the terms and phrases are defined in the context of disaster preparedness, emergency response, and disaster recovery in libraries Universal resource locators (URLs) were verified and accurate as of October 10, 2009.

acts of God. See natural disasters.

air drying. A preservation technique used to salvage materials that have been damaged by water. This requires a cool, low-humidity area with good air circulation.

alert. A warning that a disaster situation is imminent or has occurred.

alternate site. An alternate operating location to be used when the library facilities are unavailable because of a disaster.

alternate work area. A location that is used when the original work area is damaged or inaccessible; it has all necessary infrastructure such as communications and computers.

application recovery. The portion of disaster recovery that deals specifically with the restoration of computer software and data.

area command. An organization established to oversee the management of large or multiple incidents that are each being handled by emergency response organizations.

assembly area. See rendezvous location.

backup (data). A process in which data, regardless of format, is copied in another location or format. The backup can be used if the original data is lost, damaged or destroyed.

backup generator. An independent source of power, usually fueled by diesel or natural gas that can be used during an emergency.

business continuity. The ability of an organization to provide services before, during, and after a disaster.

COW. (Computers-on-Wheels). A phrase used to describe a wheeled cart designed to store, charge and facilitate delivery of multiple computer laptops to classrooms or work sites. The carts typically provide electrical power to simultaneously charge batteries in laptops when the computer is not in use. When needed, a mobile computer classroom can be created by wheeling the C.O.W. into the classroom where individual laptops are distributed to students. In some instances the cart includes a printer, LCD projector, and wireless network transmitter.

call tree. A document that depicts the order used to contact administrators, management, employees, vendors, and other key contacts in the event of an emergency or disaster.

cold site. An alternate location that has the basic infrastructure required to continue basic services, but does not have any computers, telecommunications equipment, etc.

command center. A physical or virtual location away from the area affected by the disaster where administration and managers meet in order to make decisions about the disaster response and recovery process. A library should have both primary and secondary locations in case one of them becomes unavailable or unsatisfactory. It may also serve as a central point for deliveries, services, media and all other contacts. This may also be known as the command post or incident center.

computers-on-wheels. See COW.

conservator. A person responsible for the physical preservation and restoration of collection items.

conservation. The use of procedures to preserve or repair the library's physical collections.

consortium agreement. An agreement made by a group of libraries to share collections, facilities, services and other support if one member of the group suffers a disaster.

contact list. A list of disaster response team members and key personnel to be contacted. The list will include the necessary contact information including all telephone numbers and e-mail addresses. This list is generally confidential.

contingency plan. A plan used by library unit to respond to a specific emergency or disaster.

continuity of operations plan. The Federal Government uses this term to describe activities otherwise known as disaster recovery, business continuity, business resumption, or contingency planning. These plans provide guidance on the response to emergencies.

continuity strategy. A strategy to ensure that an organization will recover and continue to provide services during and after a disaster.

crisis. An event, which, if not handled properly, may damage an organization's ability to operate.

crisis management. The management and coordination of a library response to a crisis. The goal is to minimize or avoid damage to the library's users, employees, collections, equipment and facilities, while attempting to maintain its services.

critical functions. The critical operational functions that cannot be unavailable for more than a brief time without jeopardizing the library. Such functions could include reference or interlibrary loan in the public services areas, or payroll in the fiscal services areas.

critical infrastructure. Physical assets or systems whose loss or damage would make it impossible for a library to provide basic services.

damage assessment. The process of assessing damage to the library in order to determine the extent of the disaster, and identify what can be salvaged and what must be replaced.

dehumidification. A technique for reducing the level of humidity in a building or for drying library materials that are damp.

disaster. An event that impairs a library's ability to function or provide services. Disasters range in size from small situations involving a portion of a building to major disasters that involve large geographic regions. See also emergency.

disaster recovery management team. A group responsible for directing the development, writing and implementation of the disaster planning and emergency response and recovery plan, and for implementing the plan when an emergency occurs. Similar terms include business recovery team and crisis management team.

disaster plan. A plan that includes the procedures to be followed by a library to prevent or minimize the risk of a disaster occurring, and to describe the response when a disaster happens. These plans must include contact information, building plans, and salvage priorities. Also referred to as a disaster preparedness plan and disaster recovery plan.

disaster recovery. The process of recovering and rebuilding after a disaster. This is an ongoing process that ensures that the necessary steps are taken to identify the full extent of the damage and potential losses, initiate recovery plans, and ensure resumption and continuity of services.

disaster response. The response of a library to a disaster that may damage the library, its people, collections, facilities or services. The disaster response may include evacuation of a library, initiating its disaster recovery plan, performing an initial review of damage, and any other measures required to stabilize the library's condition.

emergency. A situation that may cause injury, loss of life, destruction of property, or may cause the loss or disruption of a library's normal operations to such an extent that it poses a threat to the library. See also disaster.

emergency preparedness. The ability that enables a library to respond to an emergency in a coordinated, timely, and effective manner to prevent the loss of life and minimize damage to its facilities, collections and equipment.

emergency response. The immediate reaction and response to an emergency situation.

emergency response plan. A plan addressing the reaction and response to an emergency situation. See also disaster plan.

environmental control. The maintenance of appropriate levels of light, humidity, temperature, air movement, etc., inside a library.

environmental scan. A review of all aspects of the library's physical facilities, equipment, collections and surroundings. These scans are done in order to determine the condition of the library and identify potential vulnerabilities that need to be corrected.

evacuation. The removal of users, employees, and visitors from a library to a safe location in a controlled and monitored manner at time of an event.

exercise. An activity designed to execute and evaluate library disaster plans. They can be announced or unannounced, and are used to train employees and identify gaps in the plan.

freeze-drying. Freezing is method of stabilizing collections that have been damaged by water until they can receive conservation treatment. This process prevents the development or growth of mold.

high-risk areas. Areas that have been identified as being highly vulnerable or could be the cause of a disaster.

hot site. An alternate facility that can be used as a Command Center or Alternate Work Area that already has the communications and computing support that will allow the library to continue its crucial services.

human-caused disasters. Sometimes called man-made disasters. Disasters or crises caused by human actions such as workplace violence, riots, arson, etc.

incident. An event, natural or human-caused, that requires an emergency response to protect library users, employees, collections or facilities. Incidents may include fires, floods, hazardous materials spills, earthquakes, hurricanes, tornadoes, public health and medical emergencies, and many other events that require an emergency response.

infrastructure. The systems and structure that enable the library to perform its functions, such as the communications infrastructure.

interim site. A temporary location used to continue performing library services if a disaster makes it impossible to return to the original library facilities immediately.

interleaving. A conservation method of treating materials damaged by water that keeps pages from sticking together. Blotter paper, paper towels without printed designs, newsprint that is un-inked, freezer paper or waxed paper may be used, depending upon the nature of the materials and the extent of the damage.

intrinsic value. An item that has value beyond its intellectual content, and must be retained in its original form. Such items may have autographs or characteristics that increase its value. Such items are frequently important items that are included in the salvage priorities.

LEED. (Leadership in Energy and Environmental Design) A building rating system developed by the U. S. Green Building Council in 1998 (http://www.usgbc.org/) to promote, define and measure the design, construction and maintenance of environmentally sustainable buildings.

lead time. The time it takes to acquire equipment, services, or supplies after the library orders them. Libraries must try to minimize this time by creating agreements with companies before a crisis. See also pre-contract.

leadership in energy and environmental design. See LEED.

man-made disasters. See human-caused disasters.

mission-critical activities. The critical operational and/or support activities (either provided internally or outsourced) that enable a library to achieve its objective(s).

mitigation. The activities necessary to reduce or eliminate risks to a library or to lessen the consequences of an incident. These measures may occur before, during, or after an event.

mock disaster. A type of exercise in which a specific disaster scenario is staged. Employees conduct the activities that they would take in the event of a disaster.

off-site storage. A location that is a significant distance away from the site of the library, where back-up, duplicated and vital records or equipment may be stored for use during the disaster recovery.

natural disasters. Sometimes called acts of God. Disasters or crises caused by events such as tornados, hurricanes, earthquakes, etc.

P.I.V. (post indicator valve). A valve located above ground that controls the flow of water into a building and has an indicator showing the valve is either open or closed.

phone tree. See contact list.

post indicator valve. See P.I.V.

pre-contract. A contract between the library or its parent organization and companies that spe-

cialize in disaster response and recovery, negotiated before any emergency has occurred. Such contracts enable the library experiencing a disaster to use the services of the company immediately instead of going thru negotiations and RFPs when the emergency happens. These contracts identify the general categories of equipment, facilities, or services that will be available to the library.

preparedness. The range of tasks and ongoing activities necessary to improve the library's capability to prevent, mitigate, respond to, and recover from disasters and emergencies.

preservation. Activities associated with maintaining, repairing and preserving library materials in all formats; preservation includes conservation activities.

prevention. Actions to avoid or mitigate an emergency situation by protecting lives and library facilities, collections and equipment.

psychrometer/sling psychrometer. An instrument used to measure temperature and relative humidity. Sling psychrometers are relatively inexpensive compared to a thermohydrograph, but are accurate when used correctly.

recovery. The process and actions required to restore library services, functions and collections after a disaster

recovery timeline. The sequence of recovery activities that will be followed in order for the library to resume an acceptable level of services and activities following a disaster. The timeline may range considerably depending upon the scale of the disaster.

rendezvous location: The location(s) where employees will meet after being evacuated from the library and a roll call will be conducted.

resilience. The ability of an organization to absorb the impact of a disaster while continuing to provide an acceptable level of service.

response. The immediate, short-term reaction to an emergency to assess the damage and to determine the level of activity required to control the situation. Response includes the initial actions required to save lives and protect the library facility; begin the implementation of the library's emergency plan; and identify actions that will mitigate the losses.

restoration. The process of returning the library's services and collections to normal.

rinsing. A procedure to clean mud and dirt from materials or other items. Rinse the outside of books or items under gentle, clean running water, or gently move them in containers of water, then dry items. Scrubbing items can force dirt deeper into items. Blot off the mud and water with a soft cloth or sponge.

risk assessment/analysis. The process of identifying the risks to a library; assessing the critical functions necessary to continue regular operations; defining the measures that can reduce any vulnerabilities; and evaluating the cost for such measures.

risk management. The processes and structures that are put in place to effectively reduce risks to an acceptable level.

roll call. The process of identifying that all employees have been safely evacuated and accounted for at the designated Rendezvous Locations following an evacuation of a library.

safety warden. See warden.

salvage analysis. The act of determining the appropriate actions to be performed on damaged materials and collections. The assessment may be conducted by library personnel, insurance adjusters or authorized appraisers. Actions may include disposal, replacement, repair, or conservation. Insurance companies may hire their own appraisers or accept the documentation from the library.

salvage priorities. Collections, materials, equipment, files, or other items identified by the library as priorities to be saved in case of an emergency. These priorities should either be critical to the ongoing functioning of the library or should be its most valuable, unique materials.

security review. A regular review of policies, procedures, and practices related to security and safety to ensure that they are current and are being followed by library employees.

self-insurance. A method of managing risk in which an organization sets aside funds to compensate for a future loss instead of purchasing insurance to reimburse the organization for that loss.

thermohygrograph. A machine which records temperature and relative humidity. Sometimes called a hygrothermograph.

uninterruptible power supply. A backup electrical power supply that provides short-term continuous power to critical equipment in the event that commercial power is lost; it enough time for vital systems to be correctly powered down.

vacuum freeze drying. Frozen items are placed in a vacuum chamber and dried at below-freezing temperatures to minimize swelling and distortion. Used to salvage materials damaged by water.

vital records. Records essential to the continued functioning or reconstitution of library during and after an emergency. This may also refer to those records essential to protecting the legal and financial rights of the library.

warden. Individual(s) responsible for ensuring that all people evacuate a floor or building in the event of an emergency situation.

warm site. An alternate site which is equipped with some communications and equipment, but needs additional infrastructure in order to function as an alternative working location. See also cold site and hot site.

APPENDICES

MODEL DISASTER PREPAREDNESS, RESPONSE, AND RECOVERY PLAN

Disaster plans must be written for an individual library. The plans will vary greatly depending upon the type and size of the library. Small private libraries will have very different plans from large libraries with multiple locations reporting to a city or university. Learn what your specific institution requires and what resources are available to you.

Make the plan as detailed as possible so that your employees know what to do. Disasters often occur at the worst possible times: late at night or over a holiday weekend. Your disaster plan can guide you through the first steps of response and help reduce the level of panic that frequently comes in such situations.

You need to be able to locate sections of the plan quickly in the middle of a crisis. Use tabs or colored paper to separate sections of the plan in the print version. Create an index to your plan. Have versions that can be used on notebook computers, Netbooks and cell phones.

The first priority is the safety of the people involved: the customers and employees of the library. Everything else is secondary. Never risk anyone's safety or health. Stress that priority in your disaster plan.

In addition to the complete plan, have the most important contact numbers programmed into your cell phones. Print small cards, the size that could fit in wallets, with the most important contact numbers.

You should provide additional information in the plan's appendix on related issues such as sources of training and the environmental scan. Such support-

ing materials should not be part of the basic plan that will be used during a disaster; distribute them separately.

Model Table of Contents

Most library plans include some version of the following sections:

- Introduction and Statement of Purpose
- Contact Information—including who to call and what to say, identifying both library emergency contacts and contact information for other campus offices
- Disaster Supplies—list of supplies and locations, both internal and external
- Salvage Priorities—for collections, equipment, and other materials
- Informational/Fact Sheets—with instructions about building evacuation as well as
- best practices about how to respond to various kinds of disasters and measures to reduce their impact
- Appendix
  » List of Disaster Response Assistance Team (DRAT) members including their roles and responsibilities
  » Building floor plans including exits, areas of refuge, locations of fire alarms and fire extinguishers, utility shut-off valves, salvage priorities, etc.
  » Contact information for local, regional, and national disaster recovery and other related vendors, noting if any of these vendors has a pre-contract arrangement with

the library or parent institution; also include contact information for insurance providers, if appropriate

- » Forms for documenting the disaster
- » Links to campus emergency, safety, and disaster plan(s)
- » Environmental scan or library building survey
- » Distribution, review, and update schedule for the plan

Introduction and Statement of Purpose

Have a clear introduction to your library's disaster plan along with a concise statement of purpose. The statement of purpose might include elements such as: assigning responsibility regarding who is responsible for which tasks both during the emergency response and later during the disaster recovery stage; providing communication between, among, and across the right people at the right time; establishing contact with contractors and consultants who specialize in disaster response; documenting emergency response processes and procedures; anticipating possible disasters and developing measures to reduce their impact; ensuring that library services are reestablished as quickly as possible after a disaster; identifying the location of disaster supplies and equipment; establishing priorities to determine the order in which collections, equipment, and other materials are to be rescued and removed from damaged facilities; and soliciting feedback at multiple levels to evaluate the effectiveness of the library's disaster plan.

Contact Information
Library

For all people, list all potential methods of reaching them:

- Office phone
- Home phone
- Cell phone
- Office e-mail
- Other e-mail

- Chat or text messaging
- Social networking sites

Review the information regularly and update the lists rapidly when information changes.

Include contact information for:

- Library Director
- Disaster Response Assistance Team Leader
- Disaster Response Assistance Team Members
- Building Directors and Managers
- Department Heads

Each department head must have contact information for all their employees, including their student employees. They will be responsible for communicating with their personnel through phone/e-mail trees.

Police, Fire, and Others

Police and Fire Emergencies: 911, or your institutional emergency number. Some large organizations have phone numbers that are used in addition to 911. When calling 911 on a large campus from a cell phone, you may reach your city emergency contact rather than your campus contact. Verify in advance of the disaster which numbers work from which type of phones. If possible, program the main emergency number into all your work phones.

Police and Fire Additional Numbers

In addition to the emergency contact information, you need the direct contact information for the individuals in charge of specific units or operations. Ask for all appropriate information, assuring everyone that you will use it only in a crisis.

Utilities

Some large organizations have divisions that handle all utilities, while other libraries may deal directly with the utility companies. You need to know contact information for problems with:

- Water
- Gas
- Electricity

- Telecommunications
- Sewer

Deliveries

You may need to stop deliveries for a time. Include contact information for the U. S. Postal Service, campus mail systems, delivery companies such as FedEx and UPS, scheduled deliveries from other libraries, and any other delivery services.

Security Alarm System

If your library has a security alarm system, you need to know contact information for the system.

Institution and Community

Library Governing Body

Include contact information for both work and home for individuals in your parent organization including university or school administration; city, state or federal government; private association; library trustees; advisory board, etc. The contacts need to include those people and organizations who are responsible for the library in the broadest sense. Notify the people who are likely to be contacted by the media for comments as well as those who will be appropriately upset to learn about a disaster from the media rather than from the library.

Insurance and Risk Management

The insurance companies need to be involved at a very early stage of a major disaster. Determine your institutional policies concerning contact with these companies. If the organization has personnel responsible for handling these areas, you need to include the contact information for these people in your contact list. If you will be responsible for working directly with the insurance companies, you need to include the contact information for the companies.

Major Vendors

If a disaster is major, you may need to have shipments stopped, notify vendors of delayed payments, or ask to have invoices reissued. Notify your vendors as quickly as possible so that they can help you.

Media

Even in a large organization with a media relations unit, the media will want to work directly with individuals from the library. Learn your organizational policies about media relations. If you will be responsible for communications, have appropriate contact information for the major media outlets in your area.

Regional and Consortial Libraries

Libraries in your area and in your consortia may be able to assist during a disaster by offering services for your users and assistance during your recovery. Many state library associations have electronic mailing lists that can be used for communicating your situation. Include the contact information for all appropriate libraries and for the consortia of which you are a member.

Disaster Supplies

Depending upon the size of your library, each building or area should have basic emergency supplies. Your plan must describe what is available, where the supplies are located and how to obtain them. The supplies must be checked at regular intervals and replaced as needed.

- *Command Center Supplies:*
    - » Identification—badges and/or badge holders, brightly-colored vests
    - » Communication and safety devises—cell phones, walkie-talkies, megaphone/bullhorn, whistles, air horns, caution tape
    - » Documentation—tape or digital recorders, disposable digital cameras, cam-corders and supplies, portable flash drives
    - » Technology support—regular and heavy-duty extension cords in various lengths, surge protectors
    - » Miscellaneous—folding chairs, blankets, emergency snacks and bottled water, cash and/or credit card access

- *General Supplies:*
  » Paper and writing implements—clip boards with paper, larger paper for signs, poster board, pens, pencils, markers
  » Tape—transparent tape, duct tape, masking tape, caution tape
  » Cleaning and sanitary supplies—paper towels (without dyes that can leave stains), white towels, rags, sponges, mops, brooms, buckets, garbage bags, all purpose-cleaners, antimicrobial soap, alcohol-based hand cleaner, eye wash, toilet paper, disposable wipes, wet-dry shop vacuum
  » Scissors, utility knives with extra blades
  » Tools such as screwdrivers, hammers, nails, crow bar
  » Plastic crates, folding wheeled carts, wheeled garbage cans
- *First Aid Supplies, per ANSI Z308.1-2003:*
  » Adhesive tape
  » Adhesive bandages and sterile scissors
  » Antiseptic
  » Burn treatment
  » Gloves
  » Sterile pads
  » Absorbent compresses
  » Bandages in variety of sizes
  » And may also include: eye covering that can be attached, eye wash, cold packs, rolled bandages
- *Safety Supplies:*
  » Lighting—flashlights with extra batteries, small temporary hanging lights
  » Protective clothing (in various sizes)—rubber or nitrile rubber gloves, disposable latex gloves, booties to cover shoes in various sizes, safety-toed boots, protective coats/smocks, disposable overalls, plastic aprons, hard hats, protective safety glasses and eye covering
  » N-95 respirators (which many people call dust masks, but these respirators are fitted to the face and have double elastic bands to hold them in place) and NIOSH-compliant respirators
  » Object protection, drying, packing and salvage—plastic sheeting in large rolls, unprinted newspaper to protect surfaces and wrap materials, blotting paper, waxed paper, transparent tape, packing tape, scissors, clothes line and pins, cardboard sheets and boxes, plywood
- *Moderate to Major Disaster*—supplies typically not stored in the library (supplied by recovery and salvage vendors or available through campus physical plant or other campus areas):
  » generator, industrial fans, large humidifier/dehumidifier, large water pumps, portable devices that measure moisture in solid objects such as Aqua Boy®, pallets, fork lift, crane, freezer space, extensive temporary emergency lighting, sandbags, etc.

Salvage Priorities

Depending upon the nature of the emergency, you may have time to salvage some materials. Identify: What are your most valuable materials? What is irreplaceable? What is vital for your continued operation?

List the salvage priorities by building and area, in priority order. Identify the most crucial items and their locations very thoroughly. The initial salvage operation may be done by personnel who do not know your building or are working in very poor physical conditions; therefore, the information in your disaster plan needs to be very clear. Include the top priorities with their locations on your building plans as well as listing the information in your salvage priorities.

After materials are salvaged, you must deal with the protection and preservation of materials. There are many sources of information about how to preserve types of materials such as paper, film, photographs, computer files, etc. Before a disaster occurs, identify the resources appropriate for your library and include those contacts in your list of emergency contacts.

Informational/Fact Sheets

Safety is always the most important consideration. When there is any doubt, activate the alarms, evacuate the building, and alert the authorities. Other responses are governed by the type and size of disaster. If a fire is small and contained in a wastebasket, an employee may be able to extinguish it if they have had training and have access to a nearby fire extinguisher. Afterwards, the fire department can determine the cause and extent of the damage. If a water leak is confined to one small area, it may be possible to rope it off and call a plumber; however, if it is a larger leak that is near electrical wiring, then you will need to consult with the experts who deal with your utilities and plumbing to determine whether you must evacuate the area and possibly the entire building.

If you must close a building, post signs on the entrances and update your phone recording, your Web site, and social networking sites as soon as possible. Keep that information current with regular updates.

Selected Examples of Emergency

Following are some of the more frequent types of emergencies. Your plan should include those most relevant to your library. Be brief, giving the basic information that will guide people in their immediate response to an emergency. Include the appropriate titles or positions and phone numbers for your institution.

Animal in the Building

Notify the building manager. Attempt to keep the animal away from people. If library personnel cannot get the animal out easily, notify the police. If anyone is injured, notify police and emergency medical personnel.

Bomb Threat

Remain calm. Attempt to get as much information as possible: When will it explode? Where is it located? What kind is it? Who are you? Have someone else call the police while you are talking with the person making the threat. Notify the building manager and library administration.

Computer Crash

Contact the systems/technology unit for the building. Document the extent of the problem: Is it one computer or an entire system? Is it one function or everything?

Electrical Outage

Contact the building manager or the head of the electrical utility operation. Is it one area in a building, the entire building, the entire area, or the entire city? Distribute flashlights from your emergency supplies. Notify the library administration. If it is an extended outage, evacuate and close the building.

Fire

Rescue, Alert, Contain, and Evacuate = RACE:

- Rescue people in immediate danger if you are trained and able to help
- Alert people by pulling the fire alarm and calling 911
- Contain the fire by closing all doors
- Extinguish small fires only if you are trained and confident. If not, evacuate the building.

Notify the building manager, the fire department, the library administration.

Hazardous Materials

All hazardous materials must include basic information about hazards and emergency treatment. If materials are spilled, notify the building manager, library administration and local emergency or medical personnel for treatment.

Injuries or Sickness

Call 911 or emergency medical personnel. Do not attempt to move an injured or unconscious person. Notify the building manager and library administration.

Terrorism

Call 911. Notify the library administration.

Vandalism, Theft or Damage to Collections or Building Facilities

Notify the building manager or library administration. Call the police. Do not attempt to physically stop an individual. Observe carefully in order to make a full report.

Violence

Call 911. Notify the building manager and library administration. Do not attempt to stop an individual who is physically violent.

Water: Minor Leaks

Notify the building manager or library administration. Keep people away from the area. If you can turn off the water, do so. Notify the appropriate physical plant personnel or utility to turn off the water. If possible and appropriate, move affected materials to a nearby dry area. If water is falling on materials, cover the area with plastic sheeting.

Water: Major Flood

Call building manager, library administration, physical plant or utility. Evacuate and close the building.

Weather Emergencies

Blizzards, tornadoes, hurricanes, tsunamis, avalanches, floods, thunder storms and other natural disasters can force the evacuation of a library, or turn a library into a place of refuge. Work closely with your parent organization and local authorities in order to respond appropriately.

Building Evacuation Procedures

Your disaster plan must include instructions for evacuating all areas of your building(s) and securing them.

- Describe all exits.
- How do you alert people who do not know

what the alarms mean or cannot hear them?

- How do you evacuate or protect those who are in wheelchairs or with strollers? How do you notify the emergency personnel that there are individuals still in the building who need to be rescued from your "areas of refuge" that are designed to shelter those who cannot get out of the building readily? If you have special chairs designed to assist in taking disabled people down stairs, include the locations of the chairs.
- How do you close your building? How do you alert people in the building that the building is being closed?
- How do you notify the appropriate authorities that you are evacuating the building?
- How do you keep people away from the building? How do you keep them from reentering the building until they are authorized?
- Where will your staff assemble to make sure that everyone got out safely? How will you inform them when it is safe to return to the building? How will you update them if they are sent home?

Appendix

The disaster plan appendix should include:

- A list of the library's disaster response assistance team members including the roles and responsibilities for each member. These roles might include the library's dean or director, DRAT team leader, communications & media coordinator, facilities & security coordinator, human resources coordinator, administrative & financial coordinator, library services coordinator, systems/IT coordinator, and collections & preservation coordinator.
- Building floor plans including exits; areas of refuge; locations of fire alarms and fire extinguishers; fire doors; fire suppression systems; utility shut-off valves and other utility controls for electricity, water, gas, HVAC, etc.;

emergency supply caches and first aid kits; salvage priorities.

- Contact information for local, regional, and national disaster recovery and other related vendors, noting if any of these vendors has a pre-contract arrangement with the library or parent institution; also include contact information for insurance providers, if appropriate. If permitted by your institution, meet with recovery companies long before a disaster strikes.

- Forms for documenting the disaster. Forms should include at a minimum the nature of the emergency or disaster; the date and time it occurred; what areas of the building were involved; who first detected it; who was notified of it; what actions were taken—rescue, response, and recovery; who performed the actions; estimated cost and completion date for the recovery; what resources were needed during the response and recovery; and an overall assessment of the impact and resolution of the disaster. You should also create more specific forms based on your library's needs and the type of disaster you experienced. Also, take pictures and make audio/video recordings throughout the disaster response and recovery process.

- Provide links to your campus emergency, safety, and disaster plan(s).

- Include the environmental scan of your library and your building survey, if available.

- Include the distribution list for your disaster plan and the schedule for reviewing and updating it.

Appendix B

COMPANIES

Many companies are available to assist libraries in responding to emergencies. If the library experiences a relatively small emergency, local companies may be able to provide services such as cleaning or freeze-drying of damaged materials. If the library experiences a major disaster, consider contracting with one of the national or international companies that specialize in emergency recovery.

For further resources including additional companies and sources for restoration of specific type of materials, consult your state or regional libraries and associations, or consult online guides such as:

Disaster Resource.com http://www.disaster-resource.com/

Disaster Recovery Journal http://www.drj.com

Lyrasis Disaster Resources http://www.lyrasis.org/Preservation/Disaster-Resources.aspx

Florida State Library http://dlis.dos.state.fl.us/disasterrecovery/vendors http://dlis.dos.state.fl.us/disasterrecovery/#vendors

Northeast Document Conservation Center http://www.nedcc.org/resources/suppliers.php

The following is a list of selected companies that can assist libraries in recovering from a disaster:

Absolute Backorder Service, Inc. specializes in back volume fulfillment with over 30 years experience in our field. Absolute assists in filling the gaps of serials collections and offer a start-to-finish service that may include locating material, receiving, collating, binding and shipping.
Absolute Backorder Service, Inc.
475 Washington Street
Wrentham, MA 02093
508-384-0122
http://www.absolute-inc.com

American Freeze-Dry Operations provides emergency drying services for papers, books and documents.
American Freeze-Dry Operations
P.O. Box 5740
1722 Hurffville Road, Bldg. 2A
Five Points Business Center
Deptford, NJ 08096
856-939-8160
866-939-8160
http://www.americanfreezedry.com

Archival Products supplies resources and equipment for preservation. They publish a newsletter that describes preservation and conservation trends and products.
Archival Products
P.O. Box 1413
Des Moines, IA 50306-1413
800-526-5640
info@archival.com
http://www.archival.com

Backstage Library Works provides digitization, microfilming, authority control, cataloging, and related services.
Backstage Library Works
533 East 1860 South
Provo, UT 84606
800-288-1265
info@bslw.com
http://www.bslw.com/

Belfor USA is a disaster recovery company that specializes in recovery and restoration of materials and facilities.
Belfor USA
185 Oakland Ave. Suite 300
Birmingham, MI 48009-3433
248-594-1144
info@us.belfor.com
http://www.belforusa.com

BMS CAT offers a full range of restoration services for all commercial industries as well as Special Technologies for industries with strict regulations.
BMS CAT
303 Arthur Street
Fort Worth, Texas 76107
800-433-2940
info@bmscat.com
http://www.bmscat.com/

Brodart supplies office and library equipment and materials including preservation and conservation supplies.
Brodart
P.O. Box 300
McElhattan, PA 17748
888-820-4377
customerservice@brodart.com
http://www.brodart.com/

Disaster Survival Planning Network (DSPN) helps organizations develop comprehensive enterprise-wide business continuity programs by working with organizations to plan, implement or test continuity programs.
Disaster Survival Planning Network (DSPN)
5352 Plata Rosa Court
Camarillo, CA 93012
800-601-4899
Staff@Disaster-Survival.com
http://www.disaster-survival.com

Document Reprocessors specializes in the recovery and restoration of water-damaged books, documents, magnetic and micrographic media.
New York Office
Document Reprocessors
40 Railroad Avenue
Rushville, New York 14544
585-554-4500
800-437-9464-437-9464) 800-437-9464)
http://www.documentreprocessors.com

Emergency Lifeline is a source of emergency preparedness kits and supplies.
Emergency Lifeline
PO Box 15243
Santa Ana, CA 92735
800-826-2201
sales@emergencylifeline.com
http://www.emergencylifeline.com

Gaylord supplies office and library equipment and materials including preservation and conservation supplies. They also publish booklets on preservation of library materials.
Gaylord
PO Box 4901
Syracuse, NY 13221-4901
800-962-9580
http://www.gaylord.com

Munters Corporation specializes in energy efficient air treatment solutions and restoration services based on expertise in humidity and climate control technologies.
Munters Corporation
79 Monroe Street P.O. Box 640
Amesbury MA 01913
978-241-1100
info@munters.us
http://www.muntersamerica.com
.

National Archive Publishing Company (NAPC)
supplies periodical titles on microfilm.
National Archive Publishing Company (NAPC)
300 N. Zeeb Road
P.O. Box 998
Ann Arbor, MI 48106-0998
800-420-NAPC (6272)
info@napubco.com
http://www.napubco.com/catalog.html

Protext is a source of supplies, information and
resources to protect and preserve collections.
ProText
P.O. Box 864
Greenfield, MA 01302
(301) 320-7231 Fax: (301) 320-7232
Phone: (301) 320-7231
ProText@protext.net
http://www.protext.net/

PSC:Periodicals Service Company : Schmidt
Periodicals GmbH specializes in the supply of anti-
quarian backsets, back volumes, reprints and back
issues of out-of-print journals and serials.
PSC:Periodicals Service Company : Schmidt Periodicals GmbH
11 Main Street
Germantown, NY 12526
518-537-4700
psc@periodicals.com
http://www.periodicals.com

ServPro Industries, Inc., is a national franchise
specializing in cleaning and restoration after fire
and water damage.
ServPro Industries, Inc. (national headquarters)
801 Industrial Boulevard
Gallatin, TN 37066
Phone: (615) 451-0200
http://www.servpro.com

SOCIETIES AND ORGANIZATIONS

Many societies and organizations provide information and assistance about emergency preparedness, response, and recovery as well as preservation and conservation. The societies and organizations listed below comprise a selective listing. For further resources including sources for restoration of specific types of materials, consult with state or regional libraries and associations, or consult online guides such as:

Disaster Resource.com http://www.disaster-resource.com/

Disaster Recovery Journal http://www.drj.com

Lyrasis Disaster Resources http://www.lyrasis.org/Preservation/Disaster-Resources.aspx

Northeast Document Conservation Center http://www.nedcc.org/resources/suppliers.php

AAM provides information on disaster planning, preparedness and recovery for museums.
American Association of Museums (AAM) http://www.aam-us.org
1575 Eye Street NW, Suite 400
Washington DC 20005
202-289-1818
E-mail: Membership@aam-us.org

ACP provides a forum for the exchange of information through its network of local chapters to discuss the field of business continuity planning.
Association of Contingency Planners http://www.acp-international.com
7044 South 13th Street
Oak Creek, WI 53154,
414-908-4943, Ext. 450
800-445-4ACP, Ext. 450
info@acp-international.com

AIC promotes research and publications, provides educational opportunities, and fosters the exchange of knowledge among conservators, allied professionals, and the public. Its CERT, Collections Emergency Response Team, provides advice, damage assessments, salvage help, and some funding for recovery.

American Institute for Conservation (AIC) http://www.conservation-us.org
1156 15th Street NW, Ste. 320
Washington, DC 20005
Phone: 202.452.9545
E-mail: info@conservation-us.org

ALA provides resources on disaster planning, collection valuation, preservation and recovery.
http://www.ala.org/ala/mgrps/divs/alcts/resources/preserv/disasterclear.cfm
American Library Association (ALA): Disaster Preparedness and Recovery
50 E Huron St.
Chicago, IL 60611-2795
800-545-2433 ext. 5037
alcts@ala.org

APA provides short guides to managing stress after traumatic events such as tornadoes, hurricanes, fires, etc.
American Psychological Association (APA): Help Center http://www.apahelpcenter.org
750 First Street, NE
Washington, DC 20002-4242
800-374-2721 or 202-336-5500
helping@apa.org

The American Red Cross provides resources on disaster planning, preparedness, training, response and assistance
American Red Cross http://www.redcross.org/
2025 E Street, NW
Washington, DC 20006
Phone: (202) 303 5000
E-mail using a form on their web site.

Amigos is a library consortium in the Southwestern United States that provides assistance, advice and training on disaster preparedness and conservation.
Amigos http://www.amigos.org
Amigos Library Services
14400 Midway Road
Dallas, TX 75244-3509
800-843-8482
amigos@amigos.org

ARMA provides training, publications, and information on records management, including conservation and preservation.
ARMA International http://www.arma.org
13725 W. 109th Street, Suite 101
Lenexa, KS 66215, USA
800.422.2762
member@arma.org

The CCI supports the preservation of Canada's heritage collections through conservation research and development, expert services, and knowledge dissemination. Publications include information on combating pests, protecting Aboriginal heritage, etc.
Canadian Conservation Institute (CCI) http://www.cci-icc.gc.ca/index-eng.aspx
1030 Innes Road
Ottawa ON K1A 0M5 Canada
Tel.: 613-998-3721 or
in Canada 1-866-998-3721
E-mail: cci-icc_services@pch.gc.ca

CCAHA is a non-profit lab that specializes in the treatment of art and historic artifacts on paper. It publishes technical bulletins with information about conservation as well as *Art-i-facts*, a quarterly newsletter that includes brief articles and notices about Web sites and books.
Conservation Center for Art and Historic Artifacts http://www.ccaha.org/
264 South 23rd Street
Philadelphia, PA 19103
Phone: 215.545.0613
E-Mail: ccaha@ccaha.org

CoOL is a library of conservation information that includes information on preservation and salvage of damaged materials. CoOL is now part of AIC.
Conservation OnLine (CoOL) http://www.conservation-us.org
The American Institute for Conservation of Historic & Artistic Works
1156 15th Street NW, Ste. 320
Washington, DC 20005
Phone: 202.452.9545
Fax: 202.452.9328
E-mail: info@conservation-us.org

CoSA provides information concerning emergency training and preparedness.
Council of State Archivists (CoSA) http://www.statearchivists.org/prepare/index.htm
Council of State Archivists
308 E Burlington St #189, Iowa City IA 52240
319-338-0248
info@statearchivists.org

DMPA, the Disaster Mitigation Planning Assistance, is a project of Michigan State University libraries, the Center for Great Lakes Culture and the California Preservation Program, DMPA includes sample disaster plans and resources.
Disaster Mitigation Planning Assistance http://matrix.msu.edu/~disaster

The Getty Conservation Institute publishes resources on conservation of materials and emergency planning.
Getty Conservation Institute http://www.getty.edu/conservation
1200 Getty Center Drive, Suite 700
Los Angeles,
CA 90049-1684
310-440-7325
E-mail: gciweb@getty.edu

Heritage Preservation provides preservation advice from professional conservators. It conducted The Heritage Health Index survey, the first attempt to paint a national picture of the state of collections in all kinds of institutions.
Heritage Preservation http://www.heritagepreservation.org
1012 14th Street, NW
Suite 1200
Washington, DC 20005
202-233-0800
info@heritagepreservation.org

IAEM is a non-profit educational organization dedicated to promoting the goals of saving lives and protecting property during emergencies and disasters.
International Association of Emergency Managers (IAEM) http://www.iaem.com
International Association of Emergency Managers
201 Park Washington Court
Falls Church, VA, 22046-4527
703-538-1795
e-mail: info@iaem.com

ICCROM is an intergovernmental organization dedicated to the conservation of cultural heritage. It has publications on conservation and preservation, sponsors training, and has a laboratory.
International Centre for the Study of the Preservation and Restoration of Cultural Property (IC-CROM) http://www.iccrom.org

Via di San Michele 13, I-00153
Rome, Italy
tel: (+39) 06.585-531
iccrom@iccrom.org

IPI is a university-based, nonprofit research laboratory devoted to scientific research in the preservation of visual and other forms of recorded information. It provides of information, consulting services, practical tools, and preservation technology for libraries, archives, and museum collections worldwide.
Image Permanence Institute (IPI) http://www.imagepermanenceinstitute.org/
Rochester Institute of Technology/IPI
70 Lomb Memorial Drive
Rochester, NY 14623-5604
585-475-5199
ipiwww@rit.edu

Lyrasis is a regional consortium of libraries in the eastern U. S. It provides extensive information, resources, training, advice and consultation about conservation, preservation and disaster response and recovery.
Lyrasis: Disaster Resources http://www.lyrasis.org/Preservation/Disaster-Resources.aspx
1438 West Peachtree Street, NW
Suite 200
Atlanta, GA 30309
800-999-8558
membersupport@lyrasis.org.

NCDP focuses on natural disasters, pandemics and terrorism and the analysis of long-term recovery issues facing communities affected by disasters.
National Center for Disaster Preparedness (NCDP) http://www.ncdp.mailman.columbia.edu
National Center for Disaster Preparedness
Mailman School of Public Health
Columbia University
215 West 125th Street, 3rd Floor
New York, NY 10027

646-845-2300
ncdp@columbia.edu

NEDCC provides training, conservation services, and information about disaster planning and preservation & conservation techniques.
Northeast Document Conservation Center
(NEDCC) http://www.nedcc.org/home.php
Northeast Document Conservation Center
100 Brickstone Square
Andover, MA 01810-1494
978-470-1010
nedcc@nedcc.org

NFPA develops, publishes, and disseminates codes and standards intended to minimize the possibility and effects of fire and other risks.
National Fire Protection Association (NFPA)
http://www.nfpa.org
1 Batterymarch Park
Quincy, Massachusetts
USA 02169-7471
617-770-3000
custserv@nfpa.org

NNLM provides emergency preparedness information for librarians including disaster planning templates, reports of disasters, resources, etc.
National Network of Libraries of Medicine:
NNLM Emergency Preparedness and Response
Toolkit http://nnlm.gov/ep
National Network of Libraries of Medicine National Network Office
National Library of Medicine
8600 Rockville Pike, Bldg. 38, Room B1-E03
Bethesda, Maryland 20894
800-338-7657 (For all Regions)
The e-mails are divided by geographic region; see
http://nnlm.gov/about/contact_us.html to locate the relevant e-mail for your geographic area.

NPI is a nonprofit organization offering specialized information, continuing education, and pro-

fessional training in areas of historic preservation and cultural resource management.
National Preservation Institute (NPI) http://
www.npi.org
National Preservation Institute
P.O. Box 1702
Alexandria, Virginia 22313
703.765.0100
info@npi.org

NTHP, the National Trust for Historic Preservation is a private, nonprofit membership organization dedicated to saving historic places and revitalizing America's communities.
National Trust for Historic Preservation http://
www.preservationnation.org
1785 Massachusetts Ave. NW, Washington, DC
20036-2117
202-588-6000
800-944-6847
info@nthp.org

RAP provides information and resources on preservation and conservation for cultural institutions and the public throughout the United States.
Regional Alliance for Preservation (RAP) http://
www.rap-arcc.org
Since RAP is a national network of nonprofit organizations and not an overseeing organization, please direct questions to any one of their member organizations. http://www.rap-arcc.org/index.
php?page=contact

SAA provides information on disaster planning and recovery.
Society of American Archivists (SAA) http://
www.archivists.org
17 North State Street
Suite 1425
Chicago, IL 60602-3315
312-606-0722
866-722-7858
servicecenter@archivists.org

SLA's Emergency Preparedness & Recovery Advisory Council investigates and establishes ways to help organizations, governments, and individuals recover from the effects of natural disaster. It maintains the Information Professionals Alliance on Natural Disasters and Accidents (IPANDA) response network and the IPANDAnet blog: http://slablogger.typepad.com/ipandanet/
Special Libraries Association (SLA)
http://www.sla.org
331 South Patrick Street
Alexandria, Virginia 22314-3501 USA
Telephone: +1.703.647.4900
membership@sla.org

The Smithsonian provides extensive information concerning conservation and preservation of materials.
Smithsonian Institution http://www.si.edu
PO Box 37012
SI Building, Room 153, MRC 010
Washington, D.C. 20013-7012
202-633-6090
info@si.edu

UNESCO provides information and resources related to disaster preparedness and recovery.
UNESCO: Disaster Preparedness and Recovery
http://www.unesco-ci.org/cgi-bin/portals/archives/page.cgi?d=1&g=942.
7, place de Fontenoy
75352 Paris 07 SP
France
General phone: +33 (0)1 45 68 10 00
E-mail: bpi@unesco.or

U.S. FEMA provides information on disasters, relief efforts, and preparedness.
U. S. Federal Emergency Management (FEMA)
http://www.fema.gov
Disaster Assistance Information;
Federal Emergency Management Agency
P.O. Box 10055

Hyattsville, MD 20782-705
800-621-FEMA (3362)
FEMA-Correspondence-Unit@dhs.gov
General Contact Address:
Federal Emergency Management Agency
500 C Street S.W.
Washington, D.C. 20472
202)-646-2500
FEMAWebmaster@DHS.gov

U.S. LC , the Library of Congress, provides information on preservation and conservation, including the site *Learning from Katrina: Conservators' First-Person Accounts of Response and Recovery: Suggestions for Best Practice.* http://www.loc.gov/preserv/emergprep/katrinarespond.htmlhttp://www.loc.gov/perserv/emergprep/katrinarespond.html
U. S. Library of Congress (LC): Preservation
http://www.loc.gov/preserv/
Preservation Directorate
Library of Congress
101 Independence Ave.
Washington, D.C. 20540-4500
Telephone 202-707-5213
FAX 202-707-3434
E-mail using a form on their web page.

U.S. NARA provides information on preservation, preparedness, recovery, and conservation of materials.
U. S. National Archives and Records Administration (NARA) http://www.archives.gov
8601 Adelphi Road
College Park, MD 20740-6001
1-866-272-6272
E-mail using a form on their web page.
U.S. National Park Service provides information about caring for materials and historic buildings. It also develops standards and guidelines for historic rehabilitation projects and offers "how to" advice for hands-on preservationists. It has numerous publications on preservation and conservation.

U. S. National Park Service (NPS)
http://www.nps.gov/history/preservation.htm
National Park Service
1849 C Street NW
Washington, DC 20240
202-208-6843
E-mail using a form on their web page.
The Western States and Territories Preservation
Assistance Service (WESTPAS) is a collaborative project to provide preservation information,
education, and training by delivering preservation
education and training on disaster preparedness,
emergency response, and collection recovery to
libraries and archives in the region.

Western States and Territories Preservation Assistance Service www.westpas.org

Barclay Ogden
Preservation Department
20 Doe Library
University of California
Berkeley, CA 94720
bogden@westpas.org
work: 510-642-4946
E-mail: info@westpas.org

MODEL RFP FOR DISASTER RECOVERY SERVICES

This sample RFP is based on an RFP developed by University of New Mexico Physical Plant Department and Purchasing Department for disaster recovery services for the entire university; therefore, it refers to UNM and New Mexico throughout. Each institution can adapt it to fit their individual needs.

The parent institution of a library will have language describing its requirements for conflict of interest, insurance, and other legal aspects.

Request for Proposal Number: 123456
Offer Due by: xxxxxx

Title: Disaster Recovery Services
Table of Contents
Part 1   Vendor Information
Part 2   Terms and Conditions
Part 3   Instructions to Responders
Part 4   Evaluation Criteria—Scope of Work—Specifications

Part 1   Vendor Information asks for information that identifies the company responding to the RFP and will include their address, their Federal Employer ID number and the name of the person representing the company.

Part 2   Terms and Conditions will include the terms required by the parent institution that may include clauses concerning conflict of interest, indemnification, insurance, payment terms, or relevant legal requirements.

Part 3   Instructions to Responders may include clauses related to the submission of the response, the requirements for asking for clarification, changes in the RFP, or the responses.

Part 4   Proposal Evaluation Procedure and Criteria will describe the process which will be used to evaluate the proposals. Suggested evaluation criteria may include:

1. Proper Qualifications
   a. The Proposer must demonstrate that it has the management and operational experience, financial resources and personnel necessary to successfully perform the services specified in the RFP. A proposer must be financially solvent.

2. Evaluation of Proposals.

   a. Evaluation factors, grouped by relative order of importance, will be used in determining the best-qualified offers:

      i.   Initial response to the incident in less than 24 hours guaranteed.

      ii. Direct project management by the company guaranteed.

      iii. Assurance of UNM's priority position in widespread disaster.

      iv. Number and type of services provided directly by company versus the services provided by subcontractors as evidenced in table below.

      v.   Experience with electronic protected health information (EPH) and other confidential materials (both paper and electronic).

      vi. Experience with disaster recovery at libraries and data centers.

      vii. Ability to recover high priority office space, data and materials in a timely manner.

      viii. Ability to provide storage for recovered material (e.g. books) until renovated space is available.

      ix. Recommendation by references which have used the company's services.

      x.   Rates.

   b. Submittals—In consideration of the following information, please provide the following information:

      i.   Provide general information about your company and company experience.

      ii. Provide an explanation of how your company will meet the requirements of this RFP.

      iii. What services does your company provide?

      iv. What services do you subcontract?

      v.   Who are those vendors (subcontractors)? Please include contact names and phone numbers.

      vi. Provide a list of your rates including service for time, materials, labor, travel, etc., especially considering the tasks on the list of service required.

3. Scope of Services

   a. The University of New Mexico is seeking proposals from firms to provide disaster response and recovery services.

   b. This RFP is for the establishment of a Contract of Disaster Response and Recovery Services for UNM facilities located at various locations. The primary location is Albuquerque, New Mexico, but may also include UNM sites throughout the State of New Mexico. The contractor must also be willing to provide the service to other governmental entities and institutions throughout the state of NM. The service will cover all kinds of facilities. Please indicate which of the following types of facilities your company is able to service:

      i.   Libraries

      ii. Museums

      iii. Classrooms, Laboratories and Academic Offices

      iv. Administrative Offices

      v.   Athletic and Recreational Facilities

      vi. Hospitals, Clinics and Medical Research Facilities

      vii. Clean rooms

      viii. Maintenance Facilities

ix. Residential Units

x. Food Service Preparation, Serving and Dining Areas

xi. Bookstores

xii. Historical buildings

xiii. Theaters

xiv. Video and Audio Production and Broadcast Facilities

xv. Storage Facilities

xvi. Observatory

xvii. Student Union building (including Food Court, Shops and Meeting Rooms)

xviii. Parking Garages

xix. Other: _____

c. UNM may award multiple contracts to multiple vendors depending upon the services offered. In the event that the contract services are engaged, some variation in service requested should be expected depending upon the extent of the disaster and the response needed.

d. UNM seeks a contract for the sole purpose of securing one or more environmental or other relevant service contractor(s) for disaster recovery. The contractor will be responsible for responding to those events where the services are deemed necessary by University or local authorities and shall be responsible for providing the services within a minimum of 4 hours from the time of initial contact. The contractor will be responsible for salvaging items damaged by water and fire—both man-made and natural. The contractor may also be required to provide services such as water extraction, drying of structure and contents, debris removal etc. The contractor will not be responsible for any structural construction.

e. Services and capabilities to be provided by contractor shall include, but not be limited to the following:

i. Stabilization of the building infrastructure and environment.

ii. Facilities, personnel and oversight to effectively and efficiently provide professional advice and packing, freezing, and drying service to campus units affected by a disaster.

iii. Air treatment, smoke neutralization, sanitization, deodorization and the treatment and removal of mold for document collections and facilities.

iv. Decontamination and restoration, mitigation, cleanup and containments resulting from chemical, biological, and radiological incidents.

v. Expertise, equipment, and personnel to salvage facilities damaged by disasters.

vi. Ability to salvage and recover damaged documents, books, artifacts, electronics, stored data, lab equipment or other equipment.

vii. Flexibility to deploy additional resources should the need arise.

viii. Ability to work closely with campus personnel, and local, state, and federal agencies responding to a disaster in a manner that will ensure the successful recovery of damaged resources and the successful completion of any investigations, clean-ups, or other specialized situations.

ix. Ability and experience to safely, confidentially, and effectively, handle classified or restricted documents, hazardous materials, animal research facilities, research, or data damaged in the course of a disaster.

x. Ability to provide a standardized rate schedule for necessary services and the ability to obtain all necessary equipment.

xi. Waste disposal service in compliance with applicable state and federal laws.

xii. Vacuum freezing

Not all services will be required in all situations. However, the Contractor(s) must be particularly responsive to the security needs of a disaster site. If a disaster site has been designated a crime scene due to a criminal activity or terrorism, security is paramount and must be given full consideration without negatively impacting the interests of the University.

JOURNALS

Articles about emergency preparedness and recovery appear in a wide variety of journals. The following is a selected list of magazines and journals that focus on various aspects of emergency management. Pricing is for 2009 subscriptions.

Australian Journal of Emergency Management
Australia, Emergency Management, PO Box 1020 Dickinson, Australian Capital Territory 2602, Australia.
The official publication of Emergency Management Australia; scholarly yet practical in its orientation with a balance between academic and practitioner papers.
Free. http://www.ema.gov.au/agd/EMA/emaInternet.nsf/Page/AJEM
http://www.ema.gov.au/ajem

Contingency Planning and Management
CPM Group, 3141 Fairview park Dr., Suite 777, Falls Church, VA 22042
Online newsletters with information and strategic advice on business continuity, emergency management and security issues.
Free with registration.
http://www.contingencyplanning.com/

Contingency Planning and Recovery Journal
Management Advisory Services, P.O. Box 81151, Wellesley Hills, MA 02481-0001
A business continuity journal concerned with enterprise and IT contingency planning; emergency preparedness and business resumption; a digest of key developments and literature reviews in the field.
$75
http://www.masp.com/publications/CPR-J.html

DisasterCom
The Disaster Preparedness and Emergency Response Association, PO Box 797, Longmont, CO 80502
Online newsletter of DERA, a nonprofit association linking professionals, volunteers and organizations active in all phases of disaster preparedness and emergency management.
Free.
http://www.disasters.org/dera/dera.htm

Disaster Prevention & Management: An International Journal
Emerald Group Publishing Ltd, 60/62 Toller Lane, Bradford, England, BD8 9BY
Scholarly articles and news in the fields of disaster prevention and management, both natural and man-made disasters; supporting the exchange of ideas, experience, and practice between academics, practitioners and policy-makers.
7429 Euros
http://info.emeraldinsight.com/products/journals/journals.htm?id=dpm

Disaster Recovery Journal
Disaster Recovery Journal, P O Box 510110, St. Louis MO 63151
Trade journal dedicated to the field of disaster recovery and business continuity; sponsor of conferences and seminars on disaster recovery and business continuity.
Free to personnel involved in contingency planning.
http://drj.com

Disasters: Preparedness and Mitigation in the Americas
Pan American Health Organization, Emergency Preparedness Program, 525 23rd Street NW, Washington, DC 20037
Online newsletter concerning disasters in the Americas.
Free.
http://www.disaster-info.net/newsletter/

Disasters: the Journal of Disaster Studies, Policy and Management
Wiley-Blackwell, John Wiley & Sons, 111 River Street
Hoboken, NJ 07030-5774
Scholarly journal published on behalf of the Overseas Development Institute; reporting on all aspects of disaster studies, policy and management; providing a forum for academics, policy-makers and practitioners for research and practice related to natural disasters and complex political emergencies.
$88 personal subscription; $592 institutional subscription
http://blackwellpublishers.co.uk/ http://www.wiley.com/bw/journal.asp?ref=0361-3666

Emergency Preparedness News
Business Publishers Inc., 8738 Colesville Road, Suite 1100, Silver Springs MD 20910-3928
News for the business community on legal issues, state and federal policies, technology and other developments related to disaster management such as mitigation and response strategies, emergency communication and planning techniques, and technologies to assist in disaster recovery
$409
http://www.bpinews.com/spec_epn.htm

IAEM Bulletin
International Association of Emergency Managers, 111 Park Place, Falls Church, VA 22046-4513
Information about government actions affecting emergency management; research and information sources.
Free to members of the association and emergency management officials, as well as to allied organizations and legislative representatives with a role in emergency management issues.
http://www.iaem.com http://www.iaem.com/publications/bulletin/intro.htm

International Journal of Emergency Management
Inderscience Publishers, World Trade Center Building II 29, route de Pre-Bois
Case Postale 856 CH-1215 Geneve 15 Switzerland
Addresses contingencies and emergencies as well as crisis and disaster management; information on the use of innovative methods and technologies to improve the ability to avoid, mitigate, respond to and recover from natural and technological disasters.
494 Euros
https://www.inderscience.com/browse/index.php?journalID=8

International Journal of Mass Emergencies & Disasters
International Research Committee on Disasters, School of Policy, Planning, and Development, University of Southern California, Los Angeles, California 90089-0626
Concerned with the social and behavioral aspects of disasters or mass emergencies; focused on work dealing with the human and organizational aspects of mass emergencies.
$35 personal subscription; $55 institutional subscription.
http://www.usc.edu/dept/sppd/ijmed

Journal of Business Continuity & Emergency Planning
Henry Stewart Publications, Russell House, 28 Little Russell, London WC1A 2HN, England
Scholarly articles and case studies by expert business continuity and emergency managers in areas related to business continuity and emergency management practice.
$415
http://www.henrystewart.com/jbcep/index.html

Journal of Contingencies and Crisis Management
Wiley-Blackwell, John Wiley & Sons, 111 River Street
Hoboken, NJ 07030-5774
Information on all aspects of contingency planning, scenario analysis and crisis management in both corporate and public sectors; it focuses on the opportunities and threats facing organizations and presents analysis and case studies of crisis prevention, crisis planning, recovery and turnaround management.
$103 personal subscription; $667 institutional subscription.
http://www.blackwellpublishers.co.uk/ http://www.wiley.com/bw/journal.asp?ref=0966-0879

Journal of Emergency Management
Weston Medical Publishing LLC/Prime National Pub. Corp., 470 Boston Post Road, Weston MA 02493
To enable those responsible for emergency preparedness and response to deal effectively with everything from acts of terror, fires, floods and weather emergencies to gas explosions and catastrophic accidents.
$197 personal subscription; $265 institutional subscription.
http://www.pnpco.com/pn06001.html

Journal of Homeland Security and Emergency Management
BePress, 2809 Telegraph Avenue, Suite 222, Berkeley, CA 94705
Articles on research and practice from a broad array of professions, including: emergency management, engineering, political science, public policy, decision science, and health and medicine.
$75 personal subscription; $225 institutional subscription.
http://www.bepress.com/jhsem/

Journal of Risk Research
Taylor & Francis, Sheepen Place, Colchester, Essex CO3 3LP, UK
Theoretical and empirical research articles within the risk field from the areas of social, physical and health sciences and engineering, as well as articles related to decision making, regulation and policy issues in all disciplines.
$296 personal subscription; $1530 institutional subscription
http://www.tandf.co.uk/journals/titles/13669877.asp

Library & Archival Security
Taylor & Francis, Sheepen Place, Colchester, Essex CO3 3LP, UK
Legal and organizational issues and incidents in libraries, archives and other information centers; information on all aspects of security, including physical security, data and communications security, legislation, disaster preparedness and recovery; studies of related social, legal and ethical issues.
$92 personal subscription; $251 institutional subscription.
http://www.tandf.co.uk/journals/titles/01960075.asp

Risk Abstracts
Cambridge Scientific Abstracts, 7200 Wisconsin Avenue, Suite 601, Bethesda, ND 20814
Published in association with the Institute for Risk Research at the University of Waterloo. A database covering publications about risk arising from industrial, technological, environmental, and other sources, with an emphasis on assessment and management of risk.
Inquire for pricing.
http://www.csa.com/ http://www.csa.com/factsheets/risk-set-c.php

Risk Analysis
Wiley-Blackwell, John Wiley & Sons, 111 River Street
Hoboken, NJ 07030-5774
Published on behalf of the Society for Risk Analysis; covers new developments in the field of risk issues and analysis.
$1426.
http://www.wiley.com/bw/journal.asp?ref=0272-4332

Risk Management Magazine
Risk and Insurance Management Society, 1065 Avenue of the Americas, 13th Floor, New York, NY 10018
Analysis, insight and news for corporate risk managers; explores existing and emerging techniques and concepts that address the needs of those who are tasked with protecting the physical, financial, human and intellectual assets of their companies.
$100.
http://www.rmmagazine.com/

RiskWire
Risk and Insurance Management Society.
Provides an executive summary of the most important current risk management stories.
Free to RIMS members
http://cf.rims.org/RWTemplate.cfm

Unscheduled Events
Center for Disaster Research & Education, PO Box 1002, Millersville University of Pennsylvania, Millersville, PA 17551
Online newsletter of International Sociological Association's Research Committee on Disasters; announcements of publications and conferences.
Free.
http://muweb.millersville.edu/~isaracdue/http://www.millersville.edu/~ue/